The

Greek Praise

of Poverty

The
Greek Praise
of Poverty

Origins of Ancient Cynicism

WILLIAM D. DESMOND

University of Notre Dame Press   Notre Dame, Indiana

Library of Congress Cataloging in-Publication Data

Desmond, William, 1974–
    The Greek praise of poverty : the origins of ancient cynicism /
William Desmond.
        p. cm.
    Includes bibliographical references (p.   ) and index.
    ISBN 0-268-02581-9 (cloth : alk. paper)
    ISBN 0-268-02582-7 (pbk. : alk. paper)
    1. Cynics (Greek philosophy) 2. Cynicism. 3. Poverty.
4. Philosophy, Ancient. I. Title.
    B508.D47 2005
    183'.4—dc22

                                        2005035126

CONTENTS

Ours is sometimes described as a cynical time. This is perhaps surprising, for from an external point of view, ours might be a golden age: land and sea give up their wealth; factories pour forth innumerable products; inhabitants of the developed world at least are generally well-fed, healthy, and rich. And yet, paradoxically, the extension of scientific knowledge, technological power, and human possibilities can sometimes seem to rob life of its radiance. All is exposed to scrutiny; all is found to be limited and imperfect. Old ideals are burst asunder. Spiritual passions are forgotten amid a scientific or hedonistic materialism; new cults proliferate, fashionable, fanatical, or escapist. The ideal of knowledge is deconstructed as a subtle will-to-power or as impossible or as humanly empty. Ideals of love, honor, and citizenship are analyzed away as cunning masks of the "selfish gene." Moral progress is a lie: witness, for instance, the pornography "industry." Material progress is a dubious blessing: mechanized agriculture not only feeds the masses but fattens them. Minute by minute, mankind pursues its petty ends by nasty means. Self-interest reigns supreme everywhere. And to what end? So a cynic might ask himself as he surveys his world. "There is no end," is his conclusion, and in response he may either rant or resign himself to a resentful detachment. Some might relegate such deep cynicism to "old Europe," but the malaise is not European alone: the scores of recent books in English on cynicism go far to corroborate Sloterdijk's contention that the contemporary era is pervaded by a deep, even nihilistic cynicism.[1]

Yet what is cynicism? For all the gloom attached to the word, wits of many periods have delighted in fashioning their own definitions of the cynic—sometimes an exercise in self-analysis. Oscar Wilde's often-quoted quip has it that a cynic is "a man who knows the price of everything and the value of nothing." H. L. Mencken sees the cynic as a person "who, when he smells flowers, looks around for a coffin," and (Mencken adds mischievously) a "cynic is right nine times out of ten." In Ambrose Pierce's *Devil's Dictionary* (originally titled *The Cynic's Word Book*), a cynic is "a blackguard whose faulty vision sees things as they are, not as they ought to be. Hence the custom among the Scythians of plucking out a cynic's eyes to improve his vision." Other definitions understand the cynic as "a parasite of civilization, [who] lives by denying it" (José Ortega y Gasset); as "intellectual dandyism without the coxcomb's feathers" (George Meredith); or cynicism as "the intellectual cripple's substitute for intelligence" (Russell Lynes). More detached is the *Oxford English Dictionary:* "Cynic. A person disposed to rail or find fault; now usually one who shows a disposition to disbelieve in the sincerity or goodness of human motives and actions, and is wont to express this by sneers and sarcasm; a sneering fault-finder." One would be inclined to go further than such dictionary definitions: the cynic is one who dismisses all "higher" ideals like justice, generosity, patriotism, love, and holiness as nonexistent, for in his view people are incorrigibly self-interested, and human nature essentially evil. At times, the cynic will act upon these principles and "cynically" employ any means for his own selfish ends: hence, Macchiavelli and Hobbes are often spoken of as the cynic's cynics.

Most modern European words for "cynic" derive from *kunikos*, the adjectival form of the ancient Greek word for dog, *kuon*. The playful nickname was given to Diogenes of Sinope in the mid-fourth century B.C., and it stuck, not only to him but to his followers and their followers after them. For centuries afterwards until the passing away of the Roman empire, his imitators continued to be known as "dogs" or "dog-philosophers" for their peculiar lifestyle. Unwashed, unhoused, poor, and outspoken, these ascetics and social rebels wandered through and between the cities of the Graeco-Roman world like stray dogs—among the people, but not quite of the people, potentially friendly watchdogs, yet also aggressive, snarling satirists.

Thus ancient Cynicism had a much more specific meaning than its modern derivative. In fact, the ancient Cynics were ultimately very different from their modern namesakes. Ancient Cynics could be "cynical" in the modern sense of seeing selfish motives at play beneath a pretty appearance: the king's generosity, the general's impressive get-up, and the scholar's erudition are dismissed as so many tricks for self-promotion. They were "cynical" also towards many social conventions: these are shams and burdens and the best one can do is to renounce them and be free. But, crucially and in marked distinction from modern cynics, the ancient Cynics did not equate renunciation with nihilism. On the contrary, renunciation is for them the path to a perfect happiness and moral goodness—and in fact, the cheapest path! For the most crippling burden of social life is the widespread infatuation with wealth. The best response, then, is to renounce wealth altogether and live a life of resolute poverty, with only the minimum of material possessions. By such a voluntary poverty (the Cynics thought), one regains everything essential—freedom, contentment, a sense of self-worth, courage, wisdom, honesty, and all the virtues. Paradoxically then, renunciation is profitable; living like a dog, one realizes one's true humanity.

In all this, far from being "cynical," the ancient Cynics were astonishingly idealistic. To say that the cynicism is idealistic may seem contradictory to us. Are not cynicism and idealism opposites? Does not the true cynic scoff at ideals as *mere* ideals, as nothing more than hollow words? Yet, the ancient Cynics insisted that there is an innate human goodness that can be recovered fully with a little effort. So too they were prophets of virtue, forever preaching to passersby that nothing else has *any* worth when divorced from honesty, temperance, bravery, and self-knowledge. The virtuous life "according to nature" is the perfect one and would bring an easy happiness if only individuals were harder on themselves. But unfortunately, most people are overly clever. To their ruin, they have "sought out many devices," and surrounded themselves with inventions, luxuries, ambitions, hypocrisy, and pettiness. Self-induced delusion threatens to engulf society, and so the ancient Cynic wages unending war against what he interprets as the folly of mankind. But again, this "cynicism" is only the negative aspect of the ancient Cynic's deep optimism: he rages only out of the conviction that moral perfection is a real possibility.

This book will explore Cynicism and its precedents in Greek culture, particularly in the so-called "Classical Period" between 450 and 323 B.C. In what forms did idealistic aspects of Greek culture filter through to the resolute optimism of the Greek Cynics? The Greekness of the first Cynics, as well as the Cynicism of the classical Greeks, will be the quarry that we will pursue into the thickets of classical literature: *ignotas animum dimitte in artes!* Yet, despite being a relatively minor phenomenon, ancient Cynicism has not been an insignificant one. Its variants outlasted Alexander and his successors, and nearly outlived the Roman empire.[2] Its influence is felt in distant centuries, in the Christian praise of poverty, in idealizations of the "natural life" and the noble savage, in countercultural movements, and in reactions against the excessive materialism and consumerism of the day. Most recently, certain economists' critique of "affluenza" and newfound interest in frugality renews ancient ideas, though in a less radical way. An exploration of the precedents, origins, and peculiarities of ancient Cynicism need not, then, be merely antiquarian. The adventure may be enjoyable in its own right, and one may reemerge into the cynical world of digitalized capitalism with a greater appreciation for a human possibility that, though hidden in the past, is not altogether lost.

ACKNOWLEDGMENTS

Many people have in sundry ways contributed to the writing of this book, and a full reckoning would extend to a veritable catalogue of names were it to include all those to whom I owe my gratitude. Although they cannot here be named, they are by no means forgotten. Among friends, teachers, and former colleagues at Yale University, I owe a special debt to Tom Cole, Victor Bers, and Tad Brennan. I would like to thank the Whiting Foundation for generous support that enabled me to complete what would become a first draft of this book. I am indebted to Barbara Hanrahan and Matt Dowd, as well as the anonymous readers for the University of Notre Dame Press, for their advice and guidance through the editorial process. Above all, I thank my family—Oisín, Hugh, William, and Maria—for their encouragement, humor and love. It is to my parents, William and Maria, that I dedicate this book.

ABBREVIATIONS

1. ANCIENT AUTHORS

Abbreviations for the names and works of ancient authors will be the same as those used in the *Oxford Classical Dictionary* (*OCD*), 3rd edition, or secondarily, Liddell and Scott's *Greek-English Lexicon,* 9th ed. I use the Romanized form of Greek proper names (e.g., Socrates rather than Sokrates).

2. MODERN SCHOLARSHIP

AET   Meikle, S. *Aristotle's Economic Thought.* Oxford: Clarendon Press, 1995.

CC   Navia, L. *Classical Cynicism: A Critical Study.* Westport, Conn.: Greenwood Press, 1996.

CF   Davidson, J. *Courtesans and Fishcakes: The Consuming Passions of Classical Athens.* London: Harper Collins, 1997.

CHCK   Höistad, R. *Cynic Hero and Cynic King.* Uppsala: C. W. K. Gleerup, 1948.

DK   Diels, H., and W. Kranz. *Die Fragmente der Vorsokratiker.* 6th ed. Berlin: Weidmann, 1951–54.

EAG   Michell, H. *The Economics of Ancient Greece.* Cambridge: Cambridge University Press, 1940.

FFS   Garnsey, P. *Famine and Food Supply in the Greco-Roman World.* Cambridge: Cambridge University Press, 1988.

GC   Zimmern, A. *The Greek Commonwealth.* New York: Modern Library, 1956.

GI   Balot, R. *Greed and Injustice in Classical Athens*. Princeton: Princeton University Press, 2001.

GPM   Dover, K. J. *Greek Popular Morality in the Time of Plato and Aristotle*. Indianapolis: Hackett Publishing, 1994.

HC   Dudley, D. *A History of Cynicism from Diogenes to the 6th Century* A.D. London: Methuen & Co., 1937.

LSJ   *A Greek-English Lexicon*. Compiled by H. G. Liddell and R. Scott, revised and augmented by Sir H. S. Jones with the assistance of R. McKenzie, 9th ed., with a revised supplement. Oxford: Clarendon Press, 1996.

ME   Ober, J. *Mass and Elite in Democratic Athens*. Princeton: Princeton University Press, 1989.

MT   Reed, C. M. *Maritime Traders in the Ancient Greek World*. Cambridge: Cambridge University Press, 2003.

PRIA   Lovejoy, A. O., and G. Boas. *Primitivism and Related Ideas in Antiquity*. Paperbacks edition. Baltimore: Johns Hopkins University Press, 1997.

SCAG   Fuks, A. *Social Conflict in Ancient Greece*. Leiden: E. J. Brill, 1984.

CHAPTER ONE

Approaches to Ancient Cynicism

Τῇ Ἑλλάδι πενίη μὲν αἰεί κοτε σύντροφός ἐστιν.
Greece has always had poverty as its companion.

—Herodotus, 7.102.1

Greek literature, like the Gospels, "is a great protest against the modern view that the really important thing is to be comfortable."
—Zimmern, *The Greek Commonwealth*, 217

In antiquity, mainland Greece and its Aegean islands were poor places. The city-states were typically located on small plains, with thin soil rising quickly into stony hills. Not surprisingly, given the rocky and semiarid terrain, probably only about 20 percent of the land was arable. Manufactures, industry, and trade also remained small-scale, and could only supplement agriculture as a source of wealth. With time, the large trading cities of Miletus, Athens, and Syracuse might have rivaled Phoenician Tyre or Carthage. But the Persians sacked Miletus in 494 B.C., the Peloponnesian War ended Athens' undisputed dominance of the Aegean, and Syracuse was torn by foreign wars and internal divisions through much of the fourth century.[1] Indeed, although almost all areas of mainland Greece are within fifty miles of the sea, primary loyalties were to the land. Classical literature contains no poem in praise of the sea as conduit of trade, wealth, adventure, or liberty, and the Greeks never developed quite the maritime zeal of such peoples as the Phoenicians, Vikings, Venetians, Portuguese, Dutch, or English.

1

The relative poverty of their landscape was apparent to the Greeks, yet their writers rarely gave it sustained attention. Some passing references almost attain the level of proverbs, but little more. Herodotus' Demaratus mentions poverty as the cause of Greek valor. In Aristophanes' *Plutus*, Poverty herself is banished from Greece, and Wealth instated as the new Zeus: this is a comic fantasy that all may enjoy, but it is a fantasy nonetheless. In Herodotus again, the Andrians refer to the "poverty and helplessness" of their island home, whereas Menander's Cnemon is "a typical Attic farmer, who struggles with rocks that yield nothing but thyme and sage, and gets nothing out of it but aches and pains." In another story, the tyrant Pisistratus was touring Attica when he passed an old peasant working the thin soil. Wondering what taxes he might be able to demand from the man, Pisistratus asked the man what his farm produced. "Terrible pains" came the reply. The peasant's laconic answer is typical of allusions to poverty among the Greek authors—succinct, oblique, and incidental.[2]

The contrast with modern economic historians is as instructive as it is striking. With their methodical and systematic approach, modern historians are quick to point to Greece's geographical poverty as a crucial factor affecting its cultural development. Many quote Herodotus' Demaratus as if it were an axiomatic statement for understanding Greek society: "Poverty has always been the companion of Greece."[3] A thoroughly materialistic narrative would derive as many facts as possible from this axiom. Culture is explained from the ground up, literally: the topography, geography, soil, and climate of various regions support a limited number of humanly useful plants and animals—notably barley, wheat, olives, figs, grapes, goats, sheep, donkeys, and cattle. Out of a limited agriculture rises a simple material culture: a simple diet (mostly vegetarian—grain, olives, figs, wine), simple dress (strips of woolen or goat-hair cloth [*sakkos*] wrapped in various ways about the body; strips of leather tied round the feet), and uncomplicated architecture prevail throughout the archaic and classical periods. Athletes exercise naked, and even among the upper classes who could afford otherwise, ostentatious jewelry and clothing were not standard fare. For the impact of economic scarcity affected social relations also. Lavish accumulations of wealth and the segregation of the classes allowed autocrats in Media or Persia to lord it over their "slaves," and living "gods" ruled Egypt. But the Greek world was scandalized when Lysander and Alexander were "divinized." The smaller, more intimate Greek communities were naturally more egalitarian, for in their narrow compass, rich and poor lived in closer proximity to each other: Alcibiades and Socrates, or Alexander and Diogenes, might exchange words on the streets.

Thus, conditions tended to temper aristocratic claims to innate superiority. That is, the poverty of the land contributed largely to the egalitarian ethos of the *polis*.

In such a way, a thoroughly materialistic approach might seek to relate a myriad of cultural phenomena to a single, all-important fact. A modern approach is also systematic and methodical in its treatment of poverty itself. Poverty may be a fact, but it is merely a fact, contingent, and therefore can be eliminated. For the modern historian, then, scarcity was the fundamental economic *problem* afflicting the classical Greeks: there were lots of people, too few ready resources, and too rudimentary a level of technical knowledge to use those resources most efficiently. Such a matter-of-fact attitude inspires industrialized societies to take a course almost unknown in antiquity— waging "war" on poverty. The metaphor of a "war" is familiar in the United States from the era of President Johnson, elsewhere from the militarization of labor by communists and by the German National Socialists. More recently, the United Nations has designated 1997–2006 as the "First United Nations' Decade for the Eradication of Poverty."

The ancient world did not contemplate the eradication of poverty in this sense, and contemporary attitudes towards wealth and poverty were largely determined by the very different economic conditions that prevailed. Jesus' statement that "the poor will always be with you" was literally true for this world, for throughout Greco-Roman antiquity a technological solution to poverty was almost unimaginable. No ancient writer, not even Aristotle, "master of those that know," seems ever to have seriously entertained the notion that pure *ideas* could make possible machines and the mastery of nature. Plato mathematized nature, but in the spirit of Pythagoras, not Descartes. Aristotle mused for a moment about the shuttle that weaves of its own accord, or the plectrum that plucks the lyre without a musician's guiding hand. We might see in these imaginings the forerunners of mechanization, the sewing machine and MP3-player, and Aristotle also recognizes that such inventions would make slave labor obsolete. But for Aristotle, a singing lyre is a poet's fancy—like the moving statues of Daedalus or the walking tripods of Hephaestus—and he hurries on to complete his definition of the slave.[4] The Greek failure to invent such simple laborsaving devices as the hand-mill (to replace mortars and pestles) remains a source of much perplexity to the contemporary world which turns so instinctively to technological solutions.

In contrast to our almost automatic assumption of technological progress, the Greeks tended to treat wealth *not* so much as a material fact, but far more as an ethical and political phenomenon. Again, the contrast between modern historians and Herodotus' Demaratus is instructive: Demaratus refers to Poverty as the constant companion of Greece to emphasize the martial valor of the race, especially the Spartans; the economic point is secondary and far from axiomatic. Twentieth-century economic scholarship has increasingly emphasized the differences between ancient and modern economic practices, though there is still debate as to the extent to which ancient economies were "embedded" in communal life as a whole. On one side of the debate, the so-called formalists or modernists stress that the laws of economics do not change. Working, buying, and selling have always been governed by the same principles of rational self-interest, supply, and demand: "For the formalists, the ancient economy was a functionally segregated and independently instituted sphere of activity with its own profit-maximizing, want-satisfying logic and rationality, less 'developed' no doubt than any modern economy but nevertheless recognizably similar in kind."[5] In opposition, substantivists or primitivists refuse to simplify economic activity as an impersonal process of exchange, regulated by "laws" and almost wholly unaffected by the cultural idiosyncrasies of the people involved. For the substantivist, cultural peculiarities—the complex web of taboos, rituals, ethical expectations, and political organizations—are more important in the ancient context than any axioms of neo-classical economics: the "land" was not a neutral resource for human production, but Gaia, "wealth-giver" (ploutodotos) and oldest of the gods. A cynic might contend that people are always motivated by self-interest, but the self-interest involved in sacrificing a hecatomb, giving lavish xenia for the sake of honor and friendship, or dying for one's city or for one's philosophy is difficult to equate with the self-interest of buying low and selling high. Indeed, a "thick" cultural explanation involves a broad erudition and humanistic nuance that can be lacking in the formalist approach.[6]

The predominantly ethical nature of Greek attitudes towards wealth only further bolsters the primitivist stance. The absence of any technological ideal forced the Greeks essentially to abandon the question of production and focus far more on issues of consumption and conservation. For nobody (except comic poets when they fantasized about giving Plutus back his sight) thought that wealth could be increased indefinitely. Indeed, the notion of increasing wealth without end was almost invariably associated with individual greed, not with waging a total "war" against poverty. For three centuries, from Theognis to Aristotle, one hears writers condemning the desire for unlimited wealth as all-consuming, dehumanizing, antisocial, even criminal.[7]

Furthermore, this desire was often attributed to the already wealthy: the poor might be forced to petty crimes like cloak-snatching, but "want is not the sole incentive to crime. . . . Men do not become tyrants in order that they may not suffer cold." Much wants more: it is the very rich who rob, confiscate, murder, and tyrannize on a grand scale.[8] Therefore, throughout Greek history, the most typical economic proposals involve curtailing invidious desires, conserving what wealth exists, and distributing it more fairly. Distribution is the object of many political actions: state-sponsored colonization and cleruchies, imported grain and shared dividends distributed to the citizen-body, state-paid doctors, publicly organized festivals, liturgies and taxes imposed on the rich, and so forth. A more just distribution was also the end of the revolutionary call for the cancellation of debts and redivision of the land; distribution was one goal of the revolutionary utopias of theoreticians like Phaleas, Plato, and Zeno.[9]

But even more important from day to day were individual responses to the fundamental fact of scarcity. Work and save—such had to be the practice of Hesiod and the average peasant or artisan, for work, particularly farm-labor, was the primary source of wealth. The energetic and virtuous might espouse what could be called an "industrious optimism": hard work will make the worker personally rich, while the poor have only their own willful laziness to blame. Furthermore, what has been sown, harvested, and made must be used sparingly. Few people can afford to overeat, festivals are a special occasion, and the majority must live by temperance and thrift. Thus, Aristophanes' Strepsiades complains that his wife uses too much wool in her weaving; and the chorus leader in the *Wasps* orders his son not to burn so much lamp-oil—far too expensive! The Greek working class was not a drinking class: "love of drink" is a disease suffered only by the rich.[10] Because scarcity was a fact of life, frugality (*eutelia*) becomes a virtue of necessity. One encounters this pride in frugality in unexpected places. Pericles' funeral oration praises the democracy for its avoidance of expense: we pursue beauty with *eutelia* and philosophy without softness. Popular values are projected onto the heavens when Antiphon writes, "the gods delight in frugality."[11]

These are not just mere stray comments: frugality was an economic necessity to such an extent that it became a cultural norm. Popular thought, and later philosophical theory, would make a virtue of this necessity and enshrine temperance as one of the human excellences: as a general rule, one should restrain one's appetite, desires, and urge for self-satisfaction. Such temperance is a mark of maturity and even of civilized behavior, ever to be opposed to the forces of barbarism, as in the sculptors' *centauromachies* and *gigantomachies*. Some, like Callicles, might sneer at the temperate—"those fools"[12]—but his was a dangerous, and decidedly minority view. An affluent, industrialized society may plausibly entertain the hope that one day mechanized production would make all commodities free; such a happy anarchism was an impossible thought for the classical Greeks, for whom frugality was one of the most typical features of life.

Indeed, so typical was frugality that it could and did develop into a cult of voluntary self-deprivation. This brings us to our main topic—Cynic asceticism as a response to the Greek experience of poverty. The asceticism of the first generation of Cynics is well known. They are said to have simplified their lives as much as possible. Their meals consisted of water, lettuce, peas, lentil soup, figs, lupines, or beans—all very cheap, and perhaps free, for in some anecdotes the Cynics seem to have grown their own food or gathered wild plants.[13] Moreover, they ate their food raw, criticizing Prometheus for corrupting mankind's natural hardiness with the gift of fire and cooking. One cloak for both summer and winter, no shoes, and perhaps a staff to imitate the club-armed Heracles—their clothing was minimal.[14] They did not shave or wash. They slept rough in the stoa, in the entrances of temples, on the ground, wherever: Diogenes most famously crept into a large unused wine-jar (*pithos*), the term that would later be translated variously as his "barrel," "tub," or even "kennel," for Diogenes was nicknamed "the Dog" by contemporaries partly for his shameless, homeless lifestyle. His insistence upon the need for a virtuous poverty inspired a small band of admirers from around the Greek world: Crates was from Thebes, Crates' wife Hipparchia and brother-in-law Metrocles came from Maroneia in Thrace, Monimus from Syracuse, and Onesicritus from Astypalaea in Aegina (or perhaps the island of that name in the Cyclades). Other famous men are said to have "listened" to Diogenes—the Athenian general and orator Phocion, and the Megarian philosopher Stilpo. Still others survive only as names or colorful nicknames: Philiscus, Menander the "Oakwood," and Hegesias of Sinope, playfully called the "Dog-Collar," perhaps for his fanatical attachment to Diogenes "the Dog."[15]

But there were other Cynic-like personalities before Diogenes. Quasi-Cynic ideas have been detected in figures as disparate as Aspendus the Pythagorean, Democritus, Heraclitus, Pythagoras, Timon of Athens, and Odysseus. Socrates philosophized barefoot and was poor, and his "student" Antisthenes has very often been referred to as the "first" Cynic, for a variety of reasons: he wrote in praise of voluntary poverty and of later Cynic heroes like Heracles and Odysseus; some anecdotes give him the contemporary nickname of "the Absolute Dog"; and he is said to have frequented the Cynosarges ("White-Dog") gymnasium. Did the Cynic movement therefore get its name, its devotion to Heracles, and its first real impetus from such circumstances?[16] If there is a Homeric question, a Socratic question, an Oxyrynchus-historian question, and the like, then the traditional "Cynic question" would be whether Antisthenes or Diogenes was the first Cynic. According to one camp, Antisthenes the Athenian should be considered the first, so that the "school" would have originated in the later fifth century. According to the other camp, Diogenes of Sinope was the first "Dog," and Cynicism was a later phenomenon, often associated with the supposed decline of the *polis*. Yet, the dichotomy—either Antisthenes or Diogenes—may ultimately be a sterile one, as the most accomplished scholars have reached opposite conclusions without any substantial progress towards a consensus.[17]

Answers to the "Cynic question" are often largely determined by when one dates Diogenes' exile from Sinope and arrival in Athens. Yet in the end such answers are impossible because no precise dates can be gleaned from the sources. The name of Diogenes' father, Hicesias, is stamped on Sinopean coins from 360–320. But the currency "devaluation" of which he or his son (or both) *might* have been guilty, *may* have been earlier. Therefore, Diogenes *might* have gone into exile in the 330s, 340s, 350s, or even before 380.[18] Again, he *may* have fled for other reasons, as when Sinope was incorporated into the satrapy of the Persian Datames between 370–365. Did Diogenes meet Antisthenes? When did Antisthenes die? These facts also are unknown, and one can only speculate from a few anecdotes. One story suggests that Antisthenes knew of the Spartan defeat at Leuctra; if so, he lived until after 371. Did Diogenes arrive in Athens before 371? Did Diogenes know Antisthenes personally and for how long? Even if he didn't, might he have come to admire Antisthenes' ideas through his books, his reputation, or the friends who outlived him? The possibilities are literally endless, and there seems little point in speculating.

Yet the question of the origins of Cynicism need not be abandoned. What is important, and surely what lies behind the friendship of Diogenes and Antisthenes (whether this was actual or a later fiction), is that both men, and many others, were reacting in a similar way to similar social conditions. Attempts to articulate these conditions and the shared outlook they inspired have been intermittent, and even the following discussion is more complete and systematic than is the bibliography. Nevertheless, in pursuit of the origins of Cynic asceticism, one might distinguish five major approaches— Hellenistic, Marxist, psychological, Orientalist, and philosophical—that are represented in previous interpretations of Cynicism.

First, the Hellenistic approach sees Cynicism as a symptom and result of the "decline of the *polis*." This approach emphasizes the centrifugal tendencies that appeared with hurricane-force after the conquests of Alexander. It was an age of kings, fluctuating empires, mercenary warfare, exile and massive emigration to places as far as Afghanistan, and new exposure to a swarm of foreign customs, beliefs, and gods—in such conditions, the city-state lost its hold upon the individual. It could no longer pretend to exist in splendid isolation, with its distinctive tutelary gods, rituals, and festivals, its own dialect, coins, citizen-armies, and proud military tradition. All this was swept away. One desperate response to the sudden sense of alienation was Cynicism: Diogenes preaches that the individual can be at home anywhere if only he can live the materially most minimalist life. Among classical scholars, Dudley is the primary representative of those who explain Cynic minimalism as an answer to the exile, poverty, wars, and slavery that afflicted the Hellenistic period: "Fortune, *Tyche*, ruling deity of the Hellenistic world, was the hostile power against whom Philosophy now erected her castles."[19]

Dudley's comments are important in that they highlight the conditions that gave Cynicism its continuing appeal throughout the Hellenistic and even the Roman periods. But a movement as widespread as Cynicism does not appear overnight, even despite the shocking defeat of the old *polis* at Chaeronea. Cynic sentiments had been brewing far in advance of the kingship of Alexander, and even of Philip. Diogenes may have come to Athens as early as 380; Xenophon's *Symposium* in which Antisthenes and Charmides praise poverty was written around 380, and has a dramatic date in the late 420s, almost a century before Alexander's death. As for Hellenistic insecurity and alienation, one should not idealize the classical period as one of unbroken serenity. Archaic and classical Greeks knew well the vicissitudes of Fortune and its many guises. The temples, proud homes of gods who know no suffering, were even more sublime to a people for whom child-mortality, disease, and early death were ever-present realities. There was a widespread fatalism, manifest in phenomena like sacrifice and divination: one's success or failure could be felt to rest "on the knees of the gods." So too, the Greek tragedians were haunted (as Aristotle recognizes) by the knowledge of how quickly fortune might be reversed: the tragedies of Oedipus, Agamemnon, Heracles, Priam, Hecuba, and Xerxes were performed before the Athenian people for the life-span of the Cleisthenic democracy, some two hundred years. Forced and voluntary exile were common long before Diogenes: Hippias, Demaratus, Themistocles, Aristides, Pausanias, Cimon, Thucydides, Alcibiades, Xenophon, and many other leaders were exiled; metics were economic exiles, by choice or necessity; and exile becomes a theme in the Attic tragedies. War also, with its many examples of prosperity ruined, demonstrated the fickleness of Fortune.[20] To Dudley's few examples of Hellenistic cities snuffed out over three centuries, one could point to the devastation of Phocaea (540), Sybaris (510), Miletus (494), Eretria (490), Histiaia (446), Agrigentum (405), Plataea (428, 373), Scione (421), Melos (416), Mycalessus (415), Olynthus (348), and others. Long before Alexander razed Thebes in 335, the prospect of slavery and extermination (*andrapodismos*) terrified the Theban chorus in Aeschylus' play.[21] The Athenians in 404 feared mass executions and exile, as just revenge for the atrocities they had committed at Scione and Melos;[22] in fact, Xerxes very nearly blotted out the city in 480. Even "undefeated" Sparta fought for its very life when Epaminondas invaded in 362. Hellenistic wars were fought by professional mercenaries, and consequently tended to be less impassioned and brutal than their classical predecessors: for the hired soldiers this was just a job, while for their noble kings it could be a kind of sport in which to demonstrate one's chivalry.[23] Finally, it was not true that the *polis* was always the all-embracing institution serving every social, psychological, and religious need: family life remained sacrosanct, its "unwritten laws" off-limits to state interference; sophists wandered in from abroad, bringing "wisdom" and excitement; Athenians had their mystery rites at Eleusis, and Orphic mystics might go from city to city, selling their exotic truths.[24] It is certainly true that in the large Hellenistic kingdoms many individuals lost a sense of immediate connection to the state. Yet the fourth century also knew a deep alienation of citizen from citizen, notably the bitter alienation between the poor and the rich. All this serves to remind us that Cynicism did not *arise* in reaction to Hellenistic conditions. Those conditions may have helped to perpetuate it, but it is indisputable that Diogenes, Antisthenes, Socrates, and others were preaching voluntary poverty, self-sufficiency, and independence from externals long before Alexander was even born.

A second theory of the origin of Cynicism is Marxist in inspiration.[25] According to this approach, Cynicism appears in those places of the Greek world—Athens, Corinth, Syracuse, Sinope—where the commercial ethos has undermined tradition and even brought about the monetarization of culture: in the trading emporium, the value of friendship, honor, patriotism, and learning is measured in coin like any commodity, and human relations are reduced to mere cash-relations. The market-economy indiscriminately pushes many victims—petty bourgeois, fallen gentry, intellectuals—into the army of surplus poor. Cynic intellectuals lashed out at the system with their diatribes and almost militant poverty. The vanguard of Cynic materialism begins the assault on the superstructure of ideals and rituals that keep the masses under; thus, the proletariat begins to awaken to consciousness of its dignity and power. As with the Hellenistic approach, there are important concepts here that need to be treated with greater historical and philological precision. Most notable are the quasi-Marxist notions that labor is the source of wealth, that the exploitation of labor is the cause of excessive private wealth, and that economic inequalities are a cause of envy, hatred, and even class-war. The Cynics were not Marxists, and would not have been sympathetic to Marx's complacent vision of utopia, but nevertheless all these ideas will be crucial especially to the Cynics' social agenda.

Different again is the psychological approach. Here a philosopher's views provide the ultimate inspiration for more detailed scholarly treatments. Nietzsche's *Genealogy of Morality* is his most powerful attack upon the figure of Socrates and what Nietzsche thought he represented. For Nietzsche, Socrates was the ugly son of a stonemason who could not compete with the likes of an Alcibiades or Plato in the traditional *agônes* of aristocratic culture. Therefore, he cunningly denigrated that culture and its heroic morality. *Aretê* is no longer a matter of physical beauty, strength, athleticism, poetry, and song. Now wisdom and moral goodness are beautiful, and to gain these prizes, one must compete in argument and dialectic. Crowns and honors are cheap baubles compared to spiritual wealth. Thus the plebeian Socrates leads the masses to revolt, and a "slave-morality" usurps the ethic of the old aristocratic masters. What before was considered dirty or diseased is now celebrated as divine. Temperance, justice, truthfulness, and eventually humility, charity, and love displace what alone is useful in a godless world: strength, cruelty, will—the virtues of a master-race. All this has been applied to the Cynics covertly. For though they might disclaim the influence of Nietzsche, some interpreters essentially sneer at the early Cynics. Thus Henne writes that the Cynic outlook developed in direct reaction to the social alienation that the early Cynics suffered. Antisthenes was the bastard son of a Thracian slave and Athenian father; not being a full Athenian citizen, he suffered the indignity of having to exercise in the Cynosarges, the gymnasium for half-breeds. Diogenes was an exile, Crates an ugly cripple, Monimus a slave. "[D]isgraced before their contemporaries and before fortune," Henne concludes, "should not all these unhappy men appeal from the laws of society to the laws of nature, before which rich and poor are equal?"[26] Müller reaches a similar verdict: Diogenes was "an outcast from his native city of Sinope; his asceticism was, in all probability, a refuge from his forfeited respectability and civic usefulness; and the socialism, which he openly preached, seemed to be inspired by the recklessness of a man who had no character to lose."[27] But Nietzsche lurks very near whenever the Cynic motto "to deface the coinage" is associated with his *Umwertung aller Werte*, a phrase itself inspired by Plato's Callicles.[28] Yet Nietzsche's views of Socrates, tragedy, and aristocratic morality are far from being the final word on Greek culture, and taken alone they do not cover all aspects of ancient Cynicism: most notably this approach wholly misses (as do the other four approaches summarized here) the martial aspect of Cynic asceticism, the psychological and physical toughness of the first Cynics that impressed soldiers like Onesicritus.

While Marxist and Nietzschean approaches would treat Cynicism as an effect of the dynamic of class struggle and of the internal politics of Greek cities, what could be termed the "Oriental hypothesis" looks outside of the Greek world altogether to stereotypes of a mystical East for the origins of Cynicism. In his *Diogenes of Sinope*, Sayre begins with the assumption that Cynicism is an essentially un-Greek phenomenon, and proceeds to manipulate the evidence to locate its true source in Indian asceticism. Sinope (as Sayre notes) occupied an important crossway for East-West trade. Since Diogenes' father was a banker and hence a money-trader, Diogenes had "at Sinope an opportunity to gain a considerable amount of information on the customs and ideas of the Indian people" and no doubt heard stories about the gymnosophists whom Onesicritus later met; Sayre suggests that these "naked sophists" were in fact Jains.[29] So Diogenes the Jain arrived in Athens, and "no one knew him" until Sayre finally exposed his real heritage: "this [Cynic] preference of inaction to action and supine acceptance of present conditions without striving to better them appears Oriental rather than Western and more Indian than Greek."[30] To support his contention, Sayre reinterprets the whole anecdotal tradition to argue that Diogenes himself was not an ascetic at all, but a hedonist who might sometimes live rough only because he was lazy and too much of a snob to work. Later Cynics exaggerated the stories of his asceticism in order to adapt their hero to the Orientalist spirit of their own, decadent age.[31]

Though Sayre's argument is generally criticized for its vehement bias, an Orientalist approach can be surprisingly common. The attempt to find not only Eastern influence but Eastern origins for Greek philosophy is at least as old as Gladisch's *Einleitung in das Verständniss der Weltgeschichte* (1841), and as new as 1996.[32] Höistad is an Orientalist at times, as is Arnold when in his influential *Roman Stoicism* he suggests a link between Cynicism and Buddhism.[33] So too in his article on Stoicism for Hastings' *Encyclopaedia of Religion and Ethics*, Arnold emphasizes the fact that the early Stoics came from the East (Citium, Tarsus, Soli, Assos). Zeno, Cleanthes, and Chrysippus were therefore not real Greeks, and Stoic ethics is at root a "Semitic morality." To quote Arnold himself:

> Rooted in the strong moral instincts of the Semites, it [Stoicism] grew to embrace the scientific knowledge of the Greeks. . . . Whether Zeno himself was of Phoenician or of Greek descent concerns us little; that at Athens he was nicknamed "the Phoenician" indicates that he brought with him to that city an atmosphere of Phoenician sentiment and morality.[34]

Again in Hastings' *Encyclopaedia*, Wenley's article on the Cynics makes Orientalist assumptions: "Running over the names, one is compelled to notice the large proportion of Cynics who came from the outskirts of Hellenic culture—Pontus, Thrace, Syria, Pamphylia, Egypt, for example; they were not nurtured in the pure Greek tradition."[35] Yet, it is not clear how "pure" the Greek tradition ever was: Abdera clung to the coast of barbaric Thrace, and Elea was a town in far western Italy, yet who would claim that Protagoras, Democritus, and Parmenides were "not nurtured in the pure Greek tradition"? In fact, the first Cynics were not Hellenized foreigners; Greek was their mother tongue. Nor were they from the periphery of the Greek world. Crates was a Theban, Monimus lived in Syracuse—two of the greatest Greek cities, particularly in the fourth century. Nor was Diogenes' Sinope a struggling outpost of Hellenism: it was the largest and richest colony of Miletus among the many Greek cities strung along the Black Sea coast, maintaining close ties with Periclean Athens and no doubt other cities that depended on grain imported from the area.[36]

Sayre's assumptions seem to have blinded him to the many Greek precedents for Cynicism, which he lists cursorily at the beginning of his chapter "The Sources of Cynicism." According to Sayre, they include Thersites, the Orphics, Heraclitus, Xenophanes, the Aristophanic Socrates, Aristippus, and literary pieces like Prodicus' "Choice of Heracles," Plato's *Protagoras*, Isocrates' *Against the Sophists*, and Xenophon's conversation between Aristippus and Socrates.[37] Sayre focuses more attention on Diodorus of Aspendus (the little-known fourth-century Pythagorean), then moves on to Odysseus, Aristides the Just, the Seven Wise Men, and so forth in random profusion. The whole forms a long list of unconnected quotations and cursory remarks. Yet in itself the list suggests that Cynicism was a rich and variegated phenomenon, that drew upon or echoed innumerable figures, themes, and works across centuries of Greek culture; that is, Diogenes' philosophy cannot be reduced to an adulterated form of Jainism, transmitted across half a continent to Sinope. Contrary to Arnold, one need only turn to parts of Hesiod, Xenophon, or even Plato (e.g., *Laws*) to find an absolutist and "stern Semitic morality." Thus, an Orientalist hypothesis perpetuates worn stereotypes about a mystical and unchanging East, and misses the true spirit of Greek Cynicism.

Höistad best succeeds in articulating some of the continuities between Greek traditions and Cynic asceticism. In his *Cynic Hero and Cynic King*, Höistad reinstates Antisthenes as the "first" Cynic who brought to prominence certain themes that were emerging especially in Attic tragedy: *ponos* (work, toil) is good, and the greatest heroes (notably Odysseus and Heracles) suffered the *ponoi* of slavery, dishonor, and exile before being recognized as the kings they were. Yet Höistad too cannot quite countenance an ascetic movement in classical Athens itself. Therefore, he suggests that neither Diogenes nor Antisthenes were radically ascetic. A "thoroughgoing asceticism" only later crept into the anecdotal tradition, under the gradual influence of Eastern religions on Hellenistic culture as a whole. In this orientalized environment, later Cynics felt the need to remodel their Diogenes and therefore made him far more ascetic, squalid, and eccentric than the follower of Antisthenes really was.[38]

Höistad's discussion of pre-Cynic treatments of *ponos* is important, but he too shows only a limited appreciation of how richly varied the Cynic rhetoric and outlook probably was. In the end, he falls back on the caricature of the Cynics as psychological and social misfits. The Cynics formed

> a philosophic sect which in its concentration on the individual loses and gradually deliberately rejects supra-individual points of view and connections, a sect which in addition, because of the social origin in circles without full political rights, was burdened by social and political discontent which formed an emotional background to a programme for the revision of values; a sect which, because of the above mentioned features, is distinctly non-intellectual and at the same time strongly emotional, attaches great importance to will and is inspired by a strong sense of mission; finally a sect which for the same reason is international and whose members were in a peculiar degree περιερχόμενοι [wanderers].[39]

The allusions to a "revision of values," to the will, to Heracles as a "Willensmensch," to the Cynic as an "ethical superman-type bent on his own perfection," and to the discontent and barely controlled emotionalism of the movement all recall Nietzsche, though once again, Nietzsche's name is never mentioned.[40]

A final approach might be termed philosophical. Here, Cynicism is a perennial human possibility, answering what Livingstone calls "a permanent need of the human spirit." Many cultures have their Cynics: "The Cynics are the spiritual kinsmen of the Indian Fakir, of the anchorite of the desert, of the begging friar; of Rousseau in the solitudes of the Hermitage, of Thoreau in the woods of Walden; there is something of them in the muscular Christian and in the bearer of the white man's burden; and something in all caravaners and campers-out."[41] Far from being a cultural perversion or a psychological abnormality, the Cynic renunciation of the artificialities of custom answers to the universal longing for some form of authentic freedom. Thus a personality like Diogenes often becomes more symbol than historical figure: a philosophical hero, even a kind of holy-man, for Epictetus, Marcus Aurelius, and Julian; a pagan saint for early Christians. Aquinas cites a story of Crates to prove that poverty is necessary for religious perfection, while others liken the Cynics to Jesus, the Desert Fathers, and the Franciscan and Dominican friars.[42] On the other hand, those who look for a more secular freedom revere the Cynics as champions of authenticity, honesty, and even reason itself. Thus, for Rousseau, Diogenes was an example of a natural man. Nietzsche's Zarathustra and the Mad Man of the *Gay Science* (both of whom proclaim the death of God in the marketplace) are modeled partly on the story of Diogenes carrying a lamp into the marketplace, looking for an honest man. More recently, the "cheekiness" of the first *Kynics* is offered as medicine for the excessive suspicions and negative *cynicism* of a postmodern "enlightenment." That is, Diogenes' ability to laugh amidst squalor and ignominy becomes an inspiration to post-Auschwitz generations, tormented by the simultaneous longing for affirmation and the determination never to forget man's radical evil. Thus, due especially to Sloterdijk and the older Foucault, Diogenes became in the late twentieth century an icon of honesty, courage, and humanity.[43] Truly a figure for the ages, for, leaping back through centuries, one finds the same themes informing Elizabethan appropriations of Diogenes. Most famously, Shakespeare's Lear will tarry in the storm in order to speak with the naked, raving Edgar—this "poor bare forked animal," to whom Lear refers repeatedly as "this philosopher," this "Athenian," this "Theban," as if it were Diogenes "the Athenian" or Crates of Thebes who was standing on the heath, suffering with the king; "Philosopher, tell me, what is the cause of thunder?"[44]

All these different approaches—the Hellenistic, Marxist, psychological, Orientalist, and philosophical—contain important insights. Yet their one shared error is to relegate Cynicism to the edges of classical culture, either temporally, spatially, or psychologically. It is as if Cynic asceticism were incompatible with classicism a priori: were not the Greeks a sensuous people with a spontaneous delight in bodily life? Or one thinks of how many generations repeated the pronouncement of Apollo in Delphi: "Nothing in excess." Greek moderation is proverbial, but Diogenes' sleeping in the stoa or Antisthenes' declaration "I would rather be mad than feel pleasure" seem to demonstrate none of the balance and proportion of the classical ideal. Therefore (the argument goes), they should not be placed next to Sophocles, Aristotle, or Lysippus. They must have been mad eccentrics, alienated proletarian intellectuals, dispossessed metics, cripples, bastards. One scholar looks for Eastern influence, as if Diogenes were a mystical Jain. Another speaks of Hellenistic alienation, as if Diogenes were a mercenary soldier settled by a Seleucid king in farthest Afghanistan. Others abandon historical context altogether to make Cynicism and ancient *Zynismus* a rallying cry of freedom and authenticity.[45]

Yet the a priori assumptions partly inspiring these approaches are wrong, in my view: Cynicism should be seen as a purely classical phenomenon, with deep roots in many aspects of the Greek experience. Our motivating question therefore becomes: Why did Cynicism emerge during the fourth century throughout the Greek world? This question is a determinate one, and has not been answered, or even asked, in a methodical way.[46] Nor is it an insignificant one, given the geographical and temporal range of Cynicism. The first Cynics came from and frequented all corners of the Greek world and hailed from many social classes. Diogenes' birthplace was Sinope on the Black Sea Coast, but he lived later in Athens and Corinth, and appears as a visitor in Delphi, Delos, Olympia, Sparta, Aegina, Crete, and elsewhere.[47] Hegesias the "Dog-Collar" was from Sinope. Crates was a citizen of Thebes. Metrocles and Hipparchia came from Maroneia in Thrace. Monimus was a slave at Syracuse. Onesicritus was born in Astypalaea, a city in Aegina (or perhaps an island in the Cyclades). Politicians and thinkers who associated with the Cynics were from all areas: Phocion was an Athenian, Stilpo a Megarian, and Zeno who first "heard" Crates was of Phoenician background, from Citium in Cyprus. Sinope, Maroneia, Citium, Syracuse—the Cynics' cities span much of the Greek world. Similarly broad were the Cynics' backgrounds—commercial (Diogenes, Zeno), landed (Crates, Metrocles, Hipparchia), and slave (Monimus). A movement can attract such interest only if it articulates ideas, aspirations, or fears that are already fairly widespread. Its appeal must have had some depth also, for the Cynic outlook survived for up to nine hundred years, until the beginning of the Byzantine period. These considerations alone would suggest that Cynicism was not an overnight growth, and may even have been the fruit of a long development. Given its appeal, it must have tapped something significant in the Greek consciousness. Fully to answer the question of origins, therefore, one must attempt a broad interpretation of Greek culture from the Cynics' own point of view.

This point of view has been distilled into various key phrases or ideas. Some focus on the Cynic nature-custom (*nomos-phusis*) distinction and make the "dog-philosophy" a form of naturalism, primitivism, a "vigorous philosophical revolt against civilization in nearly all its essentials."[48] A slightly different variation would make Cynicism an offshoot of the Sophistic movement, with its focus on the individual, and its anti-nomianism and atheism.[49] Others would emphasize shamelessness (*anaideia*) and outspokenness (*parrhêsia*) as the core aspects of Cynicism: the Cynic *parrhesiast* takes up the cause of the Old Comic hero, and asserts the rights and talents of the common man against generals, politicians, intellectuals, and all such posers (*lalountes*). Foucault and Sloterdijk have developed such themes in a postmodern context, but the parallel with Attic comedy has not been fully explored. Finally, a scholar like Navia senses that the quips and antics attributed to the first Cynics are not random acts of humor or lunacy, but stem instead from a single vision. He would therefore base the Cynic outlook on a multiplicity of implicit concepts:

> Concepts such as "a life lived according to nature," rationality, lucidity, self-sufficiency, disciplined asceticism, freedom of speech, shamelessness, indifference, cosmopolitanism, philanthropy, and others, permeate in varying degrees the Cynic *Weltanschauung*, and constitute, as it were, the foundations of their philosophy.[50]

If one were to focus, however, on a single concept as central to ancient Cynicism, it should, I think, be their renunciation of wealth. This can be treated as the basis for their ideals of self-sufficiency, ascetic poverty, shamelessness, even cosmopolitanism and philanthropy. So too the Cynic renunciation of custom (*nomos*) is framed in economic terms. That is, the Cynic motto *paracharattein to nomisma* refers both literally to the defacing of coins (*nomismata*), and metaphorically to the defacing of custom (*nomos*): defacing actual coinage becomes the physical counterpart of Diogenes' mission as a Cynic. Moreover, the use of the ambiguous word *nomisma* (commonly meaning both coinage and custom) implies that *nomoi* (customs) are themselves inextricably bound up with the love of wealth.[51] To put coins out of currency becomes, therefore, the first and foremost act of the Cynic renunciation of custom: Diogenes defaces the coinage of Sinope; Crates sells his land and throws the money away, or gives it to the poor; Hipparchia ignores her parents' desire for a match more lucrative than her chosen Crates; Metrocles forgoes the luxury of a Peripatetic education for the free company of Diogenes; Monimus throws money about the bankers' tables in the marketplace; and so on, through the Cynic tradition. Thus, the renunciation of wealth serves almost as a rite of initiation into the Cynics' world. It remains their prime task ever afterward, as they mock the rich for their *hubris*, the poor for their petty materialism, and everyone for the greed and self-interest that ruins higher goods like friendship, virtue, and clarity of mind.

Such an equation of *nomisma* and *nomos*, economic and cultural life, is a remarkably reductive attitude to adopt. Yet the Cynics would not have been alone in espousing it. Aristotle, for instance, criticizes those who would measure all values by a monetary standard and reduce all human goods and talents to differences in wealth; Aristotle notes that these are often the wealthy.[52] At the other extreme are the indigent Cynics who in their utter contempt for such a view would in fact completely invert it: to them, everything truly valuable cannot be measured against money, and in fact, cannot exist simultaneously with wealth at all. Virtue is the only really worthy end, but to attain this one must renounce all wealth, and all activities and relations that involve wealth: the Cynic does not marry or have children,[53] does not work for a living or employ others, does not sacrifice to the traditional gods in expectation of a reward, does not accept citizenship in a state or fight its wars. All these relations are internalized and privatized, so that in his utter self-sufficiency the Cynic becomes his own family, friends, gods, fatherland, and army. But the "coin" that is brightest in their rhetorical treasure-chest is the conceit that the Cynic, in his poverty, is "rich." Utterly opposed, then, to the snobbery of the aristocrat or plutocrat—who thinks that the rich alone are good, beautiful, just, eloquent, intelligent, self-restrained, courageous, and warlike—is the Cynic, who disdains the rich for being unable to emulate *his* virtue, valor, invincibility, temperance, wisdom, fluency, honesty, and kindness. An ascetic poverty is the training ground of virtue.

How Greek are these assertions? Is Cynic asceticism not an anomaly within classical culture? For in general the classical Greeks did *not* praise poverty. Laments for the hardships and sufferings of poverty ring down the ages. For Achilles, only death itself is worse than being a serf and a land-less man. For Hesiod, "cursed poverty wastes a man's courage." Theognis cries that it is better for a poor man to fling himself from a cliff than to live. Athenian litigants appealed to their poverty to soften a popular jury. Aeschines claims that old age and poverty are "the greatest evils in the world". In Menander's *Dyskolos*, poverty is personified as an ugly old hag who sits in a corner and makes the household miserable by her mere presence.[54] But most furious is Chremylus' rant against Poverty in Aristophanes' *Plutus*:

> You—what good can you bring but blisters from the bath? and hungry children at the heel and a gaggle of old hags, a heap of lice, gnats and fleas which buzz about your head stinging, waking you and whispering "You are hungry, get up!" What else do you bring? To wear rags instead of a robe; to sleep not on a bed but on rushes and straw filled with bugs which bite you awake; to own a rotten mat instead of a carpet; to lay your head not on a pillow but on a large rock; to eat branches instead of mallow, and instead of bread, the tops of dry radishes. Yes indeed, are you not the cause of all these benefits to mankind?[55]

Not surprisingly then, no less an authority than Moses Finley has concluded, "The judgment of antiquity about wealth was fundamentally unequivocal and uncomplicated. Wealth was necessary and it was good; it was an absolute requisite for the good life; and on the whole that was all there was to it."[56]

And yet attitudes towards wealth and poverty were not so univocal as Chremylus and Finley suggest. In fact, wealth was hedged round with many social sanctions, while poverty and the working, free poor (as opposed to slaves or indigent beggars) could be and were associated with such virtues as honesty, justice, temperance, industry, courage, strength, and physical fitness. If anything, the "discovery" of the unconscious should encourage one to think through seemingly univocal statements to a deeper mindset, and to the mass of intuitions, desires, and phobias that are felt, if not always openly articulated. Thus, while not explicitly stated or systematically developed, there was a "praise of poverty" *implicit* or *latent* in Greek culture before the Cynics. This praise of poverty is subconscious in the sense that it may not be overtly espoused and asserted in its entirety, yet stray comments, associations of thought, and seemingly anomalous statements slip out, suggesting that unequivocally materialistic statements lie just at the surface of far more nuanced feelings. Moreover, one must posit such a general outlook if one is to explain the general appeal of Cynicism. Cryptic here, these remarks will hopefully become clearer when we turn in the individual chapters to the several components that make up the Greek praise of poverty, and that ground the various aspects of Cynic asceticism. But before turning to a survey of these components and chapters, a few words about asceticism in general.

Misunderstandings of Cynic asceticism can arise from the mistaken view that all asceticism is religious asceticism. For this is perhaps its most common guise: the holy man rushes into the wilderness to mortify the flesh and earn a glimpse of the divine fire. Historical examples abound: the Hebrew prophets, Essenes, Yogis, Jains, Buddhist monks, Muslim sufis and zahids, Christian *flagellantes*, hermits, monks, friars, and all those who emulate the poverty and passion of Christ. But religious ascetics are rare in the Greek context. We hear from Homer about the Silloi of Dodona, priests of Zeus who slept on the ground and did not wash their feet—hardly an austere group if one compare them, say, to the Irish monks of Sceilig Michael. The Silloi do not appear again in archaic or classical literature, and other religious ascetics are rare: Pythagorean mysticism had a slight ascetic component, Plato's philosopher-kings endured poverty in order to train for the vision of the Good, and the Platonic Socrates states that he was poor "in service" of Apollo in Delphi.[57]

But the relative absence in Greece of the ideal of religious asceticism does not make asceticism itself a foreign or "Oriental" entity. Ascetics are not always inspired by love of the divine or the religious longing to transcend the body. A more inclusive definition of the ascetic is one who consistently forgoes immediate pleasure for the sake of some greater good. Where one draws the line between the ascetic and nonascetic is as arbitrary as where one separates pleasure from pain: some are less sensitive than others, and the plump Trimalchio might die of shock just to hear stories of zealots eating insects and sleeping on nails. Such stories are indeed astounding, particularly when ascetics are overcome by a sudden sense of shame. Feeling that they have grown soft and self-indulgent, they redouble their efforts in fury. The leather lash now has studs of iron or glass; the straw-mat goes out, and they sleep on broken stones; they wander higher into the mountains, away from their complacent brethren, ardent for a more intense transcendence. Again, religious asceticism may provide the most inspiring or lurid cases of self-deprivation, but these should not blinker one to the existence of other ascetic types, who seek a different "good." I will call these categories the social, military, and intellectual forms of asceticism.

The social ascetic subordinates immediate personal pleasure to the good of the community. This may be the asceticism of parents who go hungry so that their children may eat. Or it is the asceticism of reformers and rebels who sacrifice personal wealth and advancement for some idealistic end—revenge, justice, equality, the coming utopia. Modern instances might include Marx living in poverty and writing furiously to further a proletarian revolution, or men like Tolstoy and Kropotkin who all but renounced their inherited rank out of solidarity with the working classes. Such social idealism is an important motive in fourth-century Greece, when various political figures, including the Cynics, propose renunciation and even poverty as a means to more harmonious class-relations.

The greatest action of a Greek man's life was to fight in battle for his city, ancestors, family, and gods. Therefore, the rhetoric of military asceticism is prevalent, even pervasive. Older men chastise their juniors, telling them to be ashamed of themselves, to remember their forebears and the glorious traditions of the state. One must not languish in luxury, making speeches and enjoying symposia, while the enemy is mustering for battle: where is your *aretê*, young men? In response, the military ascetic renounces present pleasure to harden himself for the rigors of campaign—the hot summers, cold winters, long marches, baggage, weariness, hunger, wounds. Roman militarism made military ascetics the quintessential Roman patriots.[58] Spartan militarism also produced many generations of military ascetics, among whom King Agesilaus might be mentioned with distinction.[59] In Athens, the funeral oration seeks to inspire the patriot to love his city before all else, and for her sake to enthusiastically expose his body to dangers, toils, and death. The heroes of the *epitaphioi logoi* were by rule unnamed, but one can single out other individuals as military ascetics—Timoleon, Epaminondas, Phocion, Xenophon's Cyrus, Plato's philosopher-kings, the fashionable Spartophiles in Athens (*hoi Lakonizontes*), even perhaps Socrates, or at least some people's view of him.[60] So too, the Cynics described their asceticism in military terms: poverty makes them "invincible" against the onslaughts of Fortune.

Finally, intellectual ascetics live in a garret, eat little, and save their money for their studies. Thus, Chaucer's Oxford clerk

> Would rather have at his bed's head
> Some twenty books, all bound in black and red,
> Of Aristotle and his philosophy
> Than rich robes, fiddle, or gay psaltery.[61]

This category could include many philosophers—Democritus, Socrates, Archimedes, Spinoza, Nietzsche, Wittgenstein—as well as many more poets and starving artists. The Greek tradition knew something of the bohemian poet: Hipponax at least dons the persona of the scrounging artist.[62] Diogenes and Crates fall into this class of ascetics, too, when they fling away their money and live rough for the sake of the wisdom of the "dog."

Thus Cynicism has aspects of intellectual, military, and social asceticisms; it even had a religious subtext, to be emphasized by some later interpreters,[63] even though the Cynics themselves denied any divine inspiration for their poverty. Indeed, sometimes the Cynics would deny that they are motivated by any external or "higher" goods. Their explicit asceticism, then, can take on a paradoxical tone: the Cynic ascetic renounces immediate pleasure in order to gain—immediate pleasure! It is not for religious revelation that the Cynic trains himself, nor for war, nor for some subtle intellectual discovery, nor even for the common good. All these externally given ends are so much "smoke" (*tuphos*): the traditional gods are unreal; war is evil, patriotism and duty mere words; Academics and other intellectuals are fakes or snobs; the masses are fools too often deluded by whatever they are told. Not seeking a higher truth or the common safety, the Cynic is a thorough individualist. Having nothing is the key to personal happiness, because, paradoxically, "despising pleasures is the greatest of pleasures."[64] Diogenes had more fun in his tub than Xerxes in luxurious Babylon,[65] and one later literary Diogenes can enthuse to Lady Happiness about the pleasures of pain:

"I [Diogenes] will remain, O Happiness, on account of you and drink water and eat water cress and sleep on the ground." She answered me and said, "I will make hardships more pleasant for you than the benefits to be obtained from wealth, which men prefer and ask of me, not perceiving that they are entrusting themselves to a tyrant." When I heard Happiness say that eating and drinking these things was not training but pleasure, it impelled me to this way of living.[66]

And yet, once again, one need not take such pronouncements at their face value. It is a mistake both to accept Cynic asceticism as an "end-in-itself" or, at the other extreme, to reject it as a cover for hypocritical sensualism.[67] With regard to the second extreme, the fact that Cynic asceticism is known darkly through the glass of the later anecdotal tradition should not lead one to dismiss those stories as outright fabrications or distortions of an unrecoverable original. There is no smoke without fire, and Aristotle would hardly have referred to Diogenes without explanation as "the Dog" if he were not already a fairly notorious character around Athens.[68] Nor was Cynic asceticism a foreign import. The ascetic ideal was a living one in the fourth century, and had social, militaristic, and intellectual variants. Furthermore, one need not be wholly seduced by the occasional Cynic claim to choose asceticism as an end-in-itself. Asceticism is never such an end; pain is rarely chosen for its own sake. Some other motive is also operative, whether it be the desire to assert one's toughness, test one's limits, or prove a point. Other previous ascetics, mentioned briefly above, sought some social, military, or philosophical goods, and it is these general types (rather than the religious ascetic) that the first Cynics most resemble.

All the various strands of this proto-Cynic ascetic tradition I here include under the rubric of the Greek praise of poverty. This praise of poverty will take us through three essential spheres of Greek culture—work, war, and philosophical wisdom—that in turn yield precedents to the social, military, and intellectual components of Cynic asceticism. How did some Greeks sense that poverty and the poor were worthy of praise? In economic life, industriousness, usefulness, frugality, temperance, justice, and honesty are virtues typically associated with the working poor. Rich oligarchs may claim to be the "best" or the "good and beautiful," and may vilify the poor with a torrent of names (the "bad," the "lesser"), but theirs is a minority view. Here, quasi-Marxist themes are prevalent: the Cynics' voluntary frugality becomes at times an almost public avowal of solidarity with the ideally virtuous worker. Chapter 3, on war, moves away from social asceticism and poverty as class phenomena, and focuses on traditional notions of heroism and patriotism, which often transcend class. Many legends and wars could corroborate the view that what is important in battle is not material resources, but strength, courage, valor, and discipline. For instance, Croton defeated Sybaris, Greece Persia, Sparta Athens, Thebes Sparta, and Macedonia Persia: from a limited viewpoint, therefore, history seems to demonstrate that personal "virtue" is superior to all external supports. The philosophers, and ultimately the Cynics, capitalize on these typical associations of Greek poverty and martial valor. In the fourth chapter, I discuss how the Greek tradition, particularly after Parmenides, tends to identify philosophical wisdom with a nonsensual reality. The philosopher is understood to be a creature apart: he accepts physical poverty to gain intellectual "riches," for it is only by transcending the body's trivial demands that one rises above one's parochial origins to knowledge of eternal and universal truths. There are many variations on the Eleatic dichotomy between the Way of Truth and the Way of Seeming. The Platonic sage is in some ways a religious ascetic who gives up money, honor, and pleasure for the divine music of mathematics and dialectic: "God always does geometry." Operating in the same general cultural rubric, the Cynic sage renounces the things of external Fortune to gain an absolute internal freedom. Here the Cynics are at their most negative and most idealistic at once. Their wisdom is a total skepticism with regard to externality: nothing can be known or possessed except the inner self, and so one should renounce all externals in order to gain an absolute "wealth" in one's own self-certainty.

Taken into the thickets of Greek literature, historiography, and philosophy, all this will, paradoxically, make a simple philosophy seem quite complicated. But there are still more complications. For just as the notion of a praise of poverty is paradoxical and counterintuitive, so too Cynicism was a paradoxical philosophy. Again, this paradoxomania is not the idiosyncrasy of a few philosophers but perhaps the crowning proof of the Greek creative intelligence. Their love of subtlety, argument, contradiction, and paradox reaches back to the mythmakers with their subtle Hermes, Prometheus, and Sisyphus. Here Odysseus is the canonical hero, that canny "No Man" who yet plays so many roles and whose cunning triumphs in every situation. Elsewhere, intense realizations uncover the contradictions of a situation, as in the lamentations of Attic tragedy, Heraclitus' union of opposites, or funeral encomia. But most of all, the lover of argument knows how a position can slip by imperceptible degrees into its opposite. Hence, the Sophistic "wise man" makes a practice of arguing *sic et non:* see especially the *Dissoi Logoi*, Thucydides' paired speeches arguing opposite sides, the *agôn* of the Old Comedy (e.g., *Clouds, Plutus*), or the antic display of Euthydemus in the Platonic dialogue bearing his name. Other Sophists showed off their rhetorical prowess by praising the unpraiseable: Alcidamas wrote a praise of death; Polycrates composed encomia of mice, pebbles, Clytaemnestra, a pot. He may even have written a *laus inopiae*, that in turn may have served as the basis for the arguments of Poverty in Aristophanes' *Plutus*. Prodicus' allegorical "Choice of Heracles" praises toil and pain, leading Zeller to construe it as equivalent to a "praise of poverty."[69] Plato's *Phaedo* praises philosophical death; in the *Gorgias*, Socrates defends the counterintuitive proposition that "it is better to suffer than to commit injustice"; Plato, the Cynics, and the Stoics emphatically maintain that "nothing external can harm the good man." The Cynics too had their own quasi-Sophistic *paignia* and *spoudogeloia:* Crates wrote songs in praise of the Cynic's beggar-bag (*pêra*), frugality (*eutelia*), and lentil soup (*phagês enkômion*).[70] Such paradoxomania remained part of Greek culture, not only in later Cynics like Bion and Lucian, but in general, for Juvenal complains about the clever *Graeculus esuriens* who can conquer anything with his rhetoric: well might the more stolid Roman say—*timeo Danaos et dona ferentes*.[71] Cynic-like paradoxes remain popular in postmodern circles: Larre, for instance, entitles a recent book *Diogène ou la science du bonheur*, even though the ancient Cynics repudiated both science and societal honor.

The Cynics then were thoroughly Greek in their willingness to surprise traditional expectations; these anarchists were not the first to flout the "laws" of thought. In the following chapters, we will treat four paradoxes as defining the Cynic position: poverty is wealth, idleness is work, powerlessness is power, and wisdom is foolishness.

Before explicating these paradoxes, a word about methodology. The statements, themes, and sources for Cynic asceticism and the Greek praise of poverty are various, interrelated, and overlapping. Sometimes the same or similar sources will be treated from different angles, but I have tried to avoid all unnecessary repetition. With regard to use of the sources, I do not try to engage in the precise *Quellenforschung* of, say, Höistad: given the state of the evidence, it is impossible to know which anecdotes might really be historical or not, what Diogenes or Crates may have said or done at any precise moment.[72] Indeed, this type of precision may not be necessary: the notion of asceticism itself is an elastic one and admits various degrees, as we have seen. Rather, I seek here to demonstrate the more general point that Greek economic conditions and historical experience provided a fertile ground for various forms of asceticism and therefore for Cynicism. In uncovering these conditions, I have tried to maintain a balance between factual assertions and larger intellectual considerations. The latter demand a variety of perspectives so that the challenge is not to find the single "right" approach or answer, but rather to make one's understanding as textured as possible.

While final, definitive statements about Greek culture remain elusive, an imaginative use of existing literature can still yield much. Of the many dialogues, comedies, tragedies, letters, and poems attributed to Crates, Diogenes, and the early Cynics, little remains apart from a few scattered quotations (collected in Giannantoni, *Socraticorum Reliquiae*). These are supplemented by a mass of anecdotal material in later authors such as Plutarch, Lucian, Epictetus, Dio Chrysostom, Marcus Aurelius, Julian, and the Greek Church Fathers. More important for the project of interpreting Cynicism as a Greek phenomenon is the even greater mass of classical literature. Here any author may mention something of direct or indirect relevance, but Hesiod, Herodotus, Aristophanes, Xenophon, and Plato evince perhaps the most sympathy for a proto-Cynic praise of poverty. In treating this classical material, a close attention to language is necessary. A common association of words indicates a corresponding association of ideas. Words for "wealth," for instance, are commonly associated with "hubris"; the implication, then, is that the wealthy could often act in ways that were resented as hubristic. Throughout the study, I examine as closely as is here relevant words and phrases used in connection with wealth, poverty, luxury, work, *aretê*, and related notions, while noting as much as possible how connotations changed relative to context and historical period.

But to turn from planning the journey to the road itself. The Greek praise of poverty grew out of the limits imposed by the austere Greek landscape. The relative poverty of the place ensured that great accumulations of wealth were not easy or common. Hard work and temperance were necessary not only economically, but socially, for all had to contribute to the common stock if envy, hatred, and even civil war were to be avoided. The poverty of the Greek landscape also contributed to its defense, notably during the Persian invasions; traditional hard living was celebrated as one cause of Greek virility, machismo, and military valor. Finally, many Greek thinkers looked beyond the physical world itself as a realm of limitation and finitude. Physical life is a small and poor thing, but it is only in recognizing and welcoming this fact that the human being, as mind and soul, can become something greater. Wisdom is not knowing many things, but knowing the one essential thing—one's absolute freedom from physical externals. The Cynic position synthesizes these disparate and partially articulated elements of the praise of poverty. Democratic populism, Greek heroism, philosophical yearning for some absolute affirmation—these are the major ideas that precede the emergence of Cynic asceticism and its various paradoxes. That is, the Greek *laus inopiae* preceded and conditioned the rise of early Cynicism. More succinctly still, and to revise Nietzsche, the following chapters will investigate the birth of Cynicism from the *spirit* of poverty.

CHAPTER TWO

Praise of Poverty and Work

Hail! goddess and mistress, delight of the wise—
Frugality, the child of famed Temperance.
All those who practise justice honor your virtue.
      —From Crates' "Hymn to Thrift," fr. 11 (Giannantoni, V H 77)

I do not want to heap up bright money—the happiness of the beetle,
The riches of the ant—or to become mad for wealth,
But rather would I share in justice and gather wealth
That is easy to carry, easy to acquire, and honored for virtue.
If I happen upon these, I will worship Hermes and the Muses,
Not with luxurious expenses, but with holy virtues.
      —Crates, fr. 18, in Julian. *Or.* 7.9 (Giannantoni, V H 84.20–25)

The sentiments expressed in Crates' lines are remarkable, both in themselves and for the light they shed upon widespread attitudes towards work, wealth, and the moral virtues. Crates' contrast between the Cynic and the spend-all is stark. The Cynic basks in the inspiration of the gods, while his opposite scurries to and fro, gathering and consuming endlessly. On the one side lie the "riches" of justice and virtue; on the other, the wealth of ants and beetles, dirty, difficult to acquire, and burdensome. Holiness is contrasted with luxury, virtue with expenditure. Yet such polarities play at the edge of paradox, for without some of the "beetle's wealth," a moral person will be very poor, regardless of virtue.

This seeming contradiction—that "poverty is wealth"—was central to the Cynic internalization of values. In a playful syllogism, Diogenes is said to have proved that the wise man possesses everything: the gods possess everything, friends share all things in common, the wise man is the friend of the gods, hence the conclusion follows easily.[1] As a "rich" man, Diogenes jokes that he too attracts flatterers and parasites—the mice that share his hovel.[2] Later, in Hellenized cities of the East, Cynic street-preachers would shout to passersby, "Only the poor man is rich!"[3] Cynic paradoxomania would come to infect Stoics and Epicureans as they too celebrate the "wealth" of the poor philosopher. The sixth paradox of Cicero's *Paradoxa Stoicorum* is devoted to the proposition that "the wise man alone is rich." When his trading-ship foundered off the Attic coast, Zeno came to associate with Crates; long after he used to say that he never made such a prosperous voyage as when he was shipwrecked.[4] Again, Zeno considered the beggar to be not only blessed but rich,[5] and would himself be most contented with some green figs and a sunny spot.[6] Plutarch's Stoic cries out from the colonnade, "I alone am king! I alone am rich!"[7] There may be Stoic, and thus ultimately Cynic influence in certain statements of St. Paul: "Poor, we make many rich; having nothing, we possess everything."[8] Finally, the Epicureans, despite their anti-teleological metaphysics, also celebrate the "wealth" of the poor sage. For Epicurus, poverty measured against natural ends is "great wealth," and therefore the sage can be supremely happy on water and cheap bread. For Lucretius, "there is no poverty in owning little."[9]

But Cynic paradoxomania does not end here. The rhetoric, heroic exemplars, and lifestyle of the Cynics all suggest another central paradox: "idleness is work." The Cynics adopted Heracles as their mythic prototype: just as Heracles' Labors led to his apotheosis, so the "labors" (*ponoi*) of the typical Cynic bring him happiness, virtue, and a god-like security. Antisthenes sets the keynote here with his maxim "toil (*ponos*) is good." This and similar sentiments have often been misinterpreted. Are these fragments of a lost Cynic "Gospel of Work?"[10] Or perhaps the Cynics were proto-Marxists proclaiming solidarity with the working class? "This is perhaps the greatest and most important historical contribution of the otherwise much maligned Cynics: that they exalted the dignity and worth of honest toil by endowing it with a high moral significance."[11] In fact, a "gospel" of work would give the highest significance to manual labor. But the Cynics hardly preached the holiness of carpentry and tent-making. *Ponos* is not a means to salvation, and idleness is not the devil's opportunity. Nor did they "work" to prepare the way for the earthly salvation of a communist utopia. For all their rhetoric of *ponos* and Heracles, the Cynics avoided physical labor and were resolute idlers. And yet, in their view, such ascetic idleness is a form of beneficial "work." How did this paradox emerge, and what was its appeal?

In brief, these two paradoxes appealed to certain social aspects of a "Greek praise of poverty." In the context of economic life—of production, consumption, and attitudes towards wealth as both a material and a social phenomenon—this "praise of poverty" could be summarized as follows. Wealth is not an unequivocal good, and in fact can often be both morally evil and practically undesirable. For manual labor is the real source of wealth, and those who do the necessary economic work are "the salt of the earth": industrious, frugal, honest, just, generous, pious. But too often the produce of their labor is appropriated by others more powerful, cunning, or organized. As a result, peasants and artisans remain relatively poor despite their crucial economic contribution, while a few others accumulate great private fortunes by bribes, lawsuits, confiscation, or other more subtle schemes. The luxuriousness, injustice, and *hubris* of these idle rich are generally recognized. Some go further to ask, "Why would one want to be rich?" For unless a rich person turns tyrant to lord it over resentful "slaves," he must live in a community with fellow citizens who will make demands of him. The richer he is, the greater the demands, particularly in a democratic city. Here he must shoulder burdensome religious and military duties; he must pay taxes. Even so, he is still plagued by informants, thieves, and a thousand other plotters. His wealth may afford him some costly luxuries but their moral and physical benefits are dubious. Money will not buy time, leisure, and freedom from worry, because money enslaves the mind: the more one has, the more one wants. The instinct for accumulation is insatiable, and all the while one must continually scurry, like the ant, to safeguard one's pile. But if only one could see that nature provides abundantly for necessary needs, one would embrace a voluntary simplicity. Indeed, the lot of the poor man is often better. In his own city, he may even be a "king" whom none may disturb.

Such a praise of poverty is never presented as a whole in the extant literature. A few passages—Prodicus' "Choice of Heracles," the argument of *Penia* in Aristophanes' *Plutus*, the speeches of Charmides and Antisthenes in Xenophon's *Symposium*, the friendship of Pheraulas and the Sacian in Xenophon's *Cyropaedia*—broach many of the essential themes. Other ingredients of a *laus inopiae* appear elsewhere, scattered through the literature as far back as Hesiod. The following chapter will attempt to collect and reanimate these *disiecta membra* into a living whole that can be readily recognized as a predecessor to the first two Cynic paradoxes. Here, the Greek praise of poverty is intimately related to economic conditions prevalent in the late fifth and fourth centuries. In addition to this deeper structural and psychological precedent, there are more specific proximate causes for the emergence of Cynicism in the fourth century—growing population, scarcity of food, and rising inequalities between rich and poor, attended by a host of social tensions. In such an environment, the first Cynics articulated in an uncompromising way what had long been felt and partially expressed: to remain a good person, and indeed to stay happy and sane, one must to some degree forswear wealth and even the desire for wealth, for money is the "mother-city of all evil."

In pursuing the social aspects of Cynic asceticism, I will tackle our two paradoxes in turn. The paradox that "poverty is wealth" gains plausibility for two main reasons. First are moral considerations. Wealth is typically linked with injustice, hubris, lack of self-restraint, and other vices. Associations of the corresponding virtues and poverty are less explicit, but these too surface before the Cynics asserted them more boldly. A second consideration is that certain stubborn material "facts" could make Cynic renunciation a reasonable, even attractive option. In an economy of scarcity, limited production as well as limited outlets for consumption and investment ensure that money, and material wealth generally, played a small role in individual happiness: money can buy little of real value. What is truly important cannot be bought or sold like a commodity. Health, friendship, self-regard, the various virtues that distinguish one as an excellent human being and that enable one to face life's contingencies—such goods depend more on individual disposition and choice than on riches. Material wealth can come and go in a day: *Tuchê* (Fortune), and the power of the gods, is as inscrutable as it is ruthless. Thoughtful people therefore often ranked wealth fairly low in the total economy of life; the Cynic ranked it lowest, but they were only the most radical of "the wise."

The second paradox sees a gradual internalization of the virtues associated with work and poverty. Traditionally one works for a subsistence living and then gives thanks. A new work-ethic emerges in the late fifth and fourth centuries. In certain influential circles, work loses its primary economic purpose and becomes seen as *the* means to self-actualization. One "works" to complete oneself; one's characteristic activities stem from and perfect one's inner nature. Different interpretations of this new stance bring us to the *seemingly* opposite positions of the imperialist and philosopher. Each is idle according to traditional notions of work. Yet their nonproductive *ponos* is directed towards what is seen as a higher good. For the imperialist, this good is a blend of power, honor, and wealth. The philosopher shuns such worldly ends for an inner perfection. Yet, as if to prove his social worth, the philosopher also calls this inner virtue "wealth." Gathering up all these threads of thought and weaving together the language and sentiments of an inchoate praise of poverty, the Cynic proclaims explicitly that in idleness, he "works" for the sake of "wealth" and that, therefore, though "poor," he is as "rich" as kings.

"Poverty is Wealth"

What is wealth? What is poverty? Quantitative vs. qualitative wealth

To return to the first paradox: if Antisthenes or Diogenes could plausibly call poverty wealth, then one first must consider typically classical notions of these phenomena. What, according to popular attitudes, was wealth? What was poverty? One prevalent scholarly answer is, I think, misguided in its attempt to draw a sharp distinction between Greek and modern notions. It relies too heavily upon Socratic ideas, which are not wholly traditional, even though these do return to a valorization of traditional frugality. I quote from Austin and Vidal-Naquet at length, as this textbook depiction of Greek views has often been repeated or echoed:

> What, finally, was the Greek definition of wealth and poverty? For us wealth and poverty refer to two extremes which do not overlap: one is wealthy if one has more than is necessary to live an honourable life, one is poor if one has less than this minimum. Consequently there are many between the extremes who are neither wealthy nor poor. The criterion is not the need for work in itself, but whether one has attained a certain standard of wealth: one may be wealthy and work, or one may be poor and idle. The Greek definition was quite different: the two categories did not correspond to two extremes, on the contrary they touched each other and could even overlap. The criterion was not a given standard of wealth but the need for work. A Greek was wealthy if he could live without having to work, poor if he did not have enough to live on without working. From this point of view the majority of people in Greece were poor since they had to work. In addition, the Greeks drew a distinction between the poor man and the beggar who was completely destitute and was forced to live off the generosity of other people. Very often moral qualities were attached to notions of wealth and poverty: wealth was generally considered a blessing and a precondition for the development of human virtues, whereas poverty was a misfortune, which corrupted man and made him incapable of virtue. . . . All this brings one back to what was said earlier on the absence of any positive evaluation of work:

leisure and the absence of need for economic activity represented a very widespread ideal.[12]

There are several points here that need some qualification. First, there was indeed a strong element of social snobbery, as well as a disdain for work as a form of mild slavery.[13] But one should not overestimate such negative attitudes in a culture that depended largely on free peasant labor. Aristocrats and oligarchs refer to themselves as the "best," the "good and beautiful," and many other terms, while the poor are despised as "the lesser" or "the bad."[14] But this was the self-serving language of a minority. Other attitudes persisted in other classes, even if those are not as well represented in the extant, often elitist literature. Furthermore, conflicting views can coexist not only within one culture, but within one individual. Hence one should not conclude simplistically from a few rhetorically charged passages in, say, Plato or Demosthenes that the snobbery there expressed was typical of those authors, not to mind classical culture as a whole.[15] Such passages ostensibly ridicule grammar-school teachers, janitors, clerks, actors, tinkers, retail-traders, and the like, though not more economically crucial occupations like farming and craft-making. Moreover, Demosthenes begins by apologizing profusely for being forced to denigrate Aeschines: in democratic Athens, one must not mock another for his poverty or his trade. Nor did Plato condemn work or the poor per se. After all, he chose Socrates as his philosophical exemplar, that poor, barefooted, democratic hero, son of a sculptor, and himself a sculptor; later in life, Plato saw no impiety in comparing the divine not only to a craftsman (*demiourgos*), but to a metalworker, as his Demiurge hammers and melds the recalcitrant elements into a beautiful cosmos.

Broader contextualization, then, combined with sympathetic treatment of economic conditions, can uncover more positive attitudes towards work. Although these attitudes were never so emphatic as to yield a "protestant" work-ethic, they were strong and persistent enough to leave their mark on the language itself: words for "worker" and "work-loving" are terms of praise, even in supposedly antibanausic philosophical literature. On the other hand, mere talking gets nothing done, and a working culture reproaches the idler, chatter-box, and do-nothing drone: mere words (*logoi*) are nothing beside the solid evidence of facts, deeds and *erga*—literally "works."[16] Hesiod's *Works and Days* is a sustained exhortation to manual labor as necessary, profitable, and right. Prodicus' allegorical "Choice of Heracles" emphatically recommends work as the only means to all that is good. The Hesiodic phrase "Work is no shame; not working is shameful" was repeated as a proverb or slogan centuries later. In a similar spirit, Athenian law promoted the virtues of work: there were laws against idleness and laws that forbade mocking someone for his trade. Though the need for such legislation points to the fact that there *were* idlers and mockers, one must remember that here it is the majority's values that are enshrined in law.[17] So too good work is pleasing to the gods; craftsmen, weavers, sailors, and farmers did their work under the gaze of tutelary deities, whether Hephaestus, Athena, Poseidon, or Demeter.[18] Popular indignation at the hubristic rich overflows into more elaborate criticisms of oligarchy.[19] Of course, work was not popular, and never came to be seen as enjoyable or desirable per se. In themselves ploughing, rowing, hammering are painful and tiring necessities, as felt in words like *mochthos*, *mogos*, *kamatos*, and *ponos*, that last of which also means "pain." And yet, because work is necessary, it is a good thing to work.

A second qualification to the generalization of Austin and Vidal-Naquet is that the association of wealth with leisure, poverty with work, was not at all a universal one. Hesiod was relatively rich, yet worked incessantly, and recommended nothing but work. Work makes the farmer rich, and riches mean not the leisure to write poetry (something Hesiod does not discuss in his *Works and Days*) but rather possession of things—a house, oxen, a plough, a slave, and barns brimming with grain.[20] For Hesiod, even when the harvest is in, the wise farmer should not dawdle before the blacksmith's fire, but plough and repair through the winter. Pericles also, though in a different spirit, praises the ceaseless toil of his Athenians and reminds them that they inhabit the richest city in Greece.[21] Thus, contrary to Hemelrijk and others, one might be rich and yet work very hard. On the other hand, one can be poor and idle: Plato's Socrates speaks of oligarchical cities in which paupers are driven to crime and begging.[22] The Cynics were poor idlers in the eyes of many onlookers, but they were clever enough to capitalize on other common associations to claim the contrary, as we will examine below.

Finally, in distinguishing classical Greek from modern outlooks, Austin and Vidal-Naquet contrast a quantitative and a qualitative understanding of wealth: the modern understanding is that the rich are rich because they can meet a "given standard," while the Greeks saw wealth as freedom from the "need to work." But this latter, qualitative definition is most characteristic of thinkers in the Socratic tradition, especially the Cynics. Far more typical of popular attitudes is a quantitative approach: from Hesiod to Diogenes' contemporaries, Greeks popularly held that the rich are distinguished by quantity of external possessions. This differs little from contemporary notions. Again, Hesiod in the *Works and Days* writes that men in the golden age were "rich in flocks"; men in the iron age are rich if they have land, a yoke of oxen, a plough, and a slave girl, if their barns are full, and in general if they have abundant means of livelihood (*bios polus*).[23] Solon considers rich whoever has gold, silver, horses, mules, land, and a large family.[24] Herodotus' Croesus was rich because of his big treasure-rooms, not his leisure. Alcmaeon became rich by staggering out of Croesus' treasuries with as much gold as he could carry.[25] Two thousand talents of silver, and more of gold, made the Lydian Pythius the richest man in Asia, after Xerxes.[26] Aristagoras of Miletus uses magnificent polysyllabic adjectives to describe some of the wealthy nations under Persian rule: they are *poluprobatôtatoi, poluargurôtatoi*, and *polukarpotatoi*—"superlatively rich in flocks, silver, and crops."[27] So also in the 420s, quantity of money (two hundred talents) constituted the superlative wealth of Hipponicus, son of Callias.[28] The general Nicias was rich because he owned a thousand slaves; his son Niceratus laments in Xenophon's *Symposium* that Homer has corrupted him, for he does not measure his wealth in the Socratic manner, but tallies it up in numbers of tripods, talents of gold, cauldrons, and horses. To cure himself of this materialism, he must "apply for a loan" from Antisthenes' stock of self-sufficiency.[29] Karion, the slave of Aristophanes' Chremylus, describes the riches with which the god Wealth filled their house—barley, wine, silver, gold, olive oil, myrrh, figs, brass, ivory, and so on, with no mention of "freedom from work," though this is an obvious consequence of material abundance.[30] Thucydides measures a state's wealth in terms of bullion and material resources.[31] Athens is rich for Xenophon because she has a good climate, silver mines, and marble quarries, is ideally located for trade, and attracts many industrious metics.[32] Plato envisions an Atlantis extravagantly rich in land, precious metals, forests, harbors—that is, in possession of external goods; in the *Laws*, primitive men are *not* rich, partly because they have no silver or gold.[33] Diogenes throws away his cup as an item of superfluous wealth, an act that both acknowledges and renounces the customary understanding of riches as quantity of external possessions. Finally, Aristotle does little more than confirm common sense when he begins to define wealth in a wholly quantitative way: wealth consists "in abundance of money, ownership of land and properties, and further of moveables, cattle and slaves, remarkable for number, size and beauty, if they are all secure, liberal and useful."[34]

But when Aristotle proceeds to emphasize that true wealth consists not in mere possession but in the right use of one's possessions, that wealth is the actualization of potentially useful things for human ends,[35] he is only crystallizing another powerful strand of thought that had long coexisted with the quantitative definition, although it was less prevalent. According to this second, *qualitative* understanding of wealth, what is of true value is not external goods themselves but the person who shapes, maintains, and uses them. So-called "goods" are not good except with reference to a subject; things are inert and useless without someone to use them. The first seeds of this idealistic[36] thought are small and difficult to see. Nevertheless, an incipient emphasis upon the subjective factor of wealth seems present in lines like Alcaeus' "Men are a warlike tower for their city." For Sophocles' Oedipus, "Walls and ships are worth nothing if empty of men." Thucydides' statesmen echo this insight on several occasions, as if it were a popular one for orators during trying circumstances: "things do not possess men, but rather it is men that possess them." And from a fragment of Euripides: "better than wealth and deep-sown earth are throngs of just and good men."[37]

The existence of such a qualitative understanding is not wholly surprising. In a stark landscape or amid unimpressive habitations, what one notices first are other people. Next to the sea or among high mountains, a place crowded with faces, voices, and activity immediately strikes one as important and prosperous. Hence the term *poluanthrôpia* (abundance of people) is nearly synonymous with state wealth: a flourishing city is typically said to be "large and well-populated."[38] Similar is the generalization at the opening of Gorgias' *Helen*: a city's excellence consists in its men. A century later, Zeno's utopia would glory in the virtues of its citizens—not in statues, porticoes, and temples.[39] Many Greeks, then, would not have found alien the classically inspired slogan of Ruskin, "the only wealth is life."

But the Socratic philosophers are more deliberate than others in emphasizing this subjective element of "human capital." Their systematic "turn to the subject" may perhaps be traced to Socrates himself, and more distantly to the Sophistic education of the individual. Yet in quoting the passage that is often taken as the *locus classicus* for the Socratic "cultivation of the soul" (*therapeia psychês*), one should note against whom Socrates is rebelling. Socrates claims that many of his contemporaries hold the true end of endeavor to be simply external and wealth to consist merely in things. Such people, he implies, not only have no inkling of the highest ends of life: they are ignorant even of economic facts, despite their pride in being practical. For it is a fact that the virtuous alone are productive:

> Men of Athens, I honour and love you, but I shall obey God rather than you, and while I have life and strength I shall never cease from the practice and teaching of philosophy, exhorting any one whom I meet and

saying to him after my manner: You, my friend—a citizen of the great and mighty and wise city of Athens,—are you not ashamed of heaping up the greatest amount of money and honour and reputation, and caring so little about wisdom and truth and the greatest improvement of the soul, which you never regard or heed at all? And if the person with whom I am arguing says: Yes, but I do care; then I do not leave him or let him go at once; but I proceed to interrogate and examine and cross-examine him, and if I think that he has no virtue in him, but only says he has, I reproach him with undervaluing the greater, and overvaluing the less. . . . For I do nothing but go about persuading you all, old and young alike, not to take thought for your persons or your properties, but first and chiefly to care about the greatest improvement of the soul. *I tell you that virtue is not given by money, but that from virtue comes money and every other good of man, public as well as private.*[40]

For Socrates, what is of primary importance, not only in ethics but even in practical economics, is the disposition of the individual and how he uses external materials. One can elaborate on Socrates' point. For some materialistic and imperialistic Athenians who cheered for Cleon, Cleophon, and Alcibiades, and who voted to invade Sicily in the expectation of profit,[41] the soul is the tool of the body. Courage, justice, temperance, intelligence, knowledge, perhaps even piety are mere instruments to accumulate wealth, power, pleasures, and fame. But on the contrary, asserts Socrates, the soul rules the body, and the soul's proper excellences lead to material advancement. Without the various virtues, one would not work (the unjust prefer not to), nor work intelligently, nor use wisely what one gains, nor be temperate enough to accept the natural limits of bodily need. Thus, the virtuous and just should profit, for they are the actual producers of wealth. Playing on the modern "labor theory of value," one might be tempted to call Socrates' a "virtue theory of value." In Locke's phrase, labor puts the "difference of value on a thing,"[42] but who will do the labor and who will use wisely that difference of value? Only the virtuous: the unjust prefer to steal rather than to work. If they can, the intemperate and foolish will squander the "difference" on frivolous luxuries.

Such a "virtue theory of value" pervades the ethical writings of Socratics like Xenophon, Plato, and Aristotle. Xenophon is most impressed by the political implications of this theory: the courage, justice, and temperance of Cyrus, for instance, augment and preserve his nation's wealth, and are in turn preserved by his voluntary asceticism and indifference to the wealth he

wins—a topic for the next chapter. Similarly, Plato's philosopher-kings cultivate the temperance and justice that are necessary for the proper use of
wealth—in other words, satisfying necessary physical needs and concentrat-
ing on the "music" of philosophy. For (according to Plato) the truth about
wealth is this: bodily goods should serve the body, and the body serve the
soul.[43] Without the wisdom that regulates the lesser virtues and harmonizes
the activities of the corresponding classes, this natural hierarchy is disturbed.
The more wisdom fades from the ruling class, the more vulnerable the state
becomes to the desire for externals. Love of the Good that orders the ideal
state degenerates into love of honor, thence into various forms of the love of
material things—the oligarch's miserliness, the democrat's carefree prodi-
gality, and finally the tyrant's violent sensualism.[44] Thus, when the natural order is wholly subverted and wisdom wholly absent, the love of momentary
pleasure tyrannizes the individual and the state. Indeed, wastefulness, lack of
restraint, and an insatiable appetite ensure that the tyrant and his state are
ever in need of money; spiritually empty, they are also materially poor.[45] If
virtue is the basis of material wealth, vice makes one literally poor.

No Greek thinker, therefore, would agree with Mandeville's contention
that private vices increase the general wealth and tend to augment the happiness of individuals. Certainly Aristotle explicitly adopts a "virtue theory of
value." Moreover, he does so casually, as if he were mentioning something
obvious:

> Some think that a very moderate amount of virtue is enough, but set no
> limit to their desires of wealth, property, power, reputation, and the like.
> *To whom we reply by an appeal to facts, which easily prove that mankind do
> not acquire or preserve virtue by the help of external goods, but external
> goods by the help of virtue,* and that happiness, whether consisting in plea-
> sure or virtue, or both, is more often found with those who are most highly
> cultivated in their mind and in their character, and have only a moderate
> share of external goods, than among those who possess external goods to
> a useless extent but are deficient in higher qualities; and this is not only
> matter of experience, but, if reflected upon, will easily appear to be in
> accordance with reason. . . . *Again, it is for the sake of the soul that goods
> external and goods of the body are eligible at all, and all wise men ought to
> choose them for the sake of the soul, and not the soul for the sake of them.*[46]

Thus, the Socratic tradition vehemently asserts that the virtuous soul
precedes and survives the external goods that it uses: internal virtue (*aretê*) is

the ultimate source of wealth. But such a thought makes the Socratic mind susceptible to the more radical notion that the possession of virtue, or the full possession of one's own virtuous self *is* wealth. If the cause has more reality than the effect (a common assumption), then the self that is the cause of wealth is more truly "wealth" than are any of its external possessions or artifacts: to be one's own master, self-sufficient and perfect in virtue, is the highest treasure.

Plato and Aristotle do not themselves speak in this extreme vein, particularly in their more practical moments.[47] But, emerging out of the same general intellectual atmosphere, Antisthenes and the Cynics do tend to make wealth a purely internal quality. For Antisthenes, wealth is something wholly non-quantitative. It resides in one's soul, not in one's house. Therefore he is "richer" than tycoon Callias, though not so "rich" as Socrates; Socrates is his benefactor, but he did not measure out his gifts to him with scale and balance.[48] Diogenes continues this extreme interpretation of a "virtue theory of value" with his reported syllogism, that the wise man possesses everything because the gods who have everything love him and enrich him. Thus, the Socratic tendency to stress the qualitative and subjective over the quantitative and external develops into the Cynics' complete identification of wealth with the virtuous subject. The bare, unadorned "dog-philosopher" is "rich" because he is perfect in virtue, the only wealth. This subjective conception of wealth soon becomes a commonplace of Hellenistic schools.[49]

This continuity between Cynicism and Socratic thought can be expressed in an another way. Socrates made a sharp differentiation between the self and external objects as moral ends. External objects are morally neutral and hence cannot serve as ultimate ends; material wealth is neither good nor evil in itself, but wise use makes it so.[50] Aristotle adopts this view in a more complex way, opening up at least the quasi-Cynic possibility that wisdom is self-sufficient and in no need of externals. For Aristotle, the highest life we can imagine is the life of God—pure thought and actuality, self-sufficient, unmoved, wholly non-material. Such a God has no need for wealth, for Hesiod's plough, ox, and slave-girl. In certain intense moments, one may begin to "immortalize" oneself and become like this God; through contemplation, the philosopher becomes at least psychologically more self-sufficient, less dependent on community.[51] Only a god or animal may live without community,[52] and, unlike the Cynic, the Aristotelian philosopher is more god than "dog." Yet, like the Cynics, Aristotle stresses the ontological difference between this highest state and materiality. God's well-being is not caused by externals, and analogously the thinker's most powerful experiences have nothing to do with material possessions. Wealth is not constitutive of perfect virtue and well-being as such; instead, it is a merely accidental feature of human life as ordinarily experienced. Therefore, Aristotle speaks of wealth as the *material* through which virtues like magnanimity express themselves; generosity is not *caused* by wealth, but has its origin elsewhere and so is in itself autonomous of wealth.[53] One form of wealth, for example, is the slave. But slaves are "living tools" for their masters' virtuous actions: they accompany the master and wait to carry out his orders. They belong to him, like shadows to the body, but not he to them.[54] All this is in keeping with Aristotle's teleological tendency to subordinate the material cause to the non-tangible formal, final, and efficient causes: the former is an inert, sometimes almost unreal, background upon which the latter manifest their actuality.

Furthermore, Aristotle's God is perhaps the final variation on a theme that long dominated pre-Cynic ethical discussions. Self-sufficiency (*autarkeia*) was a traditional aim of the city, because poverty, isolation, and difficulty of trade made self-reliance imperative. Reflecting this tradition, Herodotus' Solon makes self-sufficiency the political and ethical ideal.[55] Thucydides' Pericles boasts that Athens is self-sufficient to a superlative degree.[56] Self-sufficiency becomes an even more explicit and emphatic goal for the fourth-century philosophers. Xenophon's Socrates sounds the keynote for what may be the "ruling-idea" of fourth-century philosophy: it is divine to need nothing, second best to lack as little as possible.[57] Antisthenes' wealth consists in "needing nothing"; Diogenes repeated the idea.[58] Plato makes self-sufficiency a defining property of the ideal Good and, in keeping with this ultimate end, would make his utopia as self-sufficient as possible.[59] For Aristotle again, God is self-sufficient thought, and the ideal human life is one that is most complete and self-sufficient.[60] Like the philosopher, though to a lesser extent, the great-souled man also approaches the divine self-sufficiency: calm, deliberate, and strong, he needs others only for bodily needs. He does not need their emotional support or friendship, and accepts their praise because they have nothing greater to give than honor, the "greatest of external goods."[61] Consistent with this, Aristotle too would make his utopia as self-sufficient as possible.[62]

Nor was self-sufficiency an ideal for teleological thinkers only. Democritus may have praised *autarkeia* and understood wealth in terms of subjective disposition, if the various sayings attributed to him are genuine: fortune (*tuchê*) gives one an expensive meal, temperance a sufficient (*autarkes*) one; if one does not need much, a few things are as good as many; the dissatisfied grasping after money is much worse than the direst poverty; the hardships of mercenary service teach self-sufficiency.[63] Some have seen in these fragments the first glints of Cynic self-sufficiency.[64] To look for a lineal succession is less fruitful, however, than noting that self-sufficiency was a time-hallowed and widespread ideal. Both teleological and materialistic thinkers gave the ideal wider application: not only the *polis*, but God, thinking, wisdom, the virtues, the individual should be self-sufficient. The Cynics' own style of self-sufficiency may have been a squalid one, but, despite detractors like Sayre, their vehemence should not distract one from the fact they too simply readapted a very pervasive ideal.[65]

The Cynics are unusual, however, in utterly internalizing that ideal and applying it solely to the individual. For Plato and Aristotle, the accomplished philosopher or great-souled man may not need the friendship or companionship of others, but he remains physically dependent on society's exchange of services; he who lives outside the city is either an animal or a god, or he will not live long. Cynic rhetoric, on the other hand, proclaims the sage as a city unto himself. He is a *kosmopolitês*, a citizen of the cosmos rather than of Athens or Corinth. Or he is a citizen of nature, feasting on sunshine and wild plants rather than the products sold in the marketplace. In another way, Crates becomes a "citizen of Diogenes." Or in yet another variation on the theme, Crates speaks of ignominy and poverty as his fatherland: home for him is the island Pêra ("Leather Bag"); the sage is at home wherever he wanders.[66] In all this, the Cynic claims to be wholly self-sufficient; he needs nothing but himself because he is his own world.

The self-sufficiency of the *polis* thus becomes a purely internal condition, as the Cynic ascetic tries to live as free of external ties as possible. One sees in Cynicism, then, a thorough internalization of traditional values like "self-sufficiency" and "wealth" via various related intermediaries. The qualitative understanding of wealth, the virtue theory of value, and the Socratic "care for the soul" serve to partly bridge the chasm between the first Cynic paradox and traditional notions: to be innerly virtuous *is* to be self-sufficient and wealthy, and therefore the sage who possesses virtue is "rich." Yet, the roots for this paradox run deeper still. A fuller understanding of Cynic asceticism in the classical context leads to other aspects of the phenomena of wealth and work. If poverty could be praised, either implicitly or explicitly, then why was wealth often censured? Was it good to be rich?

Sources, uses, and abuses of wealth

The brief answer to this question is, from a Cynic perspective, "No": wealth is morally evil and practically unrewarding. First, great accumulations of personal wealth rarely arise directly from an individual's own labor, but more often from some form of exploitation of others. Moreover, great accumulations of wealth are not healthy: according to this particular perspective, the very rich are hubristic, greedy, self-absorbed, and profligate. Nor is wealth of much practical good, for there is not much to buy that really compels admiration or respect. Setting aside all silly luxuries, what is really valuable—breath, sunshine, nourishing food, conversation—is cheap and practically free. On the other hand, the rich must be continually vigilant to protect their pile; their jealous, unenlightened neighbors are always eyeing them to get a piece. Many thoughtful Greeks of the late fifth and fourth centuries, therefore, adopted aspects of a praise of poverty: the contrast of necessary and luxury goods, the needless burdens of wealth, and the cheapness of leisure and mental freedom all become part of a general philosophical outlook that would make the greatest impression on the Cynics.

Physical labor the primary cause of wealth

That manual work is the source of wealth is *the* great moral lesson of Hesiod's *Works and Days*.[67] Hesiod tells his brother Perses "true things," and draws a sharp dichotomy between nonproductive and productive elements and their two corresponding forms of Strife. The first causes fruitless contention, such as that between Hesiod and Perses. On the other hand,

> the good Eris rouses even the lazy to work. For anyone would desire to work upon seeing a rich man, as he hurries on to plough, to plant and to order his household well. Neighbor emulates neighbor as he hurries after wealth.[68]

The contrasts between the two Strifes, between the farm and *agora*, and between honest work and injustice, makes Hesiod vehement in his praise of work. Moral admonitions to work pepper the *Works and Days*: "If your heart within you longs for wealth, then work like this: pile work upon work upon work."[69] Hesiod's poem is the classic injunction to manual labor, and its ideas can be taken as fairly constant through the archaic and classical period, if only because they were essentially true: without machines, Greek economies were dependent on constant labor. One confirmation of this appears in Aristophanes' *Plutus*, as Poverty gives the reasons why she should not be exiled from Greece. For (she reasons), if everyone were rich, who would want to work? No one. Who then would do the necessary work? The slaves, answers Chremylus. But who would capture and keep the slaves? The slave-drivers.

But they too would be rich, and so they would have no need to ply their dangerous trade. Thus, according to Poverty, without the continual spur of need, no work would be done, nothing made, no fields planted, and no wealth gotten. Greece would sink into utter destitution.[70] A certain poverty is necessary for work, just as work is necessary for production.

Injustice the means to great private wealth

Contrasted with the hard-working Hesiod is his brother Perses, an idle schemer. Around this opposition grow the host of polarities that inform the *Works and Days* as a whole: good strife is opposed to bad, peace to war, productive labor to profligate consumption, the countryside to the market, honesty to politically-sanctioned theft. For Perses has taken to politics, embracing injustice as his guiding principle in order to rob Hesiod of his share of the family farm. He haunts the agora, insinuating himself into the favors of the powerful, the "gift-devouring" (*dôrophagoi*) kings.[71] With such bribes, he has been able to seize the greater part of their father's legacy.[72] Hesiod sees universal import in his situation. Work may be the real source of wealth, but justice often seems not to pay. Industry does not reward the virtuous for, with their "crooked judgments" and belief in the rights of power, kings can live as parasites on others' labor, "eating the bread of idleness"—an almost literal translation of one description of society's drones.[73] But their injustice and idleness are hateful to the gods, who have in fact ordained work as man's lot. In the golden age, one day's work could produce enough to last a year. But Prometheus' crimes brought down the justice of Zeus, who imposed poverty and labor upon mankind as punishment. Now, like Adam, man must work "in the sweat of his brow." Some may try to live off others' labor, but in the end none can deceive Zeus—neither Prometheus, kings, nor the likes of Perses. The unjust will suffer further punishment, and so it is best to live under Zeus' rule, to submit to an honest poverty and work for a simple subsistence. In other words, "wealth ought not to be seized, since god-given wealth is better by far." "God-given wealth" refers, of course, to the products of the land, for the gods control the weather and all growth.[74]

Hesiod's dichotomy of just and unjust acquisition looks forward to Aristotle's more extended discussion of natural and artificial wealth in the first book of the *Politics*. Here is found Aristotle's notorious critique of interest, often maligned as relying upon a specious pun. The Greek word *tokos* means both "interest" and "child," and so Aristotle asserts cleverly that because money does not breed or reproduce itself (as, say, a cow), lending at interest is an unnatural—and illegitimate—form of gaining wealth.[75] But this pun occurs as the cap of a longer discussion that shows much practical sense, not always appreciated amidst the abstractions of economic theory. Aristotle improves upon Hesiod's framework by adopting the sophistic distinction between the natural and the conventional or artificial (*phusis/nomos*). Herding, farming, fishing, hunting, and even war (to procure slaves) are all species of natural acquisition. These may be supplemented by barter, also a natural activity in that by compensating for individuals' lack of self-sufficiency it helps them to procure life's necessities. Stamped coins, on the other hand, have only a conventional value; they are valuable as symbols of natural wealth, but in themselves are useless.[76] One cannot feed or clothe oneself with them; no animal hunts coins for sustenance. Money may serve a natural purpose when it simplifies barter-transactions, facilitates the exchange of goods, and thereby helps people to live. But when the link is broken between use-value and exchange-value, when the artificial value of money is sought in increasing isolation from actual goods, then one begins to engage in the unnatural activity of moneymaking for its own sake (*chrêmatismos*). The merchant and retailer buy and sell goods for money. Even more unnatural is the usurer, who trades money for money, makes money from money.

Aristotle is often criticized here for not recognizing the productive potential of money.[77] Loans (his critics note) need not be exploitative, and can often enable ventures that bring new goods to market and so increase total wealth. In its productive capacity, money is not simply a medium of exchange but a store of surplus value: a sum of money represents a certain amount of goods or labor, and one can trade back and forth between the two sides as needed. But an Aristotelian rubric may in fact implicitly reject this defense of interest. For if money does not breed, neither does it work: unlike oxen or people, money is inanimate, inert, and must be put into motion by an external hand; that is, its value is potential and derivative, not actual. Money does not itself produce anything; money does nothing unless people agree to work for money, that is, unless people agree to work. Nor can labor be "stored": the technical metaphor only obscures the fact that daily tasks must be done daily, workers continually found, and a storeroom of perishable goods continually restocked. At best, money can represent the value of existing goods, but if these perish or disappear, then money too loses its value (i.e., inflation increases), and no one wants it. Thus one might extend Aristotle's contrast of natural wealth with conventional money to formulate a broader "labor theory of value," as well as deepen the subjective conception of "wealth": nature provides materials, but it is always human labor that gives form to those materials, making them useful to people. Money does indeed facilitate the organized exchange of goods, and so serves the satisfaction of natural needs. But it depends wholly upon the convention of trusting that money somehow "represents" stored value. That is, a stable currency *can* encourage trust, generosity, and the spirit of solidarity and friendship (*koinô-nia, philia*) between agents; these are the moral qualities that Aristotle stresses as being so vital for community and trade.[78] The money-trader can tend to forget this, placing his trust wholly in the derivative and conventional value of money; at this point, his activities become unnatural, hence illegitimate and immoral.

Given such possible extrapolations, it is not surprising that Marx was so interested in the ideas in *Politics* 1.8–10. Less obvious is the slightly Cynic coloring of Aristotle's approach. First, Aristotle treats economic man as just one peculiar type of animal. Plants grow their own food, animals graze or hunt. Human beings also graze and hunt; work and exchange are only more advanced means to provide for the simple needs of life—food and shelter. These needs are easily met (cf. Hesiod on the ease of the golden age), for nature abundantly provides for her children. Therefore, the life according to nature and according to natural forms of wealth-getting is the right one. Those who abuse the benefits of the monetary system and confuse money with true wealth in fact repeat the mistake of Midas: they may have much gold, but no food. In this critique of unnatural *chrêmatistikê*, Aristotle is far more measured than the Cynics. He would not "debase the coinage" to protest its value as *merely* conventional: for Aristotle, convention is not nothing, and art may even improve upon nature. Nevertheless, *mutatis mutandis*, the Aristotelian critique of money is slightly Cynical to the extent that it treats *homo economicus* as simply an animal and affirms that the body's needs are definite and few.

Moreover, both the Cynics and Aristotle belong to a much larger group that openly distrusts moneymakers. Here, neither Aristotle nor even the Cynics can be lightly dismissed as out-of-touch philosophers with no understanding of practical affairs. Aristotle's *Politics* is unprecedented in its synthetic vision, analytical power, and empirical detail; hence, his careful generalizations should be treated with the highest respect. Moreover, with regard to moneymaking, Aristotle's sentiments had a firm enough grasp on reality that they served as inspiration for other, non-industrialized cultures. Certainly, the Aristotelian denunciation of moneymaking, usury, and the profit-motive as unjust has countless echoes in the Greek tradition, not least the Cynics. The following serves as a partial corroboration of Aristotle's critique. We will look successively at various profit-seekers—the businessman, bribe-taking politician, and tyrant—and the injustice that is often associated with them.

First, prevalent attitudes towards the businessman (merchant, banker, retailer) differed hugely from contemporary ones. Businessmen were not envied for any remarkable success or service. They did not form a commercial or financial elite; they were often relatively poor. Great wealth was not associated with business, but rather with political power, especially absolute power. Nor were businessmen celebrated as entrepreneurs who took bold risks, brought new products to market, and thereby increased total happiness or "utility." This kind of business mentality did not exist; there were no synergies of science, industry, and fashion necessitating specialists to adapt new products to potential customers; that is, conditions ensured that there was an "absence of a productive or entrepreneurial mentality."[79] Seen as middlemen who took profits by buying low and selling high, businessmen often aroused suspicion for their cunning and readiness to deceive others.

This was especially true of those middlemen with whom peasants, craftsmen, and other non-business types had most contact—the retail-trader. But it could be true to a lesser extent of the *emporos*. The *emporos*, or overseas merchant, did more dangerous and valuable work than the retailer, particularly when he transported grain to a hungry city. But his was not a particularly enviable lot. Overseas trade-routes were never standardized, and the *emporos* plied his trade in various guises, depending on the period and his own personal situation. In heroic times, an aristocrat might mix trade with travel, adventure, raiding, and even war. Later, some traded as full-time professionals, while others (like their Homeric predecessors) did so part-time or for a season or two, to supplement their income, find a better local market for their goods, finance a trip undertaken for other motives, or a variety of other personal reasons.[80] In archaic and classical times, poverty seems to have been the prominent reason for leaving home to live by trade.[81] Nor was overseas trade particularly profitable. Ships were small, at the mercy of winds and currents, and so had to hug the coast. There was no refrigeration or elaborate storage techniques. Thus, apart from the exceptions of the Athenian grain and timber market, conditions rarely allowed specialization in a single commodity. Economies of scale were not possible and so merchants filled their ships with whatever they guessed might sell highest in the next port of call.[82] Colaeus of Samos was an exception, but he simply had the good fortune to be blown off course through the Pillars of Heracles to virgin Tartessus, with its precious tin. But neither Colaeus nor other merchants attracted any noticeable envy. Compared to all other trading ventures, the Athenian grain-trade was "big business." And yet even here it seems that the grain-merchants of the fifth and fourth centuries were relatively poor.[83]

Furthermore, at times, particularly in archaic literature, the *emporos* gained a reputation for deceit and avarice. Landed aristocrats could despise the rootless, profit-grubbing wanderer.[84] In the *Odyssey*, the only mortal who outwits Odysseus is a Phoenician slave-trader.[85] It is true that there is no Greek parallel to the Roman phrase for treachery, *Punica fides*, and the Greeks seem not to have vilified the Phoenicians as the Romans did the Carthaginians. Yet there was enough prejudice or fear to enable Herodotus to rationalize the myth of Io's abduction as just another case of a Phoenician kidnapping.

The *emporos* could be said to have earned his profits by hard and dangerous voyages. But he did not stay ashore long enough or venture far enough inland to make lasting enemies or friends. He generally dealt with other middlemen and so had limited contact with the ultimate consumers. As a result, common attitudes towards the businessman and profit-motive were shaped primarily through the daily dealings with the retail-traders, who shouted out their wares in streets and marketplaces. These unfortunate sellers had to battle the continual suspicion that they were fleecing their customers, especially country-people unused to the patter and haggling of the vendors. Thus, a cobbler is said to use cheap leather, and too little of it. He stitches it cleverly so that only later does the wearer realize what a shoddy pair of shoes he has bought. Grain-dealers give short measures. The barmaid does not fill the cup full. The fig-seller promotes wild figs as if they were juicier, cultivated ones. The fishmonger is a thug and a thief. The innkeeper and pudding-seller are harridans: when Poverty herself appears in the *Plutus*, she is so shrill that Chremylus and Blepsidemus wonder whether she is one of the Furies—or is she in fact a *pandokeutria* or a *lekithopôlis*?[86] Even the grain-retailers could be criticized for ruthlessness. During the shortage of 386, a client of Lysias prosecuted some of the dealers for illegal speculation. At its climax, the speech capitalizes on popular indignation and demands the death-penalty for the dealers, as if they were in fact not merely criminals but public enemies:

> For their interests are the opposite of other men's: they make most profit when, on some bad news reaching the city, they sell their corn at a high price. And they are so delighted to see your disasters that they either get news of them in advance of anyone else, or fabricate the rumour themselves; now it is the loss of your ships in the Black Sea, now the capture of your vessels on their outward voyage by the Lacedaemonians, now the

blockade of your trading ports, or the impending rupture of the truce; and they have carried their enmity to such lengths that they choose the same critical moments as your foes (*polemioi*) to overreach you. . . . And thus at times, although there is peace, we are besieged by these men.[87]

Philosophical writers generalize from such attitudes. For Aristotle, the market-type (*agoraios*) differs from others in seeking wealth by any means; he is capable only of mercenary friendships.[88] Equally critical is Plato's assessment of middlemen in the *Republic*: retail-traders have no distinguishing talent; not very strong or intelligent, they can contribute only by sitting in the market all day, buying and selling other peoples' goods for them.[89] Later, in *Republic* 8, the economic man reappears in the figure of the oligarch, a joyless miser who (like Aristotle's *chrematistês*) worships money in itself, and not as a mere means of exchange. He lives ascetically, deprives himself of all luxuries and hoards his coins so that he can lend at high rates of interest.[90] To increase demand for his "product," he cleverly encourages his customers' desires. But when this "drone," this "disease of the city," has ruined a neighbor or fellow-citizen with his extortionate rates, he passes him in the streets without a word or a glance, hurrying on, hunched over with his eyes on the ground. Socrates claims to be describing contemporary characters as well as a perennial human type. Equally severe is an image in the Platonic *Axiochus*. Here Socrates can find no better simile for death than to describe it as a moneylender (*obolostatis*) who mercilessly recalls all life's lendings—sight, hearing, health, memory, intelligence.[91]

The usurer (*obolostatês, daneistês*) was disliked partly for his perceived rapacity, partly because he was practiced a profession different from the "natural" wealth-acquisition of farmers, fishermen, or artisans. It was an unusual profession also in that the majority of loans (*eranoi*) were between friends, kin, or fellow demesmen. If these loans could strain such personal relationships, there would have been even less cordiality between debtor and professional lender.[92] The point is best captured in one of Alciphron's fictional letters, in which a countryman writes home from the city, where he has come to borrow money:

> The usurers in this city, kind friend, are a great nuisance. I do not know what was the matter with me when I ought to have gone to you or some other of my country neighbours at the time I was in need of money for purchasing a farm at Colonus. On that occasion a man of the city went with me to the house of Byrtius to introduce me to him. There I found

an old man, looking wrinkled and with brows contracted, holding in his hands an antique paper, rotted by time and half eaten by moths and insects. Forthwith he spoke to me in brusquest fashion, as though he considered talking loss of time. But when my voucher said I wanted money, he asked me how many talents. Then when I expressed surprise at his mention of so large a sum, he forthwith spat and showed ill-temper. Nevertheless he gave the money, demanded a note, required a heavy interest on the principal, and placed a mortgage on my house. A great nuisance these men who reckon with pebbles and crooked fingers. Never, ye Spirits, who watch over farmers, never may it again be my lot to behold a wolf or a usurer.[93]

Alciphron's moneylender is positively Dickensian—or Aristotelian, Platonic, or even Hesiodic. The fictional letter was composed in the second century A.D. by a consciously Atticizing author. But even if Alciphron were not eager to capture the classical language and spirit, the picture of the usurer he gives is an almost timeless one. The lender, pawn, loanshark, gombeen-man appeared among the classical Greeks as reviled as ever by those who despised his profits as unearned. As we will examine below, relations of creditors and debtors will prove crucial in the context of fourth-century *stasis*, revolutionaries' calls for debt-cancellation, and the Cynics' renunciation of wealth as the "root of evil."

There existed, then, a fairly widespread distrust of the purely commercial life. This distrust may partly be due to the fact that the majority lived in the country and did not like the bustle, noise, and competition of the big city. Athens had a large urban element, yet even here wariness with regard to the *agora* breaks forth in the comedians' regular contrast of the city and country. In the opening of the *Acharnians*, Dicaeopolis ("Honest Citizen") longs to be home, hating the noise of the town, where the hawkers are always shouting "Buy coal, buy vinegar, buy oil." The countryside does not know this "buy!" and all such frenzied competition. Another character in Aristophanes' *Islands* longs to be released from "the troubles of the market" where you have to wait for some criminal dealer to sell you three-day-old fish for a fortune: oh! to be back on the farm and see the pair of little oxen and hear the goats bleating and the song of the new wine as it is poured out![94] There is obviously an element of parody in such passages, as there is in Plato's opposition between the "city of pigs," with its wealth of natural products, and "fevered" Gotham-city luxuriating in "relishes and myrrh and incense and fancy prostitutes and cakes."[95] Aristophanes and Socrates poke fun at the country-longings of a

Dicaeopolis, Strepsiades, or Trygaios, and smile at the view that out there in the fields all is good and wholesome. But these portraits are not at all unsympathetic and point to a deep devotion to the land. To the same effect, Thucydides notes how the move into the city in 431 was very difficult for the peasant majority: war forced them to leave their homes and endure a kind of voluntary exile.[96]

The popular distaste for the middleman, the market, and even for the urban center generally as a locus of injustice gives Aristophanes much material for some brilliant caricature. The motivating idea of the *Knights* is that the qualifications for business are the same as those for politics: shout loud, talk fast, flatter and fool one's customers, be shameless, do anything for profit. In the comic fantasy, then, the succession of post-Periclean demagogues—Eucrates the oakum seller, Lysicles the sheep-seller, Cleon the leather-seller—culminates in the champion Agoracritus ("Market-man") himself, a *palinkapêlos*, who sells sausages and other leftover tripe at the outer gates, the toughest, roughest, foulest-mouthed braggadocio of them all. In short, the Sausage-seller is qualified to rule because he is more *agoraios* ("at home in the marketplace") than anyone else.[97]

This brings us to another prevalent association: like the businessman, the politician is also suspected of injustice and unearned profit-taking. But politics is potentially far more lucrative than business, since the magistrate may embezzle large public funds or take generous bribes. The bribe-taker is a particularly common figure. Anyone might be accused of taking bribes—or rather, to use the prevalent euphemism, of being "persuaded by gifts" (*peithesthai dôrois*). The poor were sometimes felt to be particularly susceptible to bribes, and so one means of rhetorical self-defense was to claim to be wealthy already: the accusation is ridiculous, for why would someone like *me* need to risk taking illegal money? But such arguments were double-edged, for if the accused politician is wealthy now, how did he become so but through bribes?[98] Hence, the most prominent leaders are continually prey to accusations of venality. Hesiod rages against the "gift-guzzling" kings who give "crooked judgments." Themistocles was said to give and take bribes very successfully.[99] Political rivals like Cleon and Diodotus, or Demosthenes and Aeschines, lambasted each other with endless accusations and counteraccusations.[100] The "Lycurgan" constitution may have partially immunized the traditional Spartan to money: Cleomenes and Agesilaus were celebrated for refusing to take bribes.[101] But Leotychides, Pausanias, Gylippus, and many fourth-century harmosts abused the Spartan hegemony to enrich themselves, inspiring Plato to attribute a secret passion for gold to his timarchic man.[102]

Bribery was a recognized instrument of war, used by the Persian kings and satraps, Philip of Macedon, and revolutionaries seeking to overturn a democratic or oligarchical constitution.[103] The trouble reached the gods themselves. Priests and priestesses might be bribed, as when the Alcmaeonidae paid the Pythia to deceive the Spartans.[104] If one listens to sophists and "the wise," one might criticize even the old gods for taking bribes. For under that regime, a tycoon-tyrant might sacrifice lavishly to the gods and thus "persuade" them to forget the violence that had made such sacrifices possible; those old materialistic Olympians love the externally pious tyrant more than a poor but truly just person.[105]

Bribes might be trifling or substantial, as in the Harpagus affair. But though potentially more lucrative than the retail-trader's cheating, petty corruption could not bring in really big returns. Truly superlative wealth belonged to tyrants, kings, and autocrats for, more than any other, they could employ every species of injustice to increase their fortune. "One man is great in this way, another in that, but at the peak of all are kings. Look no farther than them."[106] Pindar's saying can be applied throughout Greek history: not the businessman or middling politician, but the tyrant and king epitomize wealth in the archaic, classical, and Hellenistic periods. Furthermore, their wealth is often felt to be ill-gotten. Thus Achilles rages against Agamemnon of "much-golden Mycenae" for stealing the spoils that other hands have "toiled greatly" to win. The wealth of kings like Midas, Gyges, Croesus, and Cinyras became legendary.[107] Yet "much-golden" Gyges gained the throne by murder, while his descendant Croesus inaugurated his rise by murdering a political rival and confiscating his estate. Wealthiest of all was the Persian monarch, "king of kings," the "great king," or simply "*the* king." With the tribute list of Darius, Herodotus conveys a sense of the astounding wealth of the Persian empire and of its master.[108] None, not even a Pythius, can rival those kings who dine on gold plate even on campaign. By contrast with the Persian monarchs and satraps, the richest Greek was rich only by the lower standards of Greece, as less provincial writers realized.[109] Yet even so, Greek tyrants like Hiero, Gelo, Polycrates, and Dionysius I and II were envied for wealth that surpassed all their subjects.

From this fact arises the common question: why not be tyrant? Since royal injustice pays royally, why not pursue injustice and wealth systematically and without compunction? Such cynical questions are perhaps perennial, but they seem to have been particularly haunting for the classical Greeks. At least, many figures from the late fifth and early fourth centuries praise the unrestrained abuse of political power for self-aggrandizement—Callicles,

Thrasymachus, Glaucon, Euripides' Bellerophon—though to stem the tide of disillusion, Xenophon makes his Hiero argue that most tyrants are not happy. But for some, these arguments cannot dim the allure of tyrannical happiness. For them, the choice is self-evident, and they are incredulous that any would voluntarily choose justice over wealth:

> If I were Solon, I would have taken endless wealth and tyrannized Athens for a single day, even if they flayed me into wineskins for revenge afterwards, and snuffed out my descendants.[110]

The dichotomy between justice and wealth did not occupy intellectuals alone. Aristophanes' Strepsiades wrestles with the problems of paying his debts. At first, he submits to the Unjust Logos and the dishonest argumentation practiced in "Socrates'" *phrontistêrion*. Later, he repents and, championing the gods and the natural justice of paying one's debts, burns down the sophist's Thinkery. At the opening of the *Plutus*, Chremylos asks whether he should educate his sons to be honest. Temple-robbing orators and sycophants are rich, but Chremylos is poor, despite his just and pious ways. Wealth is blind to moral worth, so that it seems mere chance whether the good will be rewarded materially or not. Indeed, passages of the *Plutus* go even further than this and suggest that *all* the rich are unjust. In one of Aesop's fables, similarly, the deified Heracles greets the gods in Olympia, but turns away in anger from Plutus, because all the rich men he had met on earth were evil. Simplest of all is the maxim attributed to Menander, "a just man never has wealth."[111]

From Hesiod to Aristotle, then, and in a wide variety of contexts, one meets with a common association of wealth with injustice—the injustice of the usurer or retailer, of the bribe-taking politician, of the tyrant. In the Athenian context, one scholar frames a similar conclusion in Marxist terms: "most Athenians would not, I think, quarrel with defining the *plousios* generally as an individual who made his living by controlling the means of production, exploiting the labor of others, and extracting the surplus value of their labor."[112] Such prejudices are almost perennial—directed against Hesiod's "gift-guzzling kings," Plato's oligarchs, Chaucer's high-living monks, or, in the twentieth century, capitalists and Orwellian "Napoleons." The ultimate reason for the existence of the prejudice in the classical period may simply be the relative poverty of the Greek economy. Typical modes of productive work were not very lucrative: the average farmer was a small landholder, the artisan usually worked with only a handful of others. Regal wealth was possible only by appropriating the labor of others, and this inevitably involved a degree of violence and injustice.

But injustice was only one vice that could give wealth an evil reputation. Another related accusation is that of *hubris*. In general, *hubris* is the crime of self-assertion, the gratuitous display of one's power over another. The strong are hubristic towards the weak; therefore, it is particularly linked with those who are superior in status, strength, or wealth. Aristotle reflects prevalent attitudes when he writes of *hubris* as *the* vice of the rich:

> [W]ealthy men are insolent and arrogant; their possession of wealth affects their understanding; they feel as if they had every good thing that exists; wealth becomes a sort of standard or value for everything else, and therefore they imagine there is nothing it cannot buy.[113]

In Athens, *hubris* was the more particular crime of insult or unaggravated assault. In 357, Meidias' assault on Demosthenes in the theater of Dionysus seemed a vivid proof of the *hubris* of the rich. In his speech against Meidias, Demosthenes would seem to appeal to a ready hatred of "those bastards" (*bdeluroi, miaroi, kataptustoi*). Slightly more comic is the case of Konon vs. Ariston. After a wild symposium, Konon allegedly beat Ariston in the marketplace and stood in triumph over the prostrate man, flapping his arms like wings and crowing like a cock.[114] Aristophanes plays with social stereotypes when he transforms the rabidly democratic, anti-rich Philocleon into a *nouveau-riche* boor: at the symposium, even among some particularly arrogant snobs, Philocleon is easily the most hubristic, as he mocks everyone, farts freely, throws lewd shapes, and on his way home attacks everyone he happens to meet.[115] Plato too plays with traditional categories and expectations in the interchange between Alcibiades and Socrates in the *Symposium*. Here the aristocratic but spiritually impoverished Alcibiades brings a case of sorts against Socrates, who despite his bare feet and humble background is filled with a golden wisdom. "You are hubristic," Alcibiades complains, and indeed Plato's Socrates can be at times an intellectual bully, a wild satyr who assaults passersby with his undomesticated questions and doubts.[116]

Such are instances of what Fisher calls "secular *hubris*." There are also instances of *hubris* against the gods. Here, communities' efforts to curb the strong are bolstered by the promulgation of what one might call the "archaic law of wealth:" *hubris* and *atê* (moral blindness) bring down divine *nemesis* upon the sinner. This divine punishment of *hubris* is a characteristically Greek formulation. Less noticed, however, is the fact that this archaic "law" is framed in quasi-economic terms: excess (*koros*) of wealth is often said to be the cause of *hubris*:

> Excess breeds *hubris*, whenever wealth attends upon
> An evil man and upon anyone without an upright mind.[117]

Variations on the theme are heard in Solon, Pindar, Aeschylus, Sophocles, Herodotus.[118] Hesiod relies on it to frighten Perses back to honest labor. Thucydides' Cleon and Diodotus both allude to it.[119] One hears echoes of it in Xenophon, Isocrates, Plato, and others.[120] The "law" survived at least until Lucian and "Longinus," author of *On Sublimity*.[121] Those who do not fear the justice and power of the Olympian gods may tend to treat this language as a literary trope, but it would hardly have adapted itself to so many literary contexts if it were *merely* a conventional phrase. For pious Greek pagans, the "law" must have articulated a living truth and contributed to the latent sense of the virtues of the non-hubristic poor.

Summing up this critique of wealth are the many generalizations to the effect that money is the "root of all evil." The sentiment is now associated primarily with the New Testament,[122] but the number and variety of Greek instances is also remarkable. Timocreon of Rhodes wishes that blind Wealth had never appeared on land or sea, for from it "come all evils to men always."[123] In Sophocles' *Antigone*, Creon suspects that some traitor has been bribed into covering Polyneikes with dust; in an angry speech he bursts out that there is no evil greater than silver, which sacks cities, exiles innocents, and brings every form of impiety among mankind.[124] For Plato, the desire for luxuries and superfluous possessions is the cause of war and generally of all evils both public and private—selfish individualism, vice, *stasis*, unnecessary wars.[125]

Not so unclassical, therefore, is Crates' saying, "love of money is the mother-city of evils."[126] The early Cynics must have made some overt protest also, given that so many anecdotes describe Diogenes' guerilla-war against bankers, bribe-taking orators, and other petty tyrants of late Athens, as well as his contempt for kings like Alexander. Diogenes Laertius tells of Diogenes spitting in rich men's faces, even hitting Meidias. Diogenes himself speaks of all masters as "evil," and temple officials as bigger thieves than the petty thief who stole a bowl. "Why is gold pale?" Diogenes asked. Answer: "Because it has so many thieves hunting it."[127] Diogenes went into the *agora* one day with a lamp at noon, "looking for a human being" but of course he did not find one there in the "darkness," for the marketplace is where strange animals like the *kapêlos* and *palinkapêlos* go to cheat and deceive each other.[128] One need not take any of these anecdotes literally; it is unlikely for instance that Diogenes the "rich" committed an actual act of *hubris* against poor Meidias. Yet collectively they point to continuities between the Cynic critique of wealth as evil per se, and the more widespread prejudice against profit-seekers and the wealthy as immoral.

Nor was the Cynic adoption of a virtuous poverty unprecedented. With regard to bribe-taking, various leaders, generations, and institutions had been celebrated for their honesty and incorruptibility. This theme seems to have been more prevalent in the fourth century, but it extends back at least a hundred years earlier. Thus the story has it that Aristides gained his nickname, "the Just," because he resisted the temptation to steal the spoils entrusted to his care after the battle of Marathon; such trustworthiness with regard to deposits was a common understanding of the meaning of "justice."[129] He was contrasted with his cousin Callias, whose own colorful nickname, "enriched by a ditch," betrays the dirtier origin of his wealth.[130] Again, during Xerxes' invasion of 481–480, the "greatest generation" of Athenian patriots refused seductive offers to surrender to the Persians: "If we were offered all the gold in the world, or the most beautiful and fertile land imaginable, we would never be willing to join our common enemy and be party to the enslavement of Greece," the destruction of its temples, homes, and culture.[131] The Areopagus is praised in Aeschylus' *Eumenides* as "impervious to lust for gain."[132] Later, Pericles was distinguished from contemporary demagogues by the reputation of being unbribable, literally "more powerful than money."[133] Other orators boasted similar virtues. Demosthenes claimed to have a "soul upright, honest and incorruptible,"[134] unlike Aeschines and all of Philip's hirelings. In the same generation, Phocion "the Good" ostentatiously refused bribes throughout his political career, most spectacularly when he declined Alexander's gift of one hundred talents after the battle at Gaugamela; later, he was one of the few whom Harpagus could not "persuade with money."[135] Epaminondas of Thebes was a social ascetic who lived frugally and did not abuse power for personal gain. Timoleon similarly maintained a sense of modesty despite his superlative military success in Sicily. Such men seem to approximate the moral triumph of Solon and Plato's philosopher-kings: they could have become tyrants but were good enough to refuse the allure of absolute wealth.[136] The theme of a virtuous poverty appears in high literature also. In an Aeschylean ode, Justice shines forth from the smoky houses of the poor, while, hating the power of dishonorable wealth, she turns away from those palaces that unclean hands have spangled with gold.[137] Fragments of

Euripides assert that though poverty is a hard teacher, it makes children energetic and industrious.[138] This is only a partial inventory; the long-lived Isocrates can claim to have many other examples, drawn from both private and public life, of the general truth that the poor "have self-restraint and moderation," and consequently a happier life than the rich.[139]

The burdens and benefits of wealth

The burdens of wealth: Leitourgiai

Given the moral opprobrium that was often attached to great accumulations of wealth, what were its compensating benefits? Lavish prosperity could, in general, be used in two main ways—for public expenditures and private luxuries. In both cases, however, the egalitarian forces at work in a democratic culture like that of Athens could foster the perception, appropriated finally by the Cynics, that it is better, practically speaking, to be poor than rich.

We know most about state-services (*leitourgiai*) in Athens, and there may have been similar arrangements in other cities. If so, the attitudes towards *leitourgiai* expressed by Lysias, Isocrates, Demosthenes, and other Athenians might offer a glimpse of similar views in analogous circumstances elsewhere. Yet one is confined primarily to the Athenian case. As in other areas of its administration, the Athenian state tended to rely heavily on the energy and initiative of its citizens. In particular, it delegated important and expensive tasks to wealthier individuals.

These *leitourgiai* were of various kinds. The *hestiasis* required one to provide food for one's fellow deme-members at a festival, whereas the *trierarchia* demanded the maintenance of a warship for a year. The *gymnasiarchia* involved training athletes for gymnastic games, supplying them with food, oil, and other necessary equipment. The *chorêgia* entailed equipping a chorus for the poetic and musical performances in the festivals. The *architheôria* required maintaining one of the delegations sent to holy sites like Delphi or Dodona, or to the Panhellenic games at Olympia, Nemea, Corinth, and Delphi.

By far the most burdensome and difficult was the *trierarchia*. The state assigned a ship (with mast) to a citizen, who then had to make it seaworthy by supplying ropes, pitch, and the like, and carrying out any necessary repairs. In addition, using the lump-sum given by the state, he hired oarsmen and crew. He was required to sail with the ship himself, or else hire a proxy. All this ensured that the *trierarchia* was a task of great responsibility, requiring considerable time, effort, organization, and even expertise. As a result, it could also bring the trierarch the honor and gratitude of the Athenian *dêmos*. Men of the liturgic class remind popular audiences, even boast, of their many trierarchies and other services to the state: they did not care for money, but spent it lavishly, so great was their devotion to Athens and their goodwill towards the people.[140] In this way, there was a certain quid pro quo between the classes: richer Athenians competed with each other to serve their country, while in turn their poorer fellows honored them for their *leitourgiai*, literally "works for the people." Private wealth was thus redeemed by being spent for the common good; the value of wealth was sublimated into public honor. In addition, there were laws in Athens to prevent the undue abuse of the rich: an individual should not have to perform more than one liturgy at a time, or undertake two in successive years, or undergo a trierarchy when he could prove (by the process of *antidosis*) that someone else could more easily afford it.

The trierarchy went through three basic phases of organization, the last of which may be of most relevance for the origins of Cynicism. From its inception probably to 411, one ship was assigned to each trierarch. But in the aftermath of the Sicilian debacle, when so many men, ships, and resources were lost, each ship was assigned to two or more citizens by an arrangement called the syntrierarchy. This system prevailed until the next low point in Athens' fortunes. In 357, Chios, Rhodes, and Cos revolted successfully from the Second Delian League. Tribute from the allies fell to a meager forty-five talents.[141] In response to the general financial crisis, the law of Periander in 357 modified the naval provisions so that the twelve hundred richest Athenians or metics, divided into symmories, would share the costs of the syntrierarchy. But, as it turned out, not all these could afford the *leitourgia*. Beginning in 354, therefore, Demosthenes began to modify the system once more, and eventually only the wealthiest three hundred inhabitants were burdened with a trierarchy. Such developments after 357 point to a growing inequality not only between the rich and the poor, but also between the extremely rich and the merely well-to-do, who, unlike their predecessors in the Peloponnesian War, could no longer afford the trierarchy. In this area, the Athenian state became more reliant on a small group of plutocrats with unprecedented wealth.[142]

By 357, Antisthenes had probably already died, and Diogenes was already beginning to berate Athenians and others for idolizing wealth. It is not surprising, then, that during this time there were others who voiced related sentiments. In some circles, the burdens of the *leitourgiai* nourished the perception that the wealthy were being hounded by the people and its demagogues. Xenophon's *Oeconomicus* includes a conversation between Socrates and the rich Critobulus. Socrates pities Critobulus as if *he*, and not Socrates, were the poor man. For a jealous *dêmos* has buried him under a heap of duties—feasting fellow-citizens, maintaining horses for the cavalry, paying choruses, overseeing gymnastic contests, fitting out triremes, and paying war-taxes—namely, all the major liturgies. Socrates, on the other hand, has none of these worries. Far from being hounded by his fellow citizens, he is "rich" in friends who will make sure that he is never in want.[143] It is difficult to divine any ulterior motive on Xenophon's part here: it would be perfectly in character for the barefooted Socrates to praise his style of poverty, urging Critobulus to renounce the distractions of wealth and public service for what is truly profitable, the philosophic cultivation of the soul.

Certainly Xenophon's Socrates was not alone in praising poverty over wealth. In 355 Isocrates wrote the following passage, with its implicit praise of poverty:

> Athens is rife with lamentations. For some are driven to rehearse and bewail amongst themselves their poverty and privation, while others deplore the multitude of duties enjoined upon them by the state—the liturgies and all the nuisances connected with the symmories and with exchange of property; for these are so annoying that those who have means find life more burdensome than those who are continually in want.[144]

An even more extreme perspective would have it that the people tyrannized over the rich not only by imposing liturgies but in a thousand other ways, formal and informal. Sycophants and litigious opportunists laid in wait to sue the wealthy.[145] In assembly or court, the fickle mob might use the slightest pretext to vote astronomical fines.[146] Diphilus, for instance, was considered the richest private person in Greece, but sometime between 345 and 325 Lycurgus, after a successful prosecution, confiscated all his possessions and divided them among the people.[147] And yet the moderation of the Athenian democracy was noteworthy; in smaller or less secure democracies, greater personal animosity and the lack of a sizable middle-class to act as a buffer may have exacerbated friction between rich and poor. Monimus' Syracuse, for instance, had a history of wild constitutional fluctuations and class-tension; one imagines that there the wealthy often felt far less secure than they did in Athens. Certainly, Aristotle generalizes concerning contemporary radical democracies: there, demagogues are to the people as flatterers are to tyrants.[148]

The degree to which the *dêmos* tyrannized the rich in Athens and elsewhere is difficult to recover. Daily social relations are even harder to assess, given that attitudes and behavior can vary considerably, depending on the situation and time, the persons involved, as well as their passing moods. A respectful word to one of the *kalokagathoi* might be followed by a covert scowl on one day, but not the next. Wealth, family, connections, and status command respect, and there are signs that Athenian egalitarianism was tempered, especially in the fourth century, by a degree of deference to one's "betters." But in larger groups, anonymity conferred a greater sense of invulnerability and strength. In the court, theater, and assembly, the sovereign people might assert their dominance openly. Here, the elite had to adopt a special language to soothe that temperamental but powerful animal, *dêmos*. Thus, the trierarch was delighted to spend his money for the people, and he spent it all, they were so worthy. The orator has always devoted himself magnanimously to the Athenians. He praises their superlative virtue: the *dêmos* is wise (except when deceived by rhetors or foreigner kings); the *dêmos* is brave; the *dêmos* is valiant and has never been defeated on the battlefield (except when its leaders made mistakes); the *dêmos* is just, for they never make excessive demands, and they go to war only to protect themselves, the gods, or the weak; the *dêmos* is temperate and restrained, even though it need not be, given its power. The public language of the democracy was slightly more subtle than this parody. But stripping away the subtleties, Aristophanes depicts the Paphlagonian and Agoracritus like two ardent lovers, lying and wheedling their way to become first toady to Dêmos. If the Paphlagonian offers a cake, then Agoracritus offers loaves and a pair of shoes—so worthy is Dêmos of such honors, for its many virtues and its unsurpassable victory at Marathon.[149]

Indeed, Aristophanes' plays often portray the *dêmos*, or a typical representative of the democracy, as king, even tyrant. When the Sausage-seller Agoracritus is first called to power, he stands on a table as on a dais, and surveys the islands of the Aegean. He looks from Caria in the east to Carthage in the far west, a vision of empire that would inspire the Sicilian Expedition ten years later. Later, Dêmos is told by the Paphlagonian tanner that he will soon earn five obols *per diem* for judging cases from Arcadia, that is, from cities right under the shadow of Sparta, or even from Ecbatana, capital of Media. Eventually, Dêmos is crowned "king of the Greeks." Similarly, in the *Wasps*, Philocleon rules an empire as extensive as Zeus' heavens; when he "thunders" in his court, rich defendants tremble in terror.[150]

The conceit of the *dêmos*-king is used by Xenophon's Charmides to crown a speech that in its blend of themes is crucial for the Greek praise of poverty:

Now as for my situation in our commonwealth, when I was rich, I was, to begin with, in dread of some one's digging through the wall of my house and not only getting my money but also doing me a mischief personally; in the next place, I knuckled down to the blackmailers, knowing well enough that my abilities lay more in the direction of suffering injury than of inflicting it on them. Then, too, I was forever being ordered by the government to undergo some expenditure or other, and I never had the opportunity for foreign travel. Now, however, since I am stripped of my property over the border and get no income from the property in Attica, and my household effects have been sold, I stretch out and enjoy a sound sleep, I have gained the confidence of the state, I am no longer subjected to threats but do the threatening now myself; and I have the free man's privilege of going abroad or staying here at home as I please. People now actually rise from their seats in deference to me, and rich men obsequiously give me the right of way on the street. Now I am like a despot; then I was clearly a slave. Then I paid revenue to the body politic; now I live on the tribute that the state pays to me. Moreover, people used to vilify me, when I was wealthy, for consorting with Socrates; but now that I have become poor, no one bothers his head about it any longer. Again, when my property was large, either the government or fate was continually making me throw some of it to the winds; but now, far from throwing anything away (for I possess nothing), I am always in expectation of acquiring something.[151]

Fear of theft and assault, legal threats, onerous taxes, imposed responsibilities, the people's distrust, disrespect and jostling on the streets, intrusive gossip, constant worry and therefore lack of sleep—if such are the burdens of wealth, cries Charmides, how much better to be poor! The rich live like slaves, far removed from the happiness of the *dêmos*-tyrant. The speech is tongue-in-cheek, especially as it is given by none other than Charmides, future despot and enemy of Athens' democracy. Yet then again, the fact that Charmides gives it attests to the wide exposure of the ideas expressed. Xenophon's *Symposum*, Aristophanes' plays, Isocrates' political speeches could all draw upon a set of related sentiments about the burdens of wealth. These sentiments remained recognizable enough to enable Lucian, over five hundred years later, to draw wholly upon classical Attic terms when he composed his own studied praise of poverty in the *Timon*.[152]

Nor do such criticisms of wealth require a rare and specific blend of conditions. Epicurus, perhaps thinking on the erratic fortunes of kings like Pyrrhus and Demetrius *Poliorcetês*, gives the quiet command "live hidden" (*lathe biôsas!*).[153] In different conditions again, when a jealous emperor might rob, exile, or execute prominent subjects, Juvenal's *sententiae* praise the relative tranquillity enjoyed by the poor: money has strangled many in their beds; poison is not drunk from earthenware cups; power, the prey of envy, ruined Sejanus and others; few kings descend to Hades unmurdered; soldiers rarely raid a garret; there is peace for the poor man even on a besieged road; the penniless traveler sings in the face of bandits; and so forth.[154] The Menippean style of the *De consolatione philosophiae* goes back to the Cynic Menippus, and as the former consul and consort of kings awaits execution, Philosophia herself reminds Boethius of what were originally Cynic sentiments: "Riches have often harmed their possessors. . . . You who now anxiously fear to be attacked and murdered, had you entered on this life's road an empty-handed traveler, would laugh at robbers. O marvelous blessedness of mortal wealth! When you have gained that, you have lost your safety."[155] And through the centuries, Aesop's fables warn one not to be deceived by glittering appearances. A humble contentment is better than some precarious height: lightning strikes mountaintops, reeds and brambles are happier than the pine or proud oak tree.[156] In fact, the rich cultural and political diversity of the classical Greek world reproduced all these conditions *in parvo*. The gods are traditionally envious of greatness. Tyrants with their jealousies and sudden rages make the life of the elite miserable: remember Thrasybulus and the field of wheat![157] Nor did the Greek world need to await Hellenistic times to realize that the greatest fortunes are often the most unstable: many myths, such as the fall of Priam, teach the instability of *Tuchê*, as do the histories of tyrants like Croesus, Xerxes, or Dionysius II.

Given all this, it is not surprising that Diogenes and the Cynics might praise a carefree poverty over the burdens and dangers of wealth. According to one saying, the rich man sleeps with his gold hidden under his pillow, for fear of robbers.[158] Again, Diogenes' quip about the paleness of gold can be interpreted in a different way: gold and its possessors are pale with fear, because so many thieves—and sycophants, prosecutors, and legal decrees—are hunting them.[159] By contrast, Diogenes sleeps soundly in his barrel (*pithos*). Far from fearing the reversals of a Diphilus, he might even have enjoyed a certain degree of popular regard. One story has it that when a boy smashed Diogenes' *pithos*, the Athenian people voted to flog the prankster and buy Diogenes a new one, thus honoring him as if he were a public benefactor.[160] The story is not uncharacteristic of the democracy that voted a salary for the impoverished descendants of Aristides the Just, out of sympathy for their plight and in honor of Aristides' public-spiritedness. One might even speculate that Diogenes "the Dog" was adopted by some as a kind of public mascot, a "watchdog of the people," who (like Cleon and other demagogues, Plato's philosopher-kings, and even Aristophanic heroes) snarled whenever the rich grew threatening.[161] If so, then the Cynics' sometime popularity would indeed contrast sharply with the burdens felt by the rich.

The benefits of wealth: Luxuries?

In a hostile social environment, then, the rich might attempt to hide their wealth, dressing plainly, buying property abroad, or simply putting their coins in a sack or pot and burying them in the ground. This would be safer than depositing them with a friend or "banker" who might not be as "just" as his reputation suggests. But if one wanted to spend one's money immediately, then the main alternative to funding public works was to use it for oneself or one's friends and family. The question then became: what to buy?

Some economic historians have divided Greek markets into two fairly mutually exclusive spheres—markets for basic commodities and markets for luxury goods. The former were primarily local: grain, olives, and wine were typically grown, processed, and purchased within a small area. Populous Athens, more dependent than many other cities on imported wheat, was the major exception to this rule, but she too probably continued to grow a third of her grain. Preindustrial technology ensured that overseas trade often dealt in luxury goods—expensive clothes and dyes, exotic foods, metals, ivory, curiosities—which could alone offset the risks of sailing and speculation. Mass-production and steam, or else an elaborately organized and defended trade-network, are needed to enable merchants to specialize in one commodity and sail to a set destination: apart from the grain dealers, the ancient trader typically varied his hold and included many curiosities of low bulk and high value, so that in each port of call he might entice a few high-paying customers.[162]

Thucydides' Pericles states laconically that "all the products of the earth" come streaming into the Piraeus. And yet Pericles' statement is a sophistic one, for how many Athenians could regularly afford the luxury-goods that comic poets like Hermippus delight to list?

> From Kyrene come stalks of silphium and ox-hides,
> From the Hellespont mackerel and salted fish of all varieties,

From Thessaly puddings and ribs of beef . . .
From the Syracusans pigs and cheese . . .
From Egypt rigging for sails and books, from Syria frankincense,
From lovely Crete cypress for the gods,
From Africa ivory in plenty and expensive,
From Rhodes raisins and dried figs bringing sweet dreams,
From Euboia pears and well-fleeced apples . . .
From Pagasai slaves branded and not,
From the Paphlagonians Zeus' acorns
And shiny almonds, that are the adornments of a feast,
From Phoenicia the fruit of the palm and finest flour,
From Carthage carpets and many-colored cushions.[163]

The diet of the Athenian urban poor often included salted fish from the Hellespont region.[164] But surely few of the other items on Hermippus' list could have had a wide marketability. Syracusan cheese was a dainty, gobbled down by the dog in Aristophanes' *Wasps*, as if by some "gift-guzzling" politician. How many depended on apples from Euboea or Rhodian figs? Attica had its own fruit trees, and certainly the peasant majority would not need to cart regular supplies of figs back from the city-agora or Piraeus; there were smaller, local markets for perishable foods like apples. Other cities were even more self-sufficient; the countryside dominated the town economically, because it remained the locus of essential production (food, textiles). One must remember that well into the nineteenth century, most food consumed in industrialized Europe was grown locally—despite steam, refrigeration, and the beginnings of globalization. As for other goods on Hermippus' list, one imagines that the market for ivory, Carthaginian cushions, Syrian frankincense, and the like was very small indeed.

If this rough distinction between basic and luxury goods is correct, it would seem to go far to explain why in Greek literature as a whole there is little sustained praise of money for what it can buy. Indeed, important voices rank wealth relatively low in the total economy of life. Singers of the *scolia* celebrate (in order of desirability) health, beauty, wealth *justly gotten*, and youth.[165] Herodotus' Croesus warns Solon that wealth is not happiness: Tellus the Athenian was more blessed than Croesus, because he raised good sons and was honored for his heroic death fighting for his fatherland; Cleobis and Biton were happier, because they died at the pinnacle of fame and youth. For, as Solon continues, wealth may help the rich to satisfy their desires and to weather calamities, but what is truly valuable cannot be bought, or even controlled by human means: strength, health, personal beauty, children, and a happy death are goods that luck, fate, or the gods may grant—or may not.[166] In the large scheme, then, man is "pure accident," and happiness is due less to human accomplishment than to inexplicable external forces. Only in suffering the loss of his son, kingdom, and very nearly life itself does Croesus learn Solon's wisdom: consider no man happy until he dies. In a different context, at the beginning of Plato's *Republic*, the Syracusan metic Cephalus does not praise money for its purchasing power. Wealth enables him to repay his debts honestly and to keep his promises to the gods.[167] Comic poets reflect the more popular and materialistic view that it is a glorious thing to be rich. Yet even here it is remarkable that in their most ardent panegyrics of wealth, the comic poets do not directly praise *money* and the goods it could buy in the *agora*. Rather, the comedians generally extol "god-given wealth," the "natural wealth" of the land that teems forth with good things at harvest time.[168] It is of this that the peasant dreams, and the eloquent poet rounds out his homely thoughts with a catalogue of exotic and sumptuous-sounding goods. But this is the delightful language of the comedians at holiday-time: beyond their purchasing power and normal experience, luxury goods may have been almost beyond the ken of simple farmers and even artisans.

Indeed, when one leaves the comedians' fantasies, words for luxuries become less determinate and more pejorative. Down at the port, some may see the merchants offloading Carthaginian carpets, Rhodian raisins, and Phoenician palm. But that bright spectacle is gradually transformed into an invidious rumor as one travels up into the hinterland: most words for luxury are derogatory.[169] Thus, for instance, orators regularly attack each other for spending their money on themselves rather than on liturgies for the *dêmos*: it is a shameful thing to splurge on flute-girls, acrobats, *hetairai*, boy-prostitutes, dicing, racing horses, drinking in the tavern, or holding lavish *symposia* with the most expensive delicacies (*opsa*). Aeschines claims that the only liturgies undertaken by Demosthenes were "festivals for his own pleasure";[170] Isaeus coins a phrase to censure one defendant: he "wasted his estate on boys." Even more curious is the lawsuit brought against a peacock-owner for not displaying the bird in a public place for all to enjoy and for selfishly keeping it for his own private pleasure.[171] The high degree of social sanction against prodigal self-indulgence is reflected in law, as in the Athenian ordinance that forbade a man who had squandered his patrimony from addressing the assembly from the *bêma*.[172] Luxury was inegalitarian, undemocratic, and therefore un-Athenian and potentially treasonous. A Themistocles throwing lavish feasts, an Alcibiades trailing purple robes and sending multiple chariot-teams to the Olympic games, or perhaps even a glutton splurging on expensive fish could be chastised on the street for harboring tyrannical ambitions.[173] So too, Aristophanes' horse-loving, long-haired Pheidippides becomes, under the influence of sophistic immoralists, a petty tyrant who would set his own will above all traditional customs and authorities.

This popular critique of luxury is echoed by the fourth-century philosophers, who are fairly unanimous in distinguishing sharply between necessary wants and superfluous desires. Thus, Plato contrasts the "true" with the "luxurious city": in the former, fundamental needs are satisfied by a range of natural products; in the latter, basic goods are refined and prettified, and a myriad other services provided, from prostitutes to tragic theaters to professional cooks. In the luxuries of this "fevered city," injustice arises as a disease of the soul, an illness of the tyrannical disposition. The same dichotomy between the necessary and natural and their opposites is endorsed by *all* the major thinkers—by Aristotle, Epicurus, as well as the Stoics who follow the Cynics' example.[174]

Indeed, through the fourth century, one hears only one vociferous objection to the conviction of "the wise" that desires should be limited to the natural and necessary. Callicles is Socrates' opposite, and in their argument he asserts that human nature is unlimited, titanic, insatiable in its will-to-power:

> I will frankly tell you now what by nature is good and just: he who would live properly must let his desires grow as extensive as possible and not check them. Then he must be able to serve these desires using his power and intelligence. He must be able to satisfy whatever desire may happen to arise.[175]

Nourish endless ambitions and desires, and seek the means by which to satisfy them: Callicles' statement is quite alien to the ancient world. Peculiarly modern, his ideas began to be rehabilitated along with the idea of luxury itself by the neoclassical economists; now their equivalent can be asserted uncritically by introductory economic textbooks.[176] But in the Greek context, when Callicles assumes that human desires are not only infinite but primarily bodily, he opens himself to Socrates' withering sarcasm. Callicles (Socrates says) would understand the human being to be like a leaky barrel that needs to be continually filled. For Callicles, the life of the catamite is best; happiest of all animals is the gannet, because it can eat and excrete at the same time. Aristotle also mocks those who would equate happiness with consumption: that is the life of a cow, or of the gourmand who prayed to have a neck like a crane's, so as to enjoy the food's long, delicious descent down the throat. But who could believe that all the struggles of birth and growing-up, the battles and labors of past generations, have their rightful end in some momentary titillation of the palate? That would be too shameful to countenance. The "good life" does not mean eating well.[177]

The philosophers' renunciation of luxury, then, cannot be simply dismissed as the moralizing of severe intellectuals: their emphatic espousal of the natural and necessary has an analogue in popular critiques of the luxurious. The difference, perhaps, is that "the many" do not think through their assorted opinions to construct a consistent ethical outlook. Aristophanes' characters both denigrate the rich and envy them, so that at one moment they condemn high-livers as unjust traitors, but at another time dream of feasting like the Persian king. The philosopher, by contrast, seeks a coherent and comprehensive moral system. Certainly, the Cynics were comprehensive and unequivocal in their condemnation both of high-livers and of luxury itself. Perhaps their best variation on the antisybaritic theme is Crates' parody of a rich man's account book:

> Put down ten minas for the cook, a drachma for the doctor,
> Five talents for the flatterer, smoke for the counselor,
> A talent for the whore, three obols for the philosopher.[178]

The whole reads like Falstaff's laundry list, with his vast expenditures on sack and three pence on bread. Ten minas represent one thousand drachmas, roughly three years' wages for an unskilled worker (paid at one drachma *per diem*). The prostitute's talent is sixty minas, or six thousand drachmas—a colossal sum, while the flatterer's five talents is even more astronomical. In contrast, those who offer more valuable services (health, practical advice, and inner freedom) are mentioned second in each line, as if they were only an afterthought. Their wages are a pittance: the philosopher's pay, in particular, is the same celebrated three obols received for sitting on a jury or, later, the assembly.[179] Cooks, flatterers, and prostitutes—if such are the conspicuous benefits of wealth, it would not have been surprising if the Cynics could attract the sympathies of contemporaries who resented or scorned the extravagance of plutocrats, particularly in times of increased inequality and even famine.

The benefits of wealth: Leisure?

But surely the Cynics acknowledged that wealth is necessary for leisure, and that leisure is an absolute prerequisite of philosophy? Aristotle, for example, states that leisure enabled the Egyptian priests to develop geometry.[180] Plato's Socrates contrasts the philosophers' willingness to discuss a matter thoroughly with the hurried agenda of the politician or litigant: the lover of wisdom does not time his speeches by the waterclock.[181] In the Lyceum after Aristotle, a constant refrain of Theophrastus was that time is the most valuable of all commodities.[182]

But the wealthy were not always perceived to enjoy an inevitable monopoly on leisure. Some claim that the rich are harried because of their wealth; a few go further to contend that in fact the poor have the most leisure, because they have the fewest worries. Thus, Xenophon's Antisthenes speaks of leisure as the "most luxurious" of his "possessions." Leisure gives Antisthenes his greatest pleasures—talking with whomever he likes, choosing his own company, and therefore spending the day in the company of Socrates. Such philosophical conversations are free, yet far more valuable than the expensive trifles sold in the marketplace. In the same vein, Xenophon's Charmides also plays the philosopher when he boasts that poverty liberated him for intellectual life. When rich, he had no leisure and was constantly plagued by thieves, sycophants, and liturgies. Now that he is poor, no one bothers him or cares what he does, and he can spend his time talking with Socrates without any social stigma.[183]

These *jeux d'esprit* must owe much to the language of Socrates himself, but they are not peculiar to him alone. In another instance, Xenophon's Socrates jokes that he is only a "peasant-farmer (*autourgos*) of philosophy," in contrast with the Sophists and their sophisticated students. An *autourgos* was literally one who "did his own work," without slaves or hired help: above all the external aids of books and endowed institutions, Socratic philosophizing emphasizes individual effort, memory, and personal interaction. Indeed, the cheapness of the Socratic style of philosophy makes it accessible to all classes. Socrates talks with all and sundry, rich and poor, old and young, regardless of their ability to pay. From this perspective, then, Socrates is a typically democratic figure. Analogous thoughts surface in Pericles' funeral oration, that *locus classicus* for a democratic culture, when Pericles states that the Athenians pursue beauty "with frugality." That is, they can rival the professionally cultured without the expense; the poor too may enjoy the high culture previously associated with aristocratic leisure.[184]

Other peculiarly democratic conditions might lend further plausibility to the association of poverty and leisure. Various funds were allocated by the

Athenian state, and probably also by other democracies, for those who sat in a law-court or assembly; in the Athens of Diogenes' time, during the 350s, Eubulus and Diophantus reintroduced the *theôrikon* for theatergoers. Such payments could be criticized by opponents on various grounds: the sheer expense was unnecessary and excessive; paying jurors and assembly-attendees diluted the public debate by bringing in people with little political ability or interest; and the *theôrikon* made the Athenians addicts of the theater, lazy, soft, irresponsible, and hardly capable of distinguishing the stage from real life. On the other hand, its champions defended political pay as a bulwark of popular rule; as a result, it was associated closely with democratic constitutions.[185] Most importantly for our purposes, the *theôrikon* and other funds could have contributed to the perception that at least in democracies like Athens, with its plethora of feast-days,[186] the poor enjoyed *more* leisure than the rich. Aristotle, for instance, with his broad and detailed knowledge of social conditions, states that when their daily needs are met, the poor in a radical democracy have the *most* leisure, because they have the fewest external cares.[187]

This line of thought, not altogether absent from the philosophical tradition, culminates in the Cynic paradoxes. Attributed to Democritus is the sentiment that just as freedom is superior to slavery, so poverty in a democracy is much preferable to the so-called happiness of the powerful (*dunastai*).[188] Indeed, the association of poverty with leisure need not be weakened by the qualification "in a democratic context": some may forget this proviso altogether, others may suppress it for a more punchy generalization, while others still may adopt that generalization absolutely and without condition. One imagines that the early Cynics chose one of the latter two options: observing the relatively favorable circumstances of the democratic poor, they broadcast a simple message. Certainly, Teles, the second-generation Cynic, does not hesitate to claim that the poor have more time to philosophize than the rich:

> Poverty prevents one from philosophizing, while wealth is useful for it? Not true. For how many men do you think have been kept from leisure by wealth or poverty? Do you not see that the most raggedy beggars (*hoi ptôchotatoi*) are often true philosophers, while the rich are utterly overwhelmed by work due to nothing other than their wealth?[189]

Thus (Teles continues), Crates was right to say that his cobbler-friend had more of the prerequisites of philosophy (leisure, "wealth") than the Cyprian king Themison, object of Aristotle's attentions. Certainly the Cynics themselves had plenty of leisure. Unlike the flatterers in Alexander's court,

Diogenes can eat his breakfast when he thinks fit. Diogenes once saw a clock and said it had no use except to keep one from being late for dinner.[190] Diogenes' only business (he said) was love, a codeword in the Socratic vocabulary for philosophic friendship. Indeed, the phrase attributed to Diogenes reflects his paradoxomania: love is the *work* of the leisured, as if here at least idleness and "labor" were one and the same.[191] The *dêmos* may enjoy many festival days with feasts, dancing, and free theatrical plays. But for Crates, *every* day is a holiday and life itself one perpetual festivity through which he passes laughing and joking.[192] How much more fun is this bohemian life than that of the harried rich!

The evidence we have considered so far mainly concerns conditions of the Athenian democracy. But Athens was not absorbed into itself in splendid isolation. Its influence radiated outwards in many ways, through its soldiers, embassies, merchants, cleruchs, tragedies and comedies, books, and great philosophical schools that sent their students forth to all corners of the Greek world. Moreover, conditions at Athens cannot have been wholly unique. The expensive liturgies, the assembly pay, *theôrika*, and the like, which supported in Athens an emerging praise of poverty, could have fostered similar attitudes in other democratic cities. These attitudes are not fully recoverable given the scanty evidence. Yet, a democratic context seems crucial for this social aspect of philosophical asceticism: Athens was home to Socrates, Antisthenes, Charmides, Apollodorus, Aristodemus, Plato, and other admirers of Socrates' philosophical poverty; Diogenes, Crates, and other Cynics gravitated early to Athens. Furthermore, many of the other cities of the first Cynics were democracies or had strong democratic leanings. In the late fifth and early fourth centuries (during Diogenes' youth), Sinope had political and economic ties to Athens that date at least to Pericles' visit and the installation of six hundred Athenian cleruchs there in the 440s.[193] Monimus' Syracuse had a history of precarious democracy alternating with tyranny from the middle of the fifth century. In Monimus' lifetime, Timoleon freed the city from tyranny and was said to have reestablished "democracies" throughout Sicily.[194] The politics of Crates' Thebes fluctuated from oligarchical to populist. But under Pelopidas and Epaminondas, democracy flourished in Thebes. Thebes headed a Boeotian league with democratic features, and, more dramatically, this league continued the old Athenian mission of spreading democracy: with the protection of Epaminondas' armies, democratic regimes were established in Messenia, Arcadia, Elis, and elsewhere, effectively isolating aristocratic Sparta.

Thus, although perfect precision is perhaps not possible, the general pattern seems clear. The first major Cynics appeared in and frequented cities with strong democratic tendencies; they assimilated and synthesized many of the populist elements of a previous praise of poverty. Contrary to oligarchical rhetoric, the poor are not "the bad" and the wealthy are not "the good and beautiful." Rather, the poor are industrious and (along with slaves, who are generally ignored) do most of the economically necessary work. The poor are just because they live frugally on the fruit of their own labors and do not exploit others. The poor enjoy all the basic needs of life, often with more gusto than the pampered rich: they work hard and therefore have a hearty appetite (the best sauce) and sleep soundly. Nor do they need to work endlessly, since necessary goods are relatively cheap. There is plenty of time and leisure to do other things; even when working, one can talk or sing with one's fellows. The rich, on the other hand, are distracted by a host of unnecessary evils: the envy of the unenlightened have-nots; the heavy societal demands; the enervating effects of luxurious private consumption; the continual fear of thieves, sycophants, and perhaps even divine *nemesis;* and finally their own consuming mania for more wealth, which would only intensify their unhappiness. The only escape is to renounce wealth and even the desire for it. A clever speaker, then, could draw upon many scattered thoughts to argue that wealth is not much good; from both a moral and a practical point of view, poverty is much better. Indeed, the value of poverty is so great that one should appropriate the connotations of its opposite and describe poverty as "wealth." This "wealth" is internal rather than external, more a qualitative than a quantitative good, a state of mind rather an estate or "beetle's" treasure-horde. Preaching this internal state of contentment is the Cynic beggar: he *is* rich, and his style of poverty *is* wealth because the greatest, indeed the only possible form of wealth is to possess oneself.[195]

If material possessions are a specious form of affluence, then the Cynic raises an insurmountable barrier between the internal and external, or between the sage and the things of Fortune. This Cynic dichotomy also resonates with earlier attitudes. Again, given the general fact of economic scarcity, it was quite difficult to obtain significant amounts of wealth: wealth is a wet, slippery thing, hard to grasp and easily lost, while poverty is like a burr that clings tenaciously even if one only brushes it lightly with one's outer coat. These vivid images of Lucian in the *Timon* may have a general validity, and they are particularly appropriate to the classical period, when large concentrations of wealth were quite short-lived. According to Davies, only one Athenian family remained among the *pentakosimedimnoi* for five generations; by contrast, at least three hundred and fifty-seven families passed in and out of wealth, "from shirt-sleeves to shirt-sleeves," in a single generation.[196] Therefore, a typical adjective for "wealthy" is "fortunate" (*eutuchês*); wealthy speakers often describe themselves as *eutucheis*, especially in democratic contexts where it is important to stress that one's material advantages are due to luck rather than any innate superiority to "the many." Indeed, the sources of wealth are often felt to be beyond the individual's control. For the pious majority, whether one prospers or not is a thing that lies "on the knees of the gods." Thus, for instance, when Callias' worth plummeted from two hundred talents in the 420s to merely two talents by 380, the contemporary phrase had it that "an evil spirit upset the table of Hipponicus [Callias' father]."[197] Gods like Apollo, Demeter, Dionysus, Zeus, and others are "wealth-givers" (*ploutodotai*), but what the gods give they can also take away: Hesiod's Zeus may raise the lowly or blast the proud, making some famed and powerful, others obscure and weak.[198] Those favored by the gods may stumble upon a *hermaion*, a lucky find and blessing from Hermes. Fortune may favor those like Ameinocles, who collected the flotsam after Xerxes' fleet lost ships off Cape Sepias, and so "became a man of great wealth."[199] Divine inscrutability and reversals of Fortune remained perennial themes for tragedians, epic poets, and even historians. In cultivating the soul and turning towards seemingly unchanging realities (moral truths, mathematics, the heavens, nature generally), the philosophers sought to escape the tyrannical caprice of the old gods and of Fortune, and would order the lives of "the wise" on the pattern of the changeless—a theme for chapter 4. But one application of this great theme is illustrated in the Cynic renunciation of *Tuchê* and her minions as so many clay idols. This degree of attention to Fortune may be *most* characteristic of the Hellenistic mind (as Dudley suggests), but it was prevalent in these other guises long before Alexander.

One comic interchange between Diogenes and the fallen Syracusan tyrant Dionysius II sums up many of the dichotomies contained in the first Cynic paradox—subjective "wealth" vs. external possessions, sage vs. tyrant, the inner self vs. Fortune's vicissitudes, freedom vs. slavery, the happiness of the Cynic beggar (freedom, leisure, "luxury," festive gaiety) vs. the misery of the tyrant (fears, dangers, discontent). After being deposed by Timoleon, Dionysius was allowed to reside in Corinth as a private person with very meager means. His change of fortune, from being *the* most powerful and wealthy person in the Greek world to town-fool, was an astonishing one:

> For neither art nor nature did in that age produce anything comparable to this work and wonder of fortune which showed the very same man, that was not long before supreme monarch of Sicily, loitering about

perhaps in the fish-market, or sitting in a perfumer's shop drinking the diluted wine of taverns, or squabbling in the street with common women, or pretending to instruct the singing women of the theatre, and seriously disputing with them about the measure and harmony of pieces of music that were performed there.[200]

Out of curiosity, many came to wonder at, and mock, this tragic figure. Some criticized his behavior as shameless and lazy. Others praised him for accommodating himself well to his new station as a commoner. According to Plutarch, Dionysius bore his fate with a certain degree of dignified philosophical indifference. In all these reactions, there is a implicit sense that Dionysius cut a *Cynic* pose. Indeed, Diogenes himself recognized Dionysius as an impostor and usurper of his "kingdom":

Plato had not the opportunity to see Dionysius at Corinth, being already dead before he came thither; but Diogenes of Sinope, at their first meeting in the street there, saluted him with the ambiguous expression, "O Dionysius, how little you deserve your present life!" Upon which Dionysius stopped and replied, "I thank you, Diogenes, for your condolence." "Condole with you!" replied Diogenes; "do you not suppose that, on the contrary, I am indignant that such a slave as you—who, if you had your due, should have been let alone to grow old, and die in the state of tyranny, as your father did before you—should now enjoy the ease of private persons, and be here to sport and frolic (*paizôn kai truphôn*) in our society?"[201]

"Idleness is Work": The Cynic Version of An "Industrious Optimism"

Still, however, the association of the Cynics with the working poor—or even of Socrates *autourgos* with farmers like Hesiod—is an unexpected one, and leads to our second paradox. The Cynic vagrant does little or no work yet continually preaches the need for *ponos* and takes the laboring Heracles as a heroic paradigm. This paradox can be understood as the culmination of a series of different evaluations of the nature and purpose of work. First, according to the traditional evaluation, work and economic activity are limited by the body's finite needs. One only needs so much, and therefore only need work so much. Indeed, the unpredictable power of the gods, necessity, chance, or *Tuchê* is such that one should not put much hope in amassing a great surplus: one works from season to season and gives thanks in festival times. Again, Hesiod is representative of traditional expectations that change little throughout our period. Some, however, spurn this Hesiodic quietism. Like the imperial Athenians, these would assert the individual's ability to master his environment. Their seemingly limitless ambitions are matched by limitless optimism. Through toil (they believe), one may gain wealth and power almost without end. Finally, Socratic philosophizing can be partially understood as a reaction against this "imperial work ethic." For Socrates and his later admirers, mastery of externals is either impossible or a false ideal: better to master oneself, to cultivate the inner soul and see through the glittering allure of external appearances. Returning partially to traditional values, the Socratics emphasize that bodily need is finite and therefore easily satisfied. But the Socratic reaction does not simply reject the "imperial work ethic." Instead, there is a secret love affair between Alcibiades and Socrates as the imperialist's optimism is sublimated into the thinker's boundless spiritual ambitions. For the philosopher, the inner soul and such non-material ends as knowledge and virtue are treated as infinite goods, even as moments in *the* Good. Such ultimate ends require constant vigilance and effort and so the philosopher "works" ceaselessly towards his goal. Prodicus, Xenophon, Plato, and Aristotle are among those who explore such notions of an intellectual and moral labor. In the Cynics' case, the rigors of an ascetic idleness constitute their claim to "work," and in turn their peculiar species of labor bolsters their claim to the highest justice and "wealth."

The traditional work-ethic

Traditional patterns of thought present us with four ideas to consider. First, manual labor is the source of wealth. Second, poverty is a divine punishment, acceptance of which shows one's justice and piety. Third, work is limited because human needs and desires are limited; when the work is done, one celebrates and gives thanks. Finally, piety entails a certain pessimism concerning humans' ability to secure their own happiness: mankind may work, save, and pray, but the gods' will is inscrutable and often harsh.

Hesiod's *Works and Days* is the classic text for such ideas. Once again, one hears Hesiod thundering at Perses that work, work, and work alone is the cause of wealth. Talking does not fill the barn. Therefore, on cold days, one should avoid the blacksmith's forge where lazy neighbors warm themselves and chat all day.[202] One should certainly avoid the *agora* and its useless politicking. The best treasure is a sparing tongue,[203] and Hesiod cries out against all idealistic dreamers:

> The man who is rich in fancy thinks his wagon as good as built already—the fool! he does not know that there are a hundred timbers to a wagon.[204]

Second, poverty is an expression of the divine will. "Zeus has given to men hateful poverty":[205] the line introduces the central theme in Hesiod's moral sermon, for Hesiod would explain to Perses *why* he should work for his sustenance and not resort to the "crooked" injustice of the *agora*. In the golden age, one could work for a day and be idle for the rest of the year. But then "the gods hid the means of life from mankind," for either of two reasons. According to the first, Prometheus' theft of fire brought down divine revenge. Pandora was sent as a baleful gift and—with her—toil, disease, poverty, and other evils; Hope was the only good to escape from that box of curses. A second mythic explanation presents a variation on the first. In the golden age of Cronus, people lived like gods, without sorrow, want, or toil. The earth gave up its riches freely, and everyone feasted continuously. But Zeus destroyed this happy race and all subsequent races. Now an iron people plods to and fro behind the plough, not a day without toil.[206]

Yet there are times of release when a golden age seems to return. Hesiod allows himself to be glad when he sees the harvest being safely stowed away.[207] For the summer, between spring sowing and the autumn harvests, Hesiod recommends a shaded rock, Byblian wine, goat-cheese, and the meat of a calf and kid:

> drink down the bright wine, sitting in the shade, and when your heart is satisfied with food, turning your face to the west wind, pour three libations of water from an ever-running pure spring, and then a fourth time, pour with wine.[208]

Hesiod's private celebration would be magnified in the many agricultural festivals of village, deme, and city. Thus, in the traditional ordering of life, festivals and feasting follow a season of work. When the fields are seeded or the harvest in, there is relatively little to be done. The peasant does not work on feverishly, but celebrates with the community by thanking the gods.

Finally, the traditional outlook can be shadowed by a certain fatalism to which agricultural peoples are often prone. The seasons return year after year, the crops grow or fail, generations appear and disappear: all these processes are mysterious, barely understood, inaccessible to human control. Again, the impressive hymn to the power of Zeus that opens the *Works and Days* sounds this note of archaic pessimism. Zeus can so easily elevate the weak and topple the strong, make straight the crooked man and wither the proud. Zeus is powerful, man is weak—therefore, Perses, listen and practise justice, for none may escape Zeus' notice![209] The prosperity won by crime is temporary only, for Zeus hates injustice. In the cosmic scheme, then, human striving and accomplishment shrink in importance to the power of the divine will. The best one can do is to work, save, act justly, honor the gods, and trust that they do in fact reward the good. The just may now be relatively poor, but in the long term it is literally true that "half is worth more than the whole" and that there is "great benefit in asphodel and mallow," plain food fitting for the humble but honest.[210]

One must note, however, that Hesiod himself struggles to escape this fatalism with regard to external contingencies. One notes his pluck and even adherence to what was earlier called an "industrious optimism." Poverty may be Zeus' gift or punishment, but at the same time Hesiod sees it as the fault of those who are not willing to work, due to their laziness, stupidity, or unjust desire to exploit others' labor. Thus, for instance, hunger accompanies the idle; he who does not work must soon beg at his brother's door, as Perses now begs at Hesiod's.[211] The *autourgos* of Ascra might have nodded in grave approval at Aesop's fable of the grasshopper and ant: not for Hesiod the carefree song of grasshoppers and Cynic bohemians. Pile up wealth like the industrious ant, for winter is on its way!

Thus, for Hesiod, voluntary improvement is possible. One may start poor, but by continual work, one may become rich: "If your heart within you longs for wealth, then work like this: pile work upon work upon work!" Hesiod's own father fled Cyme and poverty, and his son Hesiod fears falling back into it. In this vein, envy of a neighbor's wealth is a good thing, a positive encouragement even to the natural idler. Zeus may rule the weather, crops, and growth, but he is pleased enough by piety, justice, and honest labor to reward the good man materially. Such a man will be blessed with long-lived families, and his sheep will grow fat; famine, plague, barrenness, and war await the wicked.[212] Thus, Hesiod stresses that one may gain a certain measure of control over one's own prosperity, even under the eyes of an inscrutable god.

And yet, despite these hints of an "industrious optimism," Hesiod does not venture to hope with Virgil that *labor omnia vincit*.[213] His contemporaries were likely even more fatalistic than Hesiod himself, more willing to accept events as heaven-sent. For given the almost continual hardship and pain of life, the best response is simply to endure in silence, cast a veil of piety over one's resignation, and thus make a virtue of necessity. Solon is more representative of the pessimism typical of agricultural societies, and of archaic *amêchania*, when he writes:

> Fate brings good and evil to mortals. Ineluctable are the gifts of the undying gods. There is danger in every work, and at the start of a venture no man knows where he will come ashore. But one who struggled to work falls unwittingly into great and terrible ruin, while to the bad worker, god gives a fortune good in all respects and an escape from his folly.[214]

Solon holds that eventually the virtuous will be rewarded, and Zeus' punishment will sweep down a storm on the unjust (or his descendants).[215] Again, archaic fatalism will return in a different guise in the fourth century, when the Cynic denies that one has any power to control external events: *Tuchê* determines one's material fortunes, while a different form of "work" makes one "wealthy" in spirit.

The elements of the traditional work-ethic—that work and poverty are punishments imposed by a jealous god upon errant mankind, that work ends with the satisfaction of natural need, that one cannot fully control one's material environment—must be assumed to have remained constant in the outlook of most Greeks through the fifth and fourth centuries. Once more, Greek economies relied far more on the land than the sea; the countryside dominated the city; and agricultural conditions did not change radically in the classical period. By a common estimate, over 80 percent of fourth-century Athenian citizens were peasants. The percentage would have been higher in many smaller city-states.

In particular, the evaluation of labor as something that is imposed from the outside, either as divine punishment or by natural necessity, can be assumed to be a popular mode of thought. This is certainly true of classical representations of Heracles, the Cynics' chosen hero, in fifth-century choral lyric and tragedies like Sophocles' *Trachiniae* and Euripides' *Hercules Furens*:

> Heracles' πόνοι [labors] are represented in tragedy as something which have certainly benefited mankind, but to him personally they meant *suffering imposed from without*. . . . The drama did not advance to the

position of Antisthenes in regarding πόνος as something good. From Heracles' own point of view πόνος is an *involuntary evil inflicted on him by fate.*[216]

The imperial work-ethic

But Antisthenes was not the first to differ significantly from the Hesiodic assessment of work. Rather, his proposition that *ponos* is a good rather than an unwelcome punishment was preceded by the emergence of an "industrious optimism" especially after the late fifth century. Optimistic man sets himself above environmental forces and asserts himself in the world as an indomitable force. Rather than accepting a god-given lot, he dares to "take fate by the throat." Rather than plodding the old furrows, he strikes out in a new direction, gives himself new tasks, implements his own plans, accepts his own failures. Some are more driven than others. The most ambitious impose upon themselves the greatest tasks and work incessantly for success. Some terrible restlessness goads these imperialists on, and as they hunt victory relentlessly they stamp down the weak and scoff at talk of justice. What do they want? It is hard to tell, since no success seems to satisfy them. Each triumph inspires new undertakings, each disaster resilient hope. They seem to toil on without end, as if human desire itself were infinite.

That desire is "infinite" is often asserted as a truism by modern writers. The proposition is rarer and more contentious in Greek culture, as when Socrates denounces Callicles' doctrine as "worth nothing." Yet, on the other hand, Socrates welcomes Callicles' unusual frankness (*parrhêsia*). For Callicles articulates what many others secretly think, but are afraid or ashamed to admit. Now Socrates might speak in a quasi-Freudian manner of the subconscious Calliclean urgings of the id that, unsatisfied by any given limit, would overstep all boundaries in search of more. Grasping for more, *pleonexia*, is the human thing. One may interpret this Calliclean view in different ways. In the *Gorgias*, Socrates interprets it in a very material way, suggesting that the powerful person desires to have bigger shoes and more food than his neighbor. Callicles initially resists this: as if the heroic man goes through hell-fires in order to wear a larger coat! Nevertheless, in the end Callicles does not escape Socrates' reductio ad absurdum: wealth tied to glory, power, and empire presents itself to the Calliclean type as the highest goal. Such goods seem capable of infinite extension, and for these one might toil ceaselessly. In such a rubric, then, toil (*ponos*) becomes a voluntary manifestation of one's own inner nature. Furthermore, what is of prime importance is activity itself; the actual ends posited are secondary. "Energy is eternal delight," and must have an outlet; the proper goals of this energy are disputed by imperialist and philosopher. Many figures in Greek history might be seen as energetic, Calliclean figures in this sense—the imperial Athenians and especially Alcibiades, Dionysius I, Philip and Alexander the Great, and early Hellenistic kings like Antigonus, Demetrius, Seleucus, and Pyrrhus. We will concentrate primarily on the Athenians of the second half of the fifth century.

Thucydides often casts "the Athenians" as a particular type with a distinctive "nature." This is introduced in a quasi-programmatic way when the Corinthians seek to alarm the Peloponnesians with a vision of an implacable, indomitable race:

> [T]hey toil on (*mochthousi meta ponôn*) in trouble and danger all the days of their life, with little opportunity for enjoying, being ever engaged in getting: their only idea of a holiday is to do what the occasion demands, and to them laborious occupation (*ascholia epiponos*) is less of a misfortune than the peace of a quiet life. To describe their character in a word, one might truly say that they were born into the world to take no rest themselves and to give none to others.[217]

The Corinthians' polarity between the "imperial" and "Hesiodic" type runs deep through Thucydides' approach to the Peloponnesian War. He does not use *these* terms, yet the plethora of other dichotomies that he does draw upon express similar ideas: Athenian sea power is quick, restless, and insatiable, in contrast to the slow, deliberate, complacent juggernaut of Sparta's hoplites and the Peloponnesian *autourgoi*.[218] The specter of Callicles also haunts Thucydides' Athens, for if Callicles sneers at the so-called virtue of temperance, Thucydides never uses a form of *sophrosunê* to describe any Athenian, not even Pericles.[219]

But what is a source of alarm to Peloponnesians and other traditionalist types is a source of pride to the Athenians themselves. Pericles' funeral oration praises the Athenians' distinctive excellences—their energy, industry, invincible confidence and will-to-win, their cheerful acceptance of *ponos* for the sake of a greater Athens. Any hint of Hesiodic quietism is soon banished in this praise of ceaseless "work." For Pericles' vision is not that of Hesiod—farmers resting under their olive-trees, enjoying a moment with the gods. For Thucydides' Pericles, the numerous Athenian festivals are simply *ponôn anapaulai*: the great Dionysia, rural Dionysia, Lenaia, Anthesteria, Eleusinia, the lesser and greater Panathenaeia, and countless others festivals (such as Kronia, Sunoikia, Genesia, Charisteria, Pyanopsia, Oschophoria, Brauronia, Thargelia, Delia, Thesmophoria, and not least, the Epitaphia itself) with their comedies, tragedies, games, sacrifices, rites, and other diverse celebrations of the gods' bounty—all these are reduced to the status of "work-breaks." Pericles' phrase reverses the traditional ordering of time. The festival is no longer sacred time, affording a glimpse of the abundance and laughter of the gods' life. No longer a holy day, the festival is now a vacation, a respite to recover from work. If he could, the imperialist would work all the time: in the Corinthians' paradoxical observation, the Athenian considers pursuing the task at hand (*ta deonta praxai*) to be the finest festival of all. To him, quiet idling is a "misfortune."

The Athenian patriot, then, does not work for the sake of some seasonal festivity. A temporary escape of poverty is not sufficient; it is not enough simply to satisfy bodily need. Impatient for some greater good, this imperialist listens eagerly to Pericles as he "hymns" the power of the city. Generations have made Athens the greatest and richest city in Greece. The living generation too may become part of a proud tradition that will outlive all individual deaths. For the power, honor, and wealth of Athens, then, the citizen must not flee *ponoi*. He must endure many toils—the *ponoi* of battle and campaign, of war generally with its casualties and reversals, even the sufferings of unpredictable events like the plague. All these the patriot must not merely endure but positively welcome. The contingencies of *Tuchê* may be various and dire but the citizen greets them with the same resolute optimism. Whether in the siege of Athens or in an obscure battle on a Peloponnesian headland, the Athenian must present the same indomitable self. He should use his body as a mere tool of the state. So consuming is this vision of an ardent glory that all sacrifices are redeemed; even death comes over the hero as a painless blessing. Athens has expended the most bodies and *ponoi* in war, but her name will remain as a constant source of wonder to people yet unborn.[220]

Such high language praising *ponos* in service of the state is typical of the Athenian funeral oration and of the patriotic rhetoric in general.[221] But the Thucydidean Pericles' focus upon *power* is unusual in the funerary context and seems to foreshadow later events, when the Athenians would voluntarily undertake the greatest *ponoi* for the sake of seemingly unlimited empire. For according to an interpretation that Thucydides himself seems to endorse, the invasion of Sicily in 415 was a predictable result of the Athenians' nature, their restlessness (*polupragmosunê*) and *pleonexia*.[222] A true leader rather than a mere politician, Pericles was able to hold Athenian energies in check. But successors like Cleon and Alcibiades only incited their innate impetuosity. This becomes abundantly clear in the speeches that preceded the Sicilian expedition. Here, the older, cautious Nicias attempts to deter the Athenians from the expedition altogether. Yet he rightly fears that his advice will be in vain: "against your character any words of mine would be weak enough if I were to advise your keeping what you have got and not risking what is actually yours for advantages which are dubious in themselves."[223] The young Alcibiades is more in tune with the limitless optimism of his generation. He mocks the do-nothing policy (*apragmosunê*) of Nicias as un-Athenian and cowardly. The Athenians must live up to their ancestors' example and indeed to their own very nature by conceiving and executing large designs.[224] In contrast to the sluggish Nicias, Alcibiades represents pure energy: when he sailed to Sicily, he carried (according to Plutarch) a shield emblazoned with Eros holding a thunderbolt; Plato and the writers of the two *Alcibiades* dialogues depict him as a turbulent Dionysian figure who might be a worthy successor to Socrates' philosophical *erôs*, if only he would renounce his political aspirations.

But Thucydides' Alcibiades discountenances any such renunciation. Knowing the Athenians' "nature," he excites them to an unprecedented pitch of imperialistic ambition. Inflamed by various desires—for travel, excitement, conquest, but most of all for "power, a source of endless pay"—the Athenians vote to sail to Sicily.[225] "So excessive," Thucydides writes, "was the desire of the majority that if anyone disagreed he kept quiet, fearing that he would appear unpatriotic by voting no."[226] Excessive also (from a pre-Hellenistic perspective) are the Athenian plans for western conquests as outlined by Alcibiades to the Spartans: after conquering Syracuse, Sicily, southern Italy, and perhaps even Carthage, we will turn upon the Peloponnese with immense resources in ships and barbarian mercenaries, and thus "easily rule all Greece."[227] Profits, endless pay, and conquest of the sea and of most of the Greek world—where does it end? These ambitions are not unique to Alcibiades; Alcibiades is only the most Athenian of the Athenians. His successors and the *dêmos* persevered in the attempt to take Syracuse, as if in a tragic attempt to make good Pericles' boast fifteen years earlier: "we have forced every sea and land to be the highway of our daring, and everywhere, whether for evil or for good, have left imperishable monuments behind us."[228] Thucydides does not use the word *ponoi* to describe the "toils" of the monumental Sicilian war, yet the extrapolation is wholly appropriate to his evocation of the imperialist spirit: the huge expeditionary force, the long voyage, the laborious search for allies and supplies, the siege, the battles, the dispatch of even more reinforcements, the eventual defeat, the sufferings of the retreat, the massacre at the Asinarus river, and the mass death in the salt-mines—all these are *ponoi* that the Athenians imposed upon themselves in their hunger for empire.

The Athenians ultimately failed, but others revived their insatiable ambition. One other prominent example of the "imperial work-ethic" is from the next century. Over a period of twenty years, Philip II transformed Macedonia into the ruling power of all Greece, an unprecedented achievement that owed much to the ceaseless efforts of Philip himself. Demosthenes recognized Philip's incredible energy and even used the hallowed language of the *epitaphios* to alert the Athenians that they are failing to emulate their ancestors. We Athenians (he says) do nothing but sit debating, planning, passing decrees, and gathering to gossip in the streets. We are unwilling either to fight ourselves or to spend our money on mercenaries. Slack, soft, lazy, we wait on the initiative of others. In contrast, Philip leads his army in person. He fights all year, even in winter. Suffering hardship and danger continuously, he expends his own body in order to enlarge his kingdom. He spares no resources, either public or private. In sum, just as once our ancestors undertook many *ponoi* and dangers against the Lacedaimonians, so now Philip undergoes all *ponoi* in his bid for power. The comparison of Philip with Pericles' great generation is a shocking one, and Demosthenes in fact apologizes for his *parrhêsia*.[229]

Through Philip and the even more astonishing *ponoi* that Alexander suffered for *his* empire, the imperialistic work-ethic entered the Hellenistic world. Here the picture of a young king gazing distantly into unknown horizons becomes a typical image of the age. Masterful personalities parade across the stage of world-history—Antigonus the One-Eyed, Demetrius "Stormer of Cities," Seleucus "the Victor," each with a long story of adventures and varied fortunes. The ambitions of such kings are filled out with massive armies of mercenaries, war-elephants, many-storied siege towers, new artillery weapons, ships with twelve, twenty, forty banks of oars, and other amazing machines of war. Even the little kingdoms could display the relentless energy of the age: the forms in the *gigantomachy* sculpted around the altar of Zeus at Pergamum positively seethe with life, little Rhodes erects a Colossus to the sun-god.

In such an environment, old themes harden into fixed tropes. Most notable is the contrast between the world-conqueror and the Hellenistic sage, whether Cynic, Stoic, or Academic. Countless anecdotes pit a Cynic against an autocrat—Diogenes and Philip, Diogenes and Alexander, Bion and Antigonas Gonatas, and so forth. These stories essentially reenact the themes that had informed similar, earlier encounters, as when Herodotus' Solon taught Croesus that wealth is not happiness and that one learns wisdom through suffering, or when (tyrant and "wise man" reversing roles) Xenophon's Hiero instructs Simonides in the miseries of tyranny.

Notable here is the friendship of Cineas and Pyrrhus. Pyrrhus was king of Epirus, mercenary, adventurer, supremely brave and valiant, and (it was said) the most like Alexander of all his successors. One of his companions was Cineas the Thessalian, orator, political advisor, philosopher. If Pyrrhus best resembled Alexander, Cineas' rhetorical style was more like that of Demosthenes than any other orator. When Demosthenes was aroused, he could carry all before him with his eloquence, and so too Pyrrhus admired Cineas as invincible with words: Cineas (Pyrrhus would say) had conquered more cities with his arguments than Pyrrhus had with arms. Certainly (in Plutarch's anecdote at least), Cineas conquered Pyrrhus on the eve of his wars with the Romans. Cineas asks why Pyrrhus will take upon himself so much toil. For what good will you use your victory over the Romans, O king? To conquer Italy, comes the answer—and then Sicily, then Carthage and Africa, then my Greek rivals, and all Greece and Macedonia. And what would you do then, king? Drink and talk and laugh with my friends, replies Pyrrhus, but he is embarrassed when Cineas points out that all these advantages of leisure (*scholê*) are possible right now, without the bloodshed and immense *ponoi* that war will bring.[230]

The clash is typical of such anecdotes that depict the victory of reason over arms. But these clashes also point to a certain accord between philosopher and king. "The wise" frequent the halls of tyrants, and the philosopher pays a compliment to royalty by assuming the title of "king" himself. On the other hand, the king may sometimes listen to the philosopher as one who knows the true sources of his restlessness: Alexander would choose to be Diogenes, if he were not Alexander.[231]

The philosophical work-ethic

In comparing himself with the imperialist, the philosopher claims to have the more comprehensive and discerning outlook. In his judgment, the imperialist does not accurately distinguish between body and soul. Physical needs are finite, even minimal; only noetic and spiritual realities have an infinite dimension. Knowledge, for instance, has no easily recognizable limits. The soul knows all things and "in a sense *is* all things."[232] Its kingdom is coextensive with Being itself, and in thought one might dart from Tartessus to the Caucasus with no more effort than an Olympian god. The body has no such wings and must creep about, now, here, there. Thus, even the richest materially are in truth poor. For all his speed and travels, Alexander possesses only the ground under his feet; he owns his shadow and nothing else. The imperialist chases a cloud; subconsciously moved by philosophical ends, he does not recognize the spiritual origin of his restlessness. He mistakenly transfers his energies to material ends, as if endless conquest and concubines would bring satisfaction. They do not: when Alexander has no more kingdoms to conquer, he weeps.

The nothingness of human accomplishment did not await the Socratic philosophers for its first expression. Sophocles articulates it in his famous ode:

> There are many wonders, but the greatest wonder is man. This thing presses beyond even the grey sea in winter, piercing the breaking waves. With his plows turning ceaselessly year by year and the horses pulling, he wears away the greatest of gods, the boundless and unwearied earth.[233]

So man conquers the sea, tames animals, catches birds, builds cities, and cultivates language and thought. His daring forces a way through every element. All accomplishments he claims as his own; no eventuality finds him resourceless (*aporos*). But though he may conquer all things, there is one that cannot be overcome—death. Thus optimism is tempered by the dominant note of tragedy: great in spirit, man is the most wonderful and terrible (*deinos*) of animals, yet from a cosmic point of view, he too is just another speck blown across the ageless earth. From this tragic perspective, one pities worldly ambition: so caught up in his own plans and conceptions, the imperialist forgets that he is nothing.

This element of pessimism enters also into the general orientation of the Socratic philosophers. The thinker knows that he knows nothing, that he *is* nothing.[234] The physical world is one of constant flux, change, and death, and so the honest thinker dies voluntarily to this world, downplaying the traditional means of weathering change—power, honor, wealth, even community itself—as only temporary expedients. Yet this pessimism does not become complete nihilism. The body may be limited and poor, but with regard to the soul and its potentially infinite capacities, the philosopher can be irrepressibly optimistic. This optimism yields yet another approach towards "work" and human activity. Bodily needs are finite and easily satisfied, but moral and intellectual ends require constant attendance. Therefore, the ambitious thinker "works" constantly towards his chosen goals of self-sufficiency and self-actualization. Only by such "work" can one escape the body's inalienable poverty.

The notion that intellectual effort can reveal all secrets is common enough for comedians to allude to it.[235] But the Cynics rejected science, and so, more relevant to their paradoxes of "work" is the view that *virtue* is a product of *ponos*. Again, there are popular precedents from the "praise of poverty." The athlete accepts the *ponos* of training for the sake of a prize that was felt by some to be a human being's highest reward: to be crowned victor in the Panhellenic games was to gain glory not only before one's fellow man, but before the gods themselves, for they too were spectators of the contest. The prize was a wreath of oak, laurel, or some other plant sacred to the presiding deity. Of course, cities soon added extra, very material rewards for their victorious citizens, and these were avidly sought. Yet the official award remained a nonmaterial one, and the original idealism of the games probably still continued to survive in the many gymnasia, *palaestrai*, and running *dromoi*. An epithet for athletes is "toil-loving" (*philoponos*), as if they sought nothing but the pain of training itself; Theocritus speaks of the gymnasium's "beautiful *ponos*."[236] Idealized as wholly uneconomic, this "work" ennobles and beautifies a person.

Such notions take on a moral coloring at least as early as the Sophistic movement of the mid-fifth century. Now the imperialistic ethic of realizing one's infinite desires can be transmuted into a philosophical one; the will-to-power becomes a will-to-virtue. The intellectual becomes a soul-worker whose "labor" brings the highest, nonmaterial rewards. It is perhaps not surprising that the positive associations of work began to be internalized by the Sophists, those first intellectual specialists whose "trade" was language, ideas, and morality. These claimed to be "teachers of virtue" (*didaskaloi aretês*), masters of the "craft of words" (*logôn technê*). Such language must have been common enough for the comic poets to parody it. Aristophanes pokes fun at those intellectuals who protest that they have their own, peculiar line of work. His "Socrates" works out of a *phrontistêrion* ("thinkshop"), a neologism that may be based on the common *ergastêrion* ("workshop"): here the sophist and his students concoct all sorts of ideas that impress at least Strepsides as being extremely useful. In the *Frogs*, "Aeschylus" is a "mind-building man" who hurls forth "bolt-riveted words" while Euripides becomes a "fine-knife-worker" and "mouth-worker" who with "long labor of the lungs" files poetry down into tiny bits. Again in the *Clouds*, the sophistically trained Pheidippides is in one passage a "mover and hauler of radical new words," as if he were a docker "levering" cargo on shore. Later, Plato's Demiurge (*Dêmiourgos*, literally "craftsman") most resembles a metalworker, as he hammers anarchic matter into a beautiful cosmos.[237]

More specifically, the "work" of virtue appears in various ways in Democritus, Xenophon, Plato, and Aristotle. From a fragment of Democritus: "voluntary labors make easier the onslaught of unwanted fortune."[238] Such ideas foreshadow Cynic asceticism—willful self-deprivation trains one for the inevitable losses brought by *Tuchê*—and are elaborated in Prodicus' "Choice of Heracles." In Xenophon's summary of the allegory,[239] the young Heracles has sat down at a crossroads, not knowing which path to follow through life. As he sits deliberating, two women appear to him. Their physical appearance is a study in contrasts, and they are clearly villainness and heroine. Evil (*Kakia*) is overfed, plump, rouged, and all powdered up. She wears revealing clothes and is vain, viewing herself in a mirror and turning around to see if she is being admired. Virtue (*Aretê*), on the other hand, wears simple white; her only adornments are purity, modesty, and temperance. These apparitions proceed to give speeches in praise of the life that they can give Heracles. Evil speaks first—an ominous choice, since in such debates, the first speaker typically loses. She offers Heracles a life of free, effortless pleasure. There will be no delights that he will not taste, no difficulties that he will not avoid. He need never worry about wars and affairs. All he need trouble himself about will be what food or drink to take; what to look at, hear, smell or touch for his pleasure; what partner he might enjoy, how he might sleep softest, and how he can obtain all these with the least toil (*aponôtata*). If ever there are shortages, he will not suffer *ponos* or hardship either in body or soul. Rather "you will enjoy those things that others work to produce, and you will not hold back from profiting everywhere." Evil tells Heracles her name, but adds confidentially that to her friends she is known as Happiness (*Eudaimonia*).

Very different is the tone and substance of Virtue's argument. For while Evil would have Heracles live for himself alone and treat others as means to his self-gratification, Virtue begins by saying that she knows Heracles' parents and nature: Heracles must live up to his Olympian heritage. Therefore she will not deceive him with "hymns to pleasure." Evil's enticements are in fact contrary to the divine ordering, "for the gods have given men nothing good without *ponos* and diligence." There follows a series of emphatic verbal nouns to hammer home this truth: if you want divine favor, you must worship the gods, if you want to be admired, you must do good works for your friends; if you want to be honored, you must benefit your city and Greece; if you want the earth to bear crops, you must cultivate the land. Flocks require tending, war demands practice. And if you want strength (Heracles' trademark), you must accustom your body to serve your will, and you must train "with *ponoi* and sweat."

At this point, Evil bursts in to deplore such a harsh lifestyle. She is immediately silenced, however, as Virtue argues that duality is essential to a sense of fulfillment and even to pleasure itself. For paradoxically, *ponos* (pain, struggle) makes pleasure pleasurable. Evil's vision of happiness is one of continual and languid orgy—food without hunger, drink without thirst, sex without desire, sleep without weariness. But as experience shows, continual partying soon loses its zest, even if one goes so far as to cool expensive drinks "with snow" in summertime. By contrast, Virtue's own followers have no real trouble in satisfying their desires. They do so not by committing violence against others or living off others' labor, but by simply "holding off until they actually do desire" food or drink. Hunger is the best sauce, and it is free. Furthermore, Virtue appeals to Heracles' native idealism. What hedonists have ever accomplished any "fine work" (*ergon kalon*)? None, for no beautiful or divine deed is ever done "without me [Virtue]." Therefore, wherever there are energetic, effective people, Virtue is present: she is a helper to craftsmen, a guard of the household, a partner in peacetime *ponoi*, an ally for the works (*erga*) of war, the best support of friendship. To choose Evil would be shameful and not even extremely pleasurable, while with Virtue one will lead the most varied and honorable life.

In this transparent morality-play, Heracles' choice is clear. It is also clear that the virtue and *ponos* that he will choose are undertaken voluntarily; only they are appropriate for the son of Zeus or satisfactory to his heroic ambition. Xenophon writes that Prodicus exhibited his allegory to "many"; surely few would have bothered listening to the rhetoric, and later writers would not have admired the piece, if they had not found the matter compelling, or at least interesting. Zeller suggests that the whole piece is akin to a praise of poverty, while Höistad argues that the story sees a "spiritualization" of labor, a new outlook that is "fully consistent" with "Antisthenes' equation of πόνος = ἀγαθόν (toil, pain = good)."[240]

Höistad's "spiritualization" is too strong a term, yet he is right to begin to locate the piece within the larger context of proto-Cynic attitudes. Belonging also to this context are the many Socratic conversations that Xenophon heard or adorned. Xenophon's Socrates hints at a "gospel of labor," according to which love of work is akin to godliness.[241] Far from being an antilabor philosopher, this Socrates again and again stresses the many ethical and psychological blessings of work. First, the case of Aristarchus. During the civil war between the Thirty and the democrats, Aristarchus and his fourteen female relatives are running out of money, but are too proud to work with their hands. Socrates cures them of this false pride and persuades Aristarchus to set them weaving. "Just because they are gentlefolk and related to you, do you think that they should do nothing but eat and drink?"[242] When they set up shop weaving, the work soon improves the atmosphere of the household: apart from the obvious remuneration, the very consciousness of doing honest and useful work makes them mentally alert and kinder towards each other.[243]

Xenophon writes his own version of Prodicus' "Choice of Heracles" when he juxtaposes Socrates with the hedonist Aristippus. For Socrates, the ruler's virtues include self-mastery and the willingness to "endure *ponos*": the leader voluntarily undergoes hunger, fatigue, and other forms of self-deprivation for the sake of the greater political good.[244] Aristippus cries out in protest, wondering

> how those who are trained to the art of kingship which you seem to iden-tify with happiness—how do they differ from those who suffer under compulsion, if they will be hungry, thirsty, cold, weary and will toil vol-untarily through all other such tortures?[245]

In a similar encounter, Antiphon is even more dismissive of Socrates: Socrates is a "teacher of misery."[246] But despite such criticism, Socrates perseveres in his recommendation of "toil" (*ponos, mochthos, talaipôria*) for noneconomic ends like fitness, fame, friendship, self-esteem, justice, and the virtues neces-sary for leadership.[247] In other works, Xenophon uses *philoponos* and *philo-ponia* to praise a variety of people—Agesilaus and the Spartans, Cyrus and the old Persians, hunters, and not least Socrates, who was "the most able to endure all *ponoi*."[248] Xenophon and Prodicus would hardly have composed such works if their sentiments did not have some appeal. Given Xenophon's Panhellenic experience and contacts, one suspects that that appeal was in fact quite broad.

Yet neither Xenophon nor Prodicus develops a philosophical work-ethic with the same sustained concentration that Plato devotes to it in his major political works. The *Republic* can be seen as a complex variation on the basic theme of Prodicus' "Heracles." Glaucon challenges Socrates to praise virtue in itself and to debunk views that equate vice with the supreme happiness. For Glaucon is troubled by the common tendency to idolize the tyrant's happiness. The tyrant does indeed seem to enjoy the highest felicity—the best food, drink, and housing, flatterers and sophists thronging to his table, sumptuous gifts to distribute among retainers and the people, and rich sacrifices with which to appease the gods. Moreover, this is a life without work, since as for Prodicus' Evil, the tyrant parties while the people toil. If such a painless pleasure were the highest good in life, then no mere scruple should restrain one. If one could enjoy complete immunity, then why would one not enjoy one's hubris, and like the legendary Gyges indulge in a little adultery or murder all the way to the throne? To explode this illusion and defend justice in itself, Socrates must in effect praise the life of Prodicus' Heracles— a life of self-restraint, pain, toil, and faithfulness to the highest Olympian ideals.

One aspect of the philosophical life, therefore, is that it is one of *ponos*. Socrates himself may have used such a metaphor to describe his own activities: in Plato's *Apology*, at least, he compares his examination of poets, craftsmen, and politicians to the *ponoi* of Heracles.[249] These toils Socrates imposed upon himself, for he wanted to learn whether he was in fact the "wisest" living person. Indeed, by these labors he came to realize the paradoxical nature of his wisdom, his unique capacity to recognize his own ignorance. This metaphor of *intellectual* labor is developed more fully in the *Republic*. First, as is emphasized repeatedly, the guardians and philosopher-kings live a strenuous life. From the earliest age they are tested and put through the *ponoi, erga, gymnasia,* and *agônes* of a demanding education. Therefore, the ideal rulers must not only be supremely talented: they must be "in all ways labor-loving" (*pantê philoponos*) and eager to practice their talents to perfection. They must like physical exercise as much as any athlete, and must not be "labor-hating" (*misoponos*) in any way. The greatest *ponoi* are the ten years of higher mathematics and five of dialectic between the ages of twenty and thirty-five.[250] And the highest wage of this abstract "work" is wisdom, the mind's dialogue with itself, the flight of the winged soul into the divine, the vision of a "Good beyond essence." Again, Socrates himself approximates this ideal by philosophizing ceaselessly—in the streets and countryside, in symposia and on campaign, through poverty, obscurity and ignominy, even unto death.

The greatest paradox of the *Republic*, however, is that abstract and seemingly useless philosophical "work" can also have a social "payoff," at least in the ideal state. Here, far from being an unworldly elitist, disdainful of the working classes, Plato is remarkable for his willingness to treat all activities, including philosophy, from a single, utilitarian point of view. That is, all activities in his utopia are initially treated as so many different forms of work, which become progressively necessary for the efficient maintenance of life. Farmers, herders, and fishermen produce food. Craftsmen produce shoes, clothes, and tools. Laborers sell their strength. Merchants sell their time to facilitate exchange. Soldiers and the philosopher-kings also have a product to exchange for the benefit of all, though their contributions are necessarily indirect. First, what is produced must be defended, but since the ideal state will not depend on farmer-soldiers who leave their crops to fight for a few weeks, it will need specialists in war, professional soldiers. The ability to kill is a peculiar "trade," and a threatening one. Armies who defend a people may just as easily plunder them. And so, a final type of "craftsman" becomes necessary to oversee military-civilian relations.

Indeed, the philosopher-king oversees *all* the necessary elements of the community, bringing them into a harmonious whole. But laws and their enforcement inevitably interfere with the family, workplace, market, and public spaces. Hence, the very craft of ruling seems contrary to the principle of justice, as the ruler must mind other people's business. This is a problem for imperfect societies, in which, to varying degrees, the ruling classes make laws for their own benefit and promulgate them by force. In the ideal state, by contrast, the ruler should conduct his business of minding others' business with the impersonal professionalism of a true craftsman. The philosopher is the only person who might be able to attain such professionalism in politics and to resist the specious allure of power. Trained in the most abstract studies to attain a vision of a distant Good, the philosophical rulers become abstract people. Uninterested in their bodies and in their selves narrowly conceived, they literally do not live for themselves. Rather, they are lovers of the Good, and, indirectly, lovers of the only state that enables them to live philosophically. In this way, the philosopher-rulers are truly public people who so identify themselves with abstract ends—the Good and the common good—that they devote their laborious lives utterly to them. For these labors, they get nothing that others typically want: no wealth, for they own nothing and receive only a wage (*misthos*) for their sustenance; no honor, for politics to them is just a matter of humdrum administration, and they recognize that there is nothing glorious in having power over others. Their reward is the leisure to philosophize, though even here, they must not indulge their private pleasures too much.[251]

Plato's long exploration of the nature, training, and knowledge of the ideal ruler was motivated initially by the practical need for such figures. To this he returns in the discussion of degenerate states, where the practical contribution of the philosopher-king is brought into high relief. Their labor is the guarantor of the political hierarchy, and therefore ultimately of the economic order. Without their *ponoi* and vigilance, the harmony between the classes breaks down. The "metals" are mixed, occupations are filled in the wrong way: the very talented work in mines or the fields; a violent but charismatic soldier usurps power, or a fool and lecher inherits it. Necessary tasks are no longer done efficiently because the wrong people are doing them. People's virtues and natural excellences are not harnessed for the maximization of value. Indeed, when philosophical wisdom and its ability to order and harmonize have wholly faded away, then tyrannical types appear. People are killed and everyone distrusts everyone. The general disunity invades the individual also, so that many are torn between the contrary tendencies both to hate the tyrant and to envy his happiness. Plato may in fact not have been alone in this desire to find "cash-value" in philosophical rule: Alcidamas also argued that states were most prosperous when guided by philosophical types.[252]

The *Republic* also approaches the "philosophical work-ethic" from a slightly different angle. The first principle of utopia is that each citizen performs only that one job for which he or she is most suited by nature.[253] In the ideal state, therefore, the intelligent and wise will rule, the spirited will fight, the strong labor. Those who have no distinguishing talent will sit in the market selling what others produce.[254] The degree to which Plato pursues this principle is astonishing. For instance, philosopher-rulers may bear children, but they will then delegate the work of breast-feeding and rearing the babies to professional nurses.[255] It is as if the philosopher-queen were not qualified to feed her own child: to her belongs the welfare of the child's soul, while others should tend to its bodily needs. In all such cases, work in the *kallipolis* is not imposed from without by capricious gods, exploitative masters, or economic necessity. Rather, work is the direct expression of one's own character and abilities. Far from being a form of punishment, labor is a means to self-fulfillment. The natural farmer, for instance, is happy farming. His other social and spiritual needs are amply satisfied by the state-sponsored festivals and myths; he at least has little desire or capacity for the higher "music" of philosophy. Those born philosophers, on the other hand, do have this desire, and would become angry and rebellious if they had to spend their time weaving coats. It is only in degenerate states that philosophers are forced to fritter away their talents, or, worse, to abuse them to become an eristic sophist or even tyrant (*corruptio optimi pessima*). Many have criticized the *Republic* for its lack of freedom, but in defense of the Platonic utopia, it seems in fact that there are no slaves there, neither real slaves nor wage-slaves.[256] Everyone is happy, and Plato might defend his scheme by appealing to the other definition of freedom as following one's essential nature: all freely and gladly perform *their* tasks and want little else. Here Huxley's *Brave New World* offers a penetrating reductio ad absurdum of this aspect of Platonic society: alpha-plusses play the role of philosopher-kings while the so-called epsilon semi-morons are designed to love their low, albeit necessary, tasks. Plato and Huxley may simply differ here: certainly Plato sacrifices what he sees as an unordered freedom to the greater goods of efficiency and the justice of "doing one's own job."

In the *Laws*, details change but the same endorsement of a philosophical work-ethic remains. Gone are the mathematical training and paradoxical phrases like "philosopher-kings." But once again, each citizen will do exactly one job; again, the job peculiar to the citizen-elite will be the pursuit of virtue.[257] But now the citizen-body as a whole, rather than simply the guardians and kings, are specialists in virtue; the economically necessary labor is not done (as in the *Republic*) by an artisan and farming class naturally disposed to such work, but by slaves or metics. The scheme is reminiscent of Sparta and the Dorian cities of Crete, with their militarized citizenry and farming helots. But Plato criticizes the virtues of the Spartans as too narrowly militaristic. Complete virtue is a many-sided affair, and to attain it, the ideal citizens will have to engage in ceaseless physical and intellectual "toil":

> And to men living under this second polity there remains a work to be accomplished which is far from being small or insignificant, but is the greatest of all works, and ordained by the appointment of righteous law. For the life which may be truly said to be concerned with the virtue of body and soul is twice, or more than twice, as full of toil and trouble as the pursuit after Pythian and Olympic victories, which debars a man from every employment of life. For there ought to be no bye-work interfering with the greater work of providing the necessary exercise and nourishment for the body, and instruction and education for the soul. Night and day are not long enough for the accomplishment of their perfection and consummation; and therefore to this end all freemen ought to arrange the way in which they will spend their time during the whole course of the day, from morning till evening and from evening till the morning of the next sunrise.[258]

Even more than in the *Republic*, Plato zealously pursues his main idea into the smallest details. Citizens will be punished for engaging in crafts and money-making activities: their job is to rule, judge, and protect, not to produce. They must be the first to rise, the last to go to sleep. These labor-loving citizens should not hunt by lying down to ambush their prey with nets and snares—a lazy option; more honorable and invigorating is to ride to hounds, hunting from horseback with spear and javelin. Like invincible Sparta of old, the city should have a wall made "not of earth, but of bronze and iron" (i.e., soldiers' armor). For walls give a false sense of security and lull a people into complacency. They make citizens soft and encourage them to believe that "they were not born to *ponos*." Rather, they should be constantly vigilant, training themselves to be the living wall that defends the homeland. For, as with Prodicus' Aretê, true ease (*rastônê*) arises from *ponos* voluntarily undertaken, while a shameful, unearned indolence (*rastônê*) brings a host of unwanted *ponoi*. Therefore it is with sweat and toil that citizens should earn the festivals or work-breaks (*anapaulai ponôn*) given them by the gods. On the other hand, idle beggars have earned nothing, and will not be tolerated.[259] One wonders how Diogenes might have fared in Plato's Cretan City. And yet, despite the significant differences in details, Plato and the Cynic agree in general that "work" is the means by which one attains perfect virtue and actualizes one's highest potential.

This latter phrase is deliberately formulated in Aristotelian terms, because a similar "philosophical work-ethic" surfaces also in Aristotle, who like Plato orients human energies towards noneconomic, even transcendent ends. Similar in spirit, if not in all its details, to Plato's utopias is Aristotle's ideal state. Here, most strikingly, Aristotle describes his ideal citizens as "craftsmen of virtue" (*tês aretês dêmiourgoi*)—a phrase that could be applied equally to Lycurgan Sparta, Plato's *Republic* and *Laws*, or even the Cynics. Certainly, Aristotle gives far more importance to harbors, imports, exports, and markets than these others do, yet he too renounces the notion that the state exists simply for economic ends. The state is an association not merely for the sake of life, but for the good life. The body must serve the soul, and so Aristotle would have a rigid hierarchy of economic and political elements. There is an upper city with its free (i.e., political) *agora* and citizen-class, and a lower city with the *emporion*, commercial *agora*, and "dwellers-around" (*perioikoi*) who support the citizens economically.[260] All this is in keeping with Aristotle's determination both to recognize and limit the ethical importance of wealth. Some wealth is necessary to support the leisure of a good life and cultured state; money is needed for complex exchanges. But material "wealth" is constituted by so many inert possessions. These must be used in the proper way for proper human ends: knowing these ends is the crucial thing, and Aristotle's citizens recognize that these are not pleasure and luxurious consumption, but rather virtue and the actualization of one's highest potentialities.

Thus, when Aristotle does discuss the goals of human life, money and wealth figure little. Yet, the rhetoric of "work" remains, though in accordance with a philosophical ethic the nature and value of work are internalized. Hesiod's *Works and Days* (*Erga kai Hêmerai*) treats "works" in a simple way: *erga* are what one does on a particular day or season, as when one harvests grapes at the close of summer. Aristotle uses the term *ergon* in a more idealistic way, in that the subjective agent (rather than the contingencies of location or season) determines what its "work" is. That is, for Aristotle, the nature of an entity determines what it will do, how it will act, develop, and interact with its external environment. In short, its nature determines its *ergon*—its proper function, task, or "work." The *ergon* of the plant is to grow, flower, and reproduce. The *ergon* of the animal soul is perception and locomotion. Most complex is man, the rational animal who is distinguished from the irrational by his ability to think—that is, form universal concepts, judgments, syllogisms, and arguments. Therefore Aristotle concludes, in Platonic fashion, that it is man's *ergon*—at once his function, duty, highest nature, and end—to philosophize. Of course, this rational being is also an animal that must hunt, fish, farm, trade, rob, or make war in order to eat.[261] But manual labor serves only the body's needs, and when they are met, the body should serve the soul,[262] whose proper activity is to practice virtue with philosophy. Aristotle's exhortations to practice divine philosophy are at times uncharacteristically vehement and unqualified. "There are some who say that being mortal one should think mortal things. . . . But on the contrary, one should immortalize (*athanatizein*) oneself to the utmost of one's power."[263]

Such a view of man's *ergon* is far more ambitious than Hesiod's. It is Platonic, in the sense that Plato too exhorts one to "immortalize" oneself by philosophy and contact with the Forms. And again, one is reminded of Prodicus' Aretê, who reminds Heracles to live up to his inheritance as a son of Zeus. For human beings, uniquely rational among the animals, mere life is not enough. To live like a cow or a Sardanapallus is shameful. Nature drives man to actualize his essence in the life of God. This self-imposed *ergon* of the Aristotelian philosopher is far more in harmony with the industrious optimism of the imperialist ethic. Again, "energy is eternal delight," but now that energy is directed inward and upward. The value of work is internalized and sublimated, as the philosopher seeks to contemplate, not conquer the world. For those who could recognize it, Aristotle's own energy must have been as electrifying as that of Alcibiades or Alexander: with primitive means of storing information, Aristotle wrote close to four hundred books, many destined to become classics for their close analysis of details and overall vision. His successor Theophrastus wrote almost five hundred books and was called *philoponôtatos*, "most toil-loving."²⁶⁴ Epicurus wrote an estimated three hundred, and the early Stoics are notorious for their output. Chrysippus outdid them all, and with over seven hundred rolls to his credit earned the title *ponikôtatos*, "most industrious."²⁶⁵ In search of knowledge or enlightenment, the philosopher works unceasingly.

Nor does this philosophical work require much wealth. Aristotle's assertion that nature does nothing in vain, and provides sustenance for all her creatures, faintly echoes Hesiod's claim that one day's work used to provide enough food for a year, before Prometheus' theft brought poverty "into the world and all our woe." For Aristotle, bodily needs are limited, and so one needs only a limited amount of wealth to satisfy them. Such a statement can be stressed in different ways, and Aristotle does not, of course, speak in the manner of a Cynic. Yet, the general rubric they shared was similar. We have seen Xenophon's Socrates, Plato's philosopher-kings, and even Pericles' democrats philosophizing on a frugal budget. So too, for Epicurus, "the wise" recognize that the "wealth of nature" is gotten very easily.²⁶⁶

This brings us closer to the Cynic position, and indeed the first Cynic ascetics give a radical twist to the philosophic work-ethic. The combination of Hesiodic fatalism and imperialistic optimism, the limitation of bodily labor to the satisfaction of necessities, and the limitlessness of philosophical *ponos* that prepares one for virtue are some of the elements that precede the first Cynic paradoxes. With regard to these, the following passages are indispensable:

> He [Diogenes] would often insist loudly that the gods had given to men the means of living easily, but this had been put out of sight, because we required honeyed cakes, unguents and the like.²⁶⁷

> [Diogenes] used to affirm that training (*askêsis*) was of two kinds, mental and bodily: the latter being that whereby, with constant exercise, perceptions are formed such as secure freedom of movement for virtuous deeds. . . . Nothing in life, he maintained, has any chance of succeeding without strenuous practice (*askêsis*); and this is capable of overcoming anything (*pan eknikêsai*). Accordingly, instead of useless toils men should

choose such toils as nature recommends (*hoi ponoi kata phusin*) whereby they might have lived happily. Yet such is their madness that they choose to be miserable. For even the despising of pleasure is itself most pleasurable, when we are habituated to it; and just as those accustomed to a life of pleasure feel disgust when they pass over to the opposite experience, so those whose training has been of the opposite kind derive more pleasure from despising pleasure than from the pleasures themselves. This was the gist of his conversation; and it was plain that he acted accordingly, adulterating the currency in very truth, allowing convention no such authority as he allowed to natural right, and asserting that the manner of life he lived was the same as that of Heracles, when he preferred liberty to everything.[268]

Even through the filter of Diogenes Laertius, one glimpses here what may have been the most typical argument of the Cynics. This might be reduced to three basic sets of ideas. First, as for Hesiod, Aristotle, and Epicurus, "the gods had given to men the means of living easily." Nature is bountiful and provides for all one's needs: the trees clustered with olives, figs, and apples; cabbages and lupines and wild legumes teeming up in rough patches; thyme, mint, cumin, sage, and other herbs on the fragrant hillside.

If circumstances could speak, as we do, and had the power to state their case . . . would not Poverty say to the man reviling her, "What is your quarrel with me? Have I deprived you of any good thing? Of prudence, or justice, or courage? Or are you short of any of the necessities of life? Well, are the roads not full of herbs, and the springs of water? Do I not offer you a bed wherever there is soil, and bedding wherever there are leaves? Can you not make merry in my company? What, have you never heard an old woman singing to herself as she munches her barley-cake?" . . . If Poverty spoke in this vein, what answer would you have to make? I think I should have nothing to say. But we blame anything rather than our own bad training and disposition, age, poverty, our adversary, the day, the hour, the place.[269]

Thus, nature is generous, and man has only himself to blame for his poverty. Blinded by the "smoke" of his own superfluous ideas and desires, he is afflicted by a swarm of unnatural desires—for flavored foods, too much food, houses, and other luxuries, not to mention superfluities like honor or glory. Enslaved by these false ideals, many undertake immense but "useless toils" (*achrêstoi ponoi*), and so moral corruption brings a fall from natural bliss. In reaction, the Cynics would extirpate needless desires and forgo conventional work. From the anecdotes, it seems that the Cynics did not work: they lived by gathering wild plants, rough gardening, and begging.[270] Resolute idlers, they lived from hand to mouth.

The Cynics placed far more emphasis on their "philosophical work." Cynic *ponos* is both mental and physical. Mental "works" are those acts of will by which one rejects the superfluous. To steel the will in this way, Diogenes may have recommended reading morally inspiring works—his own writings as well as encomia of such social and military ascetics as Heracles, Agesilaus, or Epaminondas.[271] Physical *ponos* includes rolling in hot sand, embracing snowy statues, eating beans, and all the ascetic practices that made Cynicism so startling. Hunger, cold, thirst, whippings, dishonor, and exile are *ponoi*,[272] and so later the Stoics simply used the term *ponos* as their standard antonym for "pleasure" (*hêdonê*). Such "works" fill the Cynic's life, and indeed he is constantly at "work," for without these *ponoi*, he would cease to be a Cynic. Thus, in one anecdote, someone suggested to Diogenes that he should relent from his self-discipline, given that he was so old; Diogenes refused.[273]

Specialists in "virtue," like Plato's guardians or Aristotle's *dêmiourgoi aretês*, the Cynics also betray an immense optimism in the rewards of their labors: "*askêsis* can overcome everything."[274] Rather than Sicily or any empires, the Cynic conquers himself; self-mastery is the greatest empire. To this end, the Cynic ceaselessly undertakes the "natural toils" (*hoi kata phusin ponoi*) by which one extirpates superfluous desires and recovers one's original nature. These are the "works" of the "dog," that lazy animal: hence, "idleness is work." Furthermore, these ascetic *ponoi* are not economically productive in the conventional sense, like farming or shoemaking; nor are they the *ponoi* of the "imperialist work-ethic." Yet they too bring in "wealth." For by them one returns to the bounty of nature; in simplicity, one learns how little one needs; with all one's wants satisfied, one does not envy others— in the true, qualitative meaning of the word, one becomes "rich." This type of poverty, therefore, *is* wealth. The poor, idle Cynic is a king.

Such thought-patterns find a close parallel in material relating to Onesicritus. In India, Onesicritus and others were sent by Alexander as ambassadors to certain sages, whom they named the "naked wise men." In the meeting, Calanus, the leader of these *gymnosophistae*, mocks Onesicritus for his luxurious outfit:

When Calanus saw him [Onesicritus] wearing a soldier's cloak, felt cap and boots, he burst out laughing and said, "In ancient times, the world was filled with barley-meal and wheat-meal just as now it is filled with dust. Some springs used to flow with water, others with milk or honey or wine or olive-oil. But due to their overconsumption and luxury (*truphê*), mankind fell into arrogance (*hubris*). Zeus hated their condition and took all away and showed to them a life of toil (*ponos*). But when temperance and the other virtues returned, there was once more a general abundance of good things. And yet, this thing [i.e., Onesicritus' get-up] borders on excess (*koros*) and hubris: surely, another destruction of wealth is at hand."[275]

The terms of Calanus' speech are thoroughly Greek: here again is the "archaic law" of *koros*, *hubris*, and *nemesis*. *Ponos* is, as for Hesiod, divine punishment for pride, but *ponos* may also be moral labor, bringing temperance and virtue. Further, when coupled with the virtues, work is the source of material abundance, as in the "virtue theory of value." Indeed, the *gymnosophistae* are depicted almost as the Cynics' Cynics. They too engage in ascetic *ponos*, lying naked and motionless on rocks in the Indian summers, eating little, and the like, "so that their will and mind (*gnômai*) might be strengthened." These Indian "Cynics" outdo their Greek counterparts, for when Onesicritus tells the Indians that they remind him of Pythagoras, Socrates, and Diogenes, the gymnosophist Mandanis responds that the Greeks sages were wise except for one mistake: they erred in preferring *nomos* to *phusis*, for if they indeed espoused nature, they would not have been ashamed to live naked.[276]

When one turns from these later sources to the few fragments of Diogenes, one detects a similar ethic of moral and philosophical "labor." Before Diogenes, Virtue was a slave to Fortune, a mere "word." But "after dismissing wealth-making injustice and unrestraint," Diogenes cultivated her as if she were an *ergon*. Similarly, all philosophers that "engage in some real toil" (*ekmochthousi ti*) will have the strength to rule the belly, "for the frugality (*euteleia*) of the wise is a teacher of counsels." Assigned to a play entitled *Heracles* is a speech that seems to belong to someone newly impoverished. The speaker laments that his father taught him music but neglected his education in *ponos*—"as if he would always be rich and unhappy," never suffering a reversal! But to have a trim belly, to drink water like the animals, to toughen the body in winter and in summer to welcome the sun's hot arrows—these are the "source of all good things for mortal men."

Unhabituated to this Cynical wisdom, the man is forced to bear up in his new hardship.[277] Fortune teaches him what his father did not.

In a similar way, the first Cynics seem to have had a penchant for adopting "labor-loving" heroes like Odysseus, Penelope, Cyrus the Great, Agesilaus, and Epaminondas.[278] Most important of all was Heracles. Diogenes may have written a tragedy called *Heracles*, and among Antisthenes' three books on the hero is one entitled "Heracles and Midas." The title suggests a dichotomy between virtuous poverty and unjust wealth: did the Cynics dramatize anew the old quarrel between countryside and tyrants, Hesiod and Perses, Solon and Croesus, *Aretê* and *Kakia*, Socrates and Callicles? Certainly, the myths of Heracles provided material for Cynic moralizing: Heracles' entire life was one of hardship and danger, as he willingly served mankind everywhere. Moreover, here was a just man who was forced by circumstances to slave for Eurystheus, arrogant tyrant of "much-golden" Mycenae. Yet, if Eurystheus appropriated the prizes that Heracles won—Hippolyta's girdle or the hide of the Erymanthian boar—in the end, Heracles' was the greater prize. Virtue is true wealth, and through his Labors, Heracles grew massively "rich"—strong, courageous, energetic, enterprising. His virtue was all-conquering, for though he wandered through the world armed only with his hands, club, and lionskin, he overcame all enemies and adversity. Eurystheus, by contrast, is remembered only as a petty and loathsome thing. So too a Cynic like Diogenes ("Zeus-born") wanders about with his staff, folded cloak, and invincible ideas, humbling the rich and liberating mankind from its self-imposed delusions. Such Herculean virtue is indeed a godlike possession. By contrast, who would want to pile up the riches of the dung-beetle? Who would not rather be poor with Heracles than rich and contemptible with Eurystheus?

ECONOMIC BACKGROUND TO CYNIC ASCETICISM

Such polarities and paradoxes may have resonated in many fourth-century cities because of the increased tension, even *stasis* (civil conflict), between the rich and poor. In turn, these social difficulties had a host of interrelated economic causes. We will touch briefly upon the increasing inequalities between rich and poor as the immediate reason for the emergence of Cynicism.

It is obviously difficult to generalize about the economic conditions of the entire Greek world during the time of the Cynics. That world included hundreds of cities, and regions as distinct and distant as the Black Sea, Cyprus, Libya, and southern Italy. Nevertheless, it seems that throughout the

Aegean and Magna Graecia conditions became more difficult. Population increased, and as a result procuring enough food became a state problem. This is most apparent to us in the case of Athens. Athens' reliance upon imported grain may have started even before the year 500, as it began to send out colonies and fight wars for influence over the Hellespont, passageway to the rich grain-areas of the southern Ukraine. Certainly, the issue of food was a crucial one to the Athenian empire, and became even more pressing after Lysander dismantled most of the navy in 404. No longer could Athenian fleets sail to the Black Sea to shore up alliances (as Pericles did in the 440s), or to Cyprus, Egypt (450), or Sicily (420s, 415–413). In the absence of more directly military options, Athenian responses became more diplomatic and political: throughout the fourth century, grain was a mandatory item at the first Athenian assembly of each month; various laws were passed to entice grain merchants to its ports.[279] For there was competition: Corinth, various Aegean islands (including Rhodes), Miletus, Smyrna, and other cities also imported grain, and so merchants without ties to one city might flock wherever profits were greatest. Too many mouths to feed, too few merchants, many dangers at sea, and the perennial threat of bad harvests or local producers stopping supplies—in such a precarious system, there were the inevitable crises: according to Garnsey, there were sporadic shortages in the 390s, 376, 362/1, 361/0, and the "universal grain shortage" of 357.[280] Philip's conquest of Perinthus and expansion towards the Hellespont worsened the situation for Athens, particularly after Chaeronea.[281] Again, Garnsey estimates that Athens suffered five crises in 338/7, 335/4, 330/29, 328/7, and 323/2, and perhaps shortages also in 332/1, 329/8, and 325/4. Indeed, the years from 332–321 may have seen shortages throughout the eastern Mediterranean. During this decade, Egypt had two poor harvests, and in 328/7 the Athenian state for the first time spent public money to buy food; grain commissioners (*sitônai*) began to be appointed, and the number of "grain-guardians" (*sitophulakes*) increased from ten to thirty-five, probably in the 330s or 320s.[282] Other grain-importing cities without Athens' stature and attractive market must have faced difficulties even more severe.

But even while procuring necessary grain became a widespread problem, there are signs of increased luxury among the richer classes. New characters seem to come to prominence in popular literature: cook, flatterer, parasite. A "parasite" was originally a temple-assistant or political official who received his sustenance from worshippers' offerings or the state, respectively. But in the plays of the Syracusan Epicharmus, the word gains its later meaning of a person who eats at another's table, flattering and amusing the master. The figure hardly appears in Attic Old Comedy, but becomes a stock-character in Middle

and New Comedy: Alexis, Antiphanes, and Diphilus wrote plays entitled
Parasitos, and so too the parasite looms large in Plautus' *Menaechmi* and
Captivi. The flatterer plays a similar role at the rich man's table, but more
important is the cook (*mageiros*). Davidson has detailed the rise of gourmet
cooking in late fifth-century Greece and after. Appearing first perhaps in Sicily,
it spread among the wealthy classes of other cities, bringing a taste for larks'
tongues, mullet, turbot, oysters, pheasant, and other exotic delicacies. The
growing market for gourmet dining among wealthier Athenians surely helped
provoke the renewal of sumptuary legislation, introduced twice by Demetrius
of Phalerum, in 317 and 310. Such luxurious living was invidious and enjoyed
only by a small few: many writers and orators speak in starkly binary terms, as
if in fact one had to be either rich or poor, oligarch or democrat, enjoying
lavish banquets or only simple necessities.[283]

Hunger vs. sumptuous symposia—this polarity could generate terrible
hatred in the small cities with their naturally egalitarian spirit. Certainly, the
specter of *stasis* (civil conflict) haunted much of the Greek world for much of
the fourth century, and it was generally economic in character, pitting the rich
against the poor, the oligarchic "few" against the democratic "many." Trouble
became widespread in the Peloponnesian War, as Athens and Sparta promoted
regimes similar to their own in the effort to control foreign cities.[284] This
remained the general policy of the large powers of the fourth century, including Philip with his tyrant-dependents. As a result, though Athens, Sparta, or
Macedonia themselves remained staunchly democratic, oligarchic, or monar-
chic, the constitutions of other cities might fluctuate wildly. To focus on the
cities of the early Cynics: in Monimus' Syracuse, democracy yielded to the
tyranny of Dionysius I and II, and then a period of anarchy before Timoleon
restored a "democracy" in the 330s. Crates' Thebes also suffered the vicissitudes of fortune: her democrats were exiled by a Spartan-backed coup in 382,
but regained full control in 379 under Pelopidas. Epaminondas and the
Thebans capitalized on the victory at Leuctra in 371 to democratize much of
the Peloponnese, thereby depriving Sparta of her traditional subject-cities:
revolutions in Phigalea, Sicyon, Megara, Phlius, Corinth, Mantinea, and Tegea
are explicitly mentioned, but there were probably many others. One that was
probably part of the same movement was the *skutalismos* at Argos in 370, when
the *dêmos* clubbed to death 1200–1500 rich Argives, then turned upon the
demagogues who had whipped them up.[285] In turn, oligarchs could celebrate
a victory by purging the democratic leadership; some oligarchic ruling coun-
cils took oaths to the effect that they would be "an enemy to the people and
devise all possible harm against them."[286] A concise phrase like "all possible

harm" should not blind one to the brutalities of *stasis*: political life was very personal and could therefore be very vicious. Thucydides' vivid description of the *stasis* in Corcyra illustrates what might happen when popular prejudices against the unjust rich or oligarchs' hubristic disdain for "the useless" classes took a violent turn.

All this class-conflict made a marked impression upon many politicians and political writers, and a variety of solutions were proposed. Among the partisans themselves, solutions were, not surprisingly, one-sided. Democratic revolutionaries typically clamored for land-distribution and abolition of debts.[287] In turn, oligarchic rhetoric appropriated the virtue of moderation (*sophrosunê*) in the effort to discredit democrats as profligate and improvident: unlike the rich who know how to make and save money, the poor would squander hard-won capital on petty handouts. But another possible interpretation of this upper-class *sophrosunê* would put a curb upon the elite's own conspicuous consumption. Thus, for instance, in attacking rich men like Meidias, Demosthenes repeatedly harkens back to the simplicity of Miltiades, Aristides, Cimon, Themistocles, and to a better time when citizens devoted all their wealth to the common good.[288] The praise of old-fashioned frugality and *sophrosunê* may in fact be part of a larger effort to discourage egregious inequalities: moderation and even frugality become patriotic gestures.

The personal example of the Cynics seems closer to such rhetoric than to other, more fantastical remedies for *stasis*. Perhaps most radical of all these solutions was the call for war. Taking inspiration from the archaic Ionian migrations that saw the Hellenization of the Aegean and western Turkey, Isocrates for almost half a century cast about for a city, general, or king to make Thessaly or Asia Minor a part of greater Greece. That is, the Greeks should unite in a war of conquest and settle their surplus poor on conquered barbarian territory. Eventually, in the *Philippos* of 346, Isocrates set his hopes on Philip, who by annexing "Asia from Cilicia to Sinope" might become the saviour of Greece.[289] Others would find salvation in utopian schemes for a more equitable redistribution of wealth. Redistribution may be complete, as in Aristophanes' *Plutus* and *Ecclesiazusae*, or in the communistic societies set forth by Iambulus and Zeno.[290] Alternatively, the redistribution might be partial, as in Plato's Cretan city, in which the richest citizens will not possess more than four times the wealth of the poorest.

Less radical were the calls for a sort of ethical conversion. *Noblesse oblige* and the rich should learn, or be taught, "to throw their superflux" to the poor, for the lasting benefit of all. Isocrates again looks for his guidance to what he saw as the spirit of the Athenian past. Sometime before the evils of the radical democracy (Isocrates may place this happy time under Solon, or Cleisthenes, or Aristides and Themistocles, but he never makes a final decision), rich Athenians rented land and lent money at moderate rates, and in return the poor thanked them with honor and respect. Now, Isocrates laments, the poor are not gainfully employed and rely too heavily for sustenance and well-being on the promises of demagogues. Their laziness (*argia*) only exacerbates their poverty and desperation. To remedy this, Isocrates would have them "work and save." And to this end, the rich should lend enough capital to allow the poor to buy a little farm or start up a business in overseas trade.[291] Aristotle advocates the same spirit of sharing, and his wording is at times remarkably reminiscent of Isocrates. But Aristotle drew his inspiration from a wider array of sources—from Carthage with its schemes for sponsored emigration, from Tarentum, where the rich directly employ the poor, and perhaps also from cities in Rhodes and Crete. Certainly he admired the social solidarity of the Spartans. There, travelers are allowed to use fellow-citizens' slaves, horses, and dogs, and to cull crops from the fields. Such customs lie behind Aristotle's celebrated conclusion that "Property should be private, but the use of it common; the special business of the legislator is to create in men this benevolent disposition."[292]

A similar spirit motivates others again to recommend individual philanthropy. In one fragment, Democritus writes: "When the well-to-do prevail upon themselves to lend to the have-nots, and help them and benefit them, herein at last is pity, and an end to isolation, and friendship, and *homonoia*, and other blessings such as no man could enumerate." Archytas of Tarentum, the Pythagorean, makes philanthropy a direct consequence of reason (*logismos*):

> Right Reckoning (*logismos*), when discovered, checks civil strife (*stasis*) and promotes concord, for where it has been achieved, there can be no *pleonexia* and there is equality.... Through this the poor receive from the men of means, and the rich give to the needy.

Such early, theoretical justifications of wealth-sharing are followed later by a rising movement of public generosity. In his *apologia pro vita sua*, Demosthenes notes how he often "helped those in need." One hears other stories of individuals in Corinth and Mytilene, perhaps around 350 who out of pity, generosity, and scorn for wealth, renounced the debts owed to them. Aelian notes that in doing so, Theocles, Thrasonides, and Praxis managed to avoid the fate of those other creditors who were murdered by angry debtors. Many other instances of grain-donations, expensive *leitourgiai*, and renunciation of debts could be mentioned as precedents to the Hellenistic cult of rich individuals as the "bene-factors" (*euergeteis*) and "saviors" (*sôtêres*) of cities.[293]

Redolent of all these various reactions to economic inequality is Cynic asceticism. Socrates and Antisthenes spoke the democratic language of shar-ing their "wealth," philosophizing with all and sundry on the streets. Furthermore, the stories of the Cynics' first acts of renunciation have a social dimension. Crates at least is said to have sold his estates and distributed the proceeds among the poor. When he heard about Diogenes' superlative virtue, Monimus stood on his master's banking table and began to throw the money around: was this slave of a moneylender and currency-trader tossing coins into the crowd, and was this an act of solidarity with the "many"? That it was is suggested by a fragment of Crates, which recommends a social asceticism as the only practical solution to civil discord: "do not—by enlarg-ing your plate of shellfish and forgetting the lentil soup—throw us into *stasis*." So too, a century later, Cercidas of Megalopolis would exhort his au-dience to reverence a goddess like "Share" (*Metadôs*). Again, Crates' ideal "republic" of Pêra has no coinage, no parasites, and no luxuries, just natural wealth like thyme, garlic, figs, bread—and therefore no *stasis*. This Pêra is of course the Cynic himself: the sage becomes a world unto himself, sur-rounded by oceans of dark *tuphos*—the materialism of too many contem-poraries.[294] Cynic asceticism is also akin to Isocrates' exhortation to "work and save." The Cynic "works" for the sake of natural self-sufficiency, by which thrift is maximized and expense slashed to a minimum. Such "work" is the source of the Cynic's "wealth." Finally, one might hear faint echoes even of Isocrates' call for war. The Cynics seem to have declared something of a "war" upon poverty, or at least to have made much use of various mili-tary metaphors. Thus, in Crates' words, gathering beans and cockles will allow one to erect a "trophy over poverty."[295] Voluntary poverty is, paradox-ically, the greatest victory over poverty.

In this way, then, invidious inequalities of the fourth century prompted Cynics to synthesize the themes of a Greek praise of poverty into their own social asceticism. Work is the source of justly gotten wealth, and therefore the subject-oriented "labor" of self-denial makes the Cynic "rich" in a nondivisive way. As for the wealth of "the ant," the Cynic sees no real benefits there, but only a host of needless worries and dangers. Best to reject it as a false ideal, for what sane person would choose the dangers of shellfish over lentil soup and cockles? Let the ants scurry to and fro for what tomorrow will take away. The "wise" set themselves at variance with the tricks of Fortune. They declare war on wealth and other conventional notions, buoyed by the idealistic conviction that the individual may be radically self-sufficient and despite external poverty may in fact triumph over all the world. Thus, if Crates' encomium of *ponos* and lentil soup might gratify some contemporary Hesiods with their approbation of quiet work and thrift, Cynicism also bears within it the mark of the imperialistic outlook. Though the Cynic is a homeless beggar, utterly pessimistic about the worth of quantitative wealth in a world ruled by *Tuchê*, over himself he retains absolute rule and through continual *ponos* steadily increases his inner "wealth." Thus, a pessimism concerning the external is contrasted with an "industrious optimism" concerning the internal and purely subjective aspect of experience: the Cynic beggar is unchallenged master, tyrant, and king of himself. But kingship symbolizes power—bringing us to our next set of paradoxes, that weakness is strength, and that the seemingly defenseless mendicant is in fact an indomitable monarch.

CHAPTER THREE

Praise of Poverty and War

The Andrians were the first islanders to refuse Themistocles' request for money. When Themistocles sent the message that the Athenians would come with two great gods in their service, Persuasion and Force, and that the Andrians had better pay the money, they replied that the Athenians were indeed marvelously powerful and prosperous, and that with such useful gods they would always succeed. But since the Andrians were poor in land and all necessities, and since their own two useless gods, Poverty and Powerlessness (*amechaniê*) loved and would not leave their island—therefore having such gods, they would not give the Athenians the tribute. For the power of the Athenians would never prove stronger than their own powerlessness. And so, when the Andrians had made their response and refused to pay, they were besieged.

—Herodotus, 8.911

ὁ σπουδαῖος ἀήττητος.
The good man is invincible.

—Epictetus (Arrian, *Epicteti Dissertationes*, 3.6.5)

The speech of the Andrians to the Athenians gives in its most explicit form the paradox that will occupy us in this chapter: latent in the Greek popular consciousness is the notion that under certain circumstances, powerlessness is power. In the Andrians' case, it is the poverty of their rocky island home that enables them to dismiss Athenian demands for tribute: their *amechaniê* is "stronger" than any armada's power to exact payment. For the Cynics over a century later, it is not poverty caused by geography, but a voluntary asceticism that makes the weak philosopher strong. For though seemingly powerless, the Cynic self is on the contrary "invincible." He is a "king" who imperiously talks down worldly monarchs like Alexander.[1] In his perpetual enmity with *Tuchê*, the Cynic's virtue is a weapon that cannot be taken away. Surrounded by the chaotic destruction of Fortune, the Cynic describes himself as a fortress, an island where peace forever dwells unbroken.[2] Here asceticism has a militaristic flavor and becomes the means to superiority in the metaphorical "wars" that the Cynics wage against *tuphos*. Enduring hunger, sleeping rough, wearing few clothes in winter, and the like are the Cynic's means to attaining the virtues of a soldier—courage, temperance, strength, physical fitness.

Previous interpretations of ancient Cynicism have generally overlooked its martial aspect. Yet the Cynics' peculiar brand of heroism as well as the paradox that powerlessness is power have precedents in a praise of poverty that is deeply rooted in the Greek experience. This Greek praise of martial poverty can be traced through three conceptual levels—the individual or ethical, the geographical or national, and the historical. First, poverty is a natural preparation for the hardships of war. Want inures the individual to heat, cold, hunger, weariness, toil, and all that one must suffer on campaign. Therefore, the poor can make the best soldiers. Certainly wealth does not make one courageous and fit. On the contrary, wealth can be seen as the cause of both physical and moral ruin: preferring homely comforts to sleeping rough on the march, the rich hire others to do their fighting for them. Second, what is true of individuals may be equally true of nations. Geographical factors shape national characteristics, and so poor countries like Greece with its jagged mountains and small plains are distinguished by their traditions of military valor. On the other hand, in Herodotus' generalization, "soft lands breed soft men."[3] Finally, notions of geographical determinism flow into a quasi-economic philosophy of history. History runs in repeating circles: warlike nations emerging from poverty demonstrate an energy and prowess that overwhelm the superior resources of rich, decadent enemies. But while poverty can propel to conquest, victory corrupts. Great empires bring wealth, and with it complacency and arrogance. As they neglect their ancestral virtues, ruling races are overthrown by others, and the cycle begins anew. This motive for a praise of poverty is an essential theme of Herodotus' history of the Persian Wars, Xenophon's *Cyropaedia*, and Plato's *Critias*; it surfaces also in attitudes towards other wars, notably the Peloponnesian War, even as narrated by Thucydides.

These ethical, geographical, and historical aspects of the praise of martial poverty will thread through our examination of precedents to Cynic martial asceticism. As before, such precedents include a wide variety of texts, voices, periods, and themes, and once again, certain conditions of the fourth century seem crucial for the emergence of the paradoxical figure of the "invincible" Cynic tramp. But beyond these historical contingencies, there are other ingredients in the *mélange* of ideas and sentiments contributing to early Cynicism: Xenophon's Cyrus; Plato's philosopher-kings; exemplary individuals like Phocion, Timoleon, Epaminondas, and Socrates; the *Marathônomachai* of legend; Herodotus' warlike primitives; heroes like Heracles and Odysseus; and the perennial idealism of the citizen-hoplite who claimed to fight for freedom, justice, or honor, but never for profit. The Cynics put their own stamp upon this broad cultural inheritance: the indomitable Cynic hero fights unaided against all the powers of Fortune and the idols of human customs. He does not fight for money or even honor, but for an end still higher than these socially sanctioned norms. The essential themes of such an outlook can be potentially located in the earliest legends, and the Cynics explicitly adopted Heracles and Odysseus as paradigms. Yet in the figure of Homer's Achilles, there are the first glimmers of a later dissociation of heroism and wealth, and even of the Cynics' rejection of conventional attitudes towards war. And so from this unwonted vantage point, we start with a selective view of the *Iliad*.

The Praise of Martial Poverty

Achilles is a difficult and even paradoxical figure, in that this most heroic of the Achaeans was also the one who very nearly rejected the ideals of heroic life. Those goals could be summed up in a single word and concept: the *geras* or "gift of honor" was bestowed by a community in recognition of a soldier's exemplary service. The gift is expensive—a horse, tripod, talent of gold, sword, woman—but material worth is inextricably linked with symbolic value. The more costly the *geras*, the more honor done to the recipient, and though the hero seeks glory and fame first, he seeks them through an external display of wealth and personal adornment.[4] The *Iliad*'s story of Achilles' inner growth, however, sees Achilles more and more vehemently reject merely monetary rewards. In book 1 of the *Iliad*, Achilles goes wild with rage not so much because Agamemnon reappropriated his valued slave-girl, but because Agamemnon took back the *geras* that "the sons of the Achaeans gave."[5] He has been insulted before his peers, and the dishonor is more hurtful than the theft of any commodity. But after brooding in his tent, contemplating the plague and wasteful slaughters of battle, Achilles reaches a point of crisis and renunciation such that even Agamemnon's superlative gifts of recompense cannot persuade him to return: "Hateful to me are his gifts. I count them at a hair's worth." Such gifts convey no honor, for Agamemnon would try merely to buy Achilles' loyalty. Achilles refuses to be bought, and wavers between an outright rejection of war as a sordid business and a more intense involvement with its tragic heroism. What is honor? Achilles does not ask the question explicitly, yet it haunts the entire epic. What is it to be honored by one's peers, or by unborn generations? The generations of men are as transient as leaves or flowers or migrating birds; their great battles are only like the clashes of lions with hounds, or like waves crashing on rocks. Achilles would leap beyond these natural cycles and be honored by Zeus alone. Honor is his highest good, his absolute, and he will accept honor only from the highest god. And so, after rejecting Agamemnon's gifts, Achilles threatens to sail away for Phthia, his father, and home. He has no business fighting Trojans, for they never crossed the seas to harass his people or steal his flocks.[6]

In the end, Achilles does not sail but remains at Troy, choosing long fame and an early death. After Patroclus' death, he returns to battle, but profoundly changed. One aspect of this change is illustrated by Achilles' now furious rejection of any talk of ransom and gifts. In his *aristeia*, seemingly single-handedly he drives the Trojan army back to the city. Lycaon, son of Priam, does not escape, however. This Lycaon Achilles had captured twelve days previously and sold into slavery. Now he is contemptuous of Lycaon's offer of ransom: why should a Lycaon have life when Patroclus lies dead and when even the most beautiful must die? So again later, before Hector's death, Achilles brutally refuses his request for ransom. Finally, when Priam does arrive with this ransom, Achilles angrily refuses to consider it. It is not for these clothes, cauldrons, and tripods that he will release Hector's corpse. He will do so freely, out of respect for Zeus' wish rather than for any payment; his motives run deeper than any narrow calculation of profit.[7]

Such refusals are a powerful testament to Achilles' revolt from the materialism involved in more conventional notions of honor. Certainly, his treatment of Priam is in marked contrast with Agamemnon's opening rejection of Chryses' ransom: Achilles treats Priam like a father, whereas Agamemnon had terrorized Chryses with the prospect of his daughter's sexual enslavement. Such contrasts not only distinguish Achilles from his more materialistic peers, they also define the heroic type: Achilles' unbending pride furnishes the first instance of a dichotomy typical of attitudes towards war throughout Greek history. The incitements to war—whether glory, honor, love, patriotism, or aggressive self-assertion—are more admirable than profit and private enjoyment. The gourmand is a contemptible waster, the businessman a petty moneygrubber. The latter's thoughts dwell among copper coins and prices. What does he know of the ecstasy of battle?[8]

This typical dissociation of heroism and wealth-getting is evident from a variety of perspectives. First, the *via negativa*: throughout the archaic and classical periods, it is commonly asserted that only mercenaries and barbarians fight *primarily* for wealth. That there was a stigma attached to killing for profit is suggested by the many euphemisms for mercenary soldiers—"hired laborers" (*misthôtoi, mistharnêtikoi*), "wage-earners" (*misthophoroi*), "helpers" (*epikouroi*), or most common, "foreigners" (*xenoi, to xenikon*). Poetry also could lend a veneer of respectability to a brutal business, as in Hybrias' lines:

> My wealth is my heavy spear and sword,
>> And the bright breast-plate that guards my chest.
>> For with these I plough, and with these I reap,
>> With these I trod the sweet wine from the vine,
>> With these I am called lord by the serfs.[9]

Similar is Archilochus' celebrated couplet:

> On my spear (*en dori*) is my kneaded bread, and on my spear
>> my Ismarian wine; on my spear I rest and drink.[10]

Various attempts to explain the phrase *en dori* by giving Archilochus a knapsack (filled with bread and wine) to hang "on the spear" are far too literalistic.[11] Like Hybrias, Archilochus speaks of his spear as his "means of production," as if it were with this that he did all the work of ploughing, harvesting, pressing grapes, and kneading bread. The mercenary does none of these things, of course. His "work" is the unproductive business of fighting. He is paid to destroy, and to supplement his income he may plunder others' harvests and vintages; fighting only for his own profit, he is notoriously fickle and disloyal. Mercenaries were common in the archaic period, but seem to have disappeared from the Greek world between 550 and 400, only to return in force in the fourth century when poverty, overpopulation, and numerous wars forced or enticed many men from their homes.[12] This resurgence of mercenary warfare would have a notable influence on Xenophon, Plato, and the Cynics in their construction of the idealized philosopher-soldier, as we will explore below.

But until the reemergence of professional soldiers, dominant attitudes towards war developed out of the conditions peculiar to hoplite warfare.

The hoplite phalanx required above all that soldiers remain disciplined, that they stand in their place and not panic at any false alarms or even real reversals elsewhere on the field.[13] Therefore courage or fearlessness before danger becomes the canonical virtue; holding one's appointed station in the battle-line becomes a metaphor for moral duty itself.[14] Moreover, the dynamics of the phalanx-line demanded the utter subordination of the individual to the communal formation: alone a hoplite soldier was slow and clumsy, and it was only in massed formations that the thick armor, heavy shield, and thrusting spear could be effective. These simple dynamics of a hoplite battle remained essentially the same for centuries, until the fourth-century innovations of Iphicrates, Epaminondas, and Philip.

As a result of this longevity, there grew up a definite ethos and rhetoric of war that seems to have changed little through its many manifestations in epinician odes, epitaphs, funeral speeches, and other derivative literary forms. The Athenian funeral speech (*epitaphios logos*), in particular, is the crucial institution that defined the meaning of war for the largest Greek state over a span of two centuries.[15] Every year in which there were casualties in battle, a distinguished speaker was chosen to deliver an oration in praise of the dead and of the great tradition for which they died. Two themes of this tradition are important for the ultimate emergence of Cynic asceticism. First is the common boast that the patriots struggled "few against many" and prevailed despite all odds. Such hyperbole may be partly justified by the astonishing victories at Marathon and Plataea. But other battles too may have bolstered the official rhetoric. In 458, when the main army was engaged in Aegina, the Corinthians invaded Attica, only to be defeated in the Megarid by Myronides and his makeshift array of boys and old men. The victory was celebrated as yet another proof of Athenian resourcefulness and pluck.[16]

Second, a seemingly hallowed sentiment of the *epitaphios logos* was that the Athenians fight only for the noblest ends. The state as a whole goes to war for justice, honor, freedom, and in order to protect the weak from the predatory strong. Such an assertion is not unique to Athens: Sparta and Corinth, for instance, could pride themselves on fighting *solely* for freedom and against tyranny.[17] Equally noble and unselfish are the motives of the individual citizen. He forsakes all for the common good—life, family, friends, and a fortiori, his private wealth. The patriot does not act for personal gain; no calculation of profit drives him on. Indeed he scorns such calculations. He is not distracted by the pleasures of wealth at home, nor by the hope of attaining such wealth some day.[18] On the other hand, there are shirkers whom wealth tempts to cowardice and "softness" (*malakia*):[19] the wealthy can use their influence to avoid being called up, and in the last expedient can bring their own horses to serve in the cavalry—an assignment that was both less dangerous and less crucial to the battle's outcome. In the enduring popular image, then, Wealth (*Ploutos*) is a craven god.[20] In this vein, the funeral-speeches of democratic Athens are remarkable for their suppression of all class differences and their elevation of the common soldier. Cavalry, officers, even generals are not specifically mentioned. The state burial afforded to all citizens alike regardless of status was likely designed to promote egalitarian ideals and replace the aristocratic tradition of spectacular private funerals.[21] In this regard, Socrates notes with gentle sarcasm that the hyperbole of the *epitaphios* makes him giddy with a sense of his own valor: even the poorest or most undistinguished citizen is honored with a costly official burial. Socrates' sarcasm reveals how the *epitaphios* makes an indirect contribution to a praise of the martial poor. For though the hoplites were not *thêtes* from the poorest ranks, they were relatively poor, and are sometimes described as such. This is not surprising: their equipment was not *that* expensive, particularly as bronze armor does not rust and can be used for generations, fathers bequeathing it to sons. The *zeugitae* (who in Athens at least constituted the bulk of the hoplite-class) were mainly small farmers who owned little more land than could be farmed by a yoke of oxen. Hence, the *zeugitai* and *thêtes* tended to be contrasted in Athens with the wealthier *pentacosiomedimnoi* and *hippeis;* relevant here is Aristotle's gnomic remark that "the ox is the poor man's slave."[22] Thus, Socrates' sarcastic enthusiasm in the *Menexenus* suggests that some at least saw many patriots as relatively poor citizens who fought for nothing but the good of the state.

But if the typical hoplite of Athens, Sparta, and other smaller inward-looking states does not fight for profit but only in the best traditions of his city, contact with imperialistic Oriental kingdoms woke the Greek consciousness to different attitudes towards war as well as to the relative idealism of their own outlook. Herodotus' synthetic vision looks back to the archaic period and forward to the changes of the Peloponnesian War: many revealing anecdotes in his *Histories* articulate the belief that traditional Greek hoplite-wars were waged in the idealistic causes of honor or justice, while Lydians, Persians, and others fight primarily for gain. The first of these anecdotes pictures the Persian general Mardonius marveling at the stupidity of the Greek *nomos* of war:

> As I have heard, the Greeks have a custom of going to war without any plans at all, out of sheer idiocy and foolishness. For whenever they

declare war on each other, they find the finest and smoothest plain and rush onto it to fight. The result is that even the victors leave off with great loss. I do not mention the defeated, for they are destroyed altogether.[23]

Why do Greek armies so regularly slaughter each other in their paltry, dusty plains? Mardonius can see no reason why they should fight each other. He does not know that since Achilles, Sarpedon, and Hector, the Greek hero claims to fight for preeminence and honor: "always to be the best and to be superior to others."[24] The Persian Tritantaechmes is equally astonished by the Greek agonistic spirit. After the disaster at Thermopylae, he learns that the Greeks are away celebrating the Olympics, where the only prize is an olive-wreath:

> Tritantaichmes, son of Artabanos, expressed a most noble sentiment which caused him to be accused of cowardice by the king. When Tritantaichmes heard that the prize was a wreath and not money, he could not restrain himself and stay silent but burst out in the presence of all: "My god! Mardonius, against what kind of men are you leading us, these men who compete not for money but excellence (*aretê*)?"[25]

Herodotus' dichotomy between money and something as idealistic as *aretê* often becomes more pronounced in the fourth century. The Spartan king Agesilaus, for instance, claimed to invade Asia not for plunder but in reprisal for Xerxes' atrocities a century before. Throughout his long life, Isocrates advocated a crusade of sorts to avenge Xerxes' burning of the Athenian acropolis and attack on Delphi; Isocrates' expedition would thus be a kind of holy war, not at all an organized booty raid.[26] That is, Agesilaus and Isocrates seek justice for the Persians' initial crime. Again, in the Hellenistic period, the best soldier claims to fight for honor and glory rather than money or pleasure. After his victory at Issus in 333, Alexander spared Darius' mother, wife, and daughters, reassuring them that "they need not fear any harm from Alexander, who made war upon him [Darius] only for dominion."[27] Alexander claims to fight solely for political power and honor. So too, when Darius offered Alexander ten thousand talents and all Persian lands east of the Euphrates, Alexander refused: a man like Parmenio might accept such an offer, but not Alexander.[28] But Parmenio, Ptolemy, Demetrius Poliorcetes, and others did emulate Alexander's yearning for an absolute glory. In Plutarch's anecdotes at least, after the battle at Gaza (312), Ptolemy returned Demetrius' captured tent, money, furniture, and private belongings, along with a "humane and courteous message, that they were not fighting for anything else but honour and dominion."[29] Later, Demetrius repaid the "debt" in kind. For these chivalrous kings, money should be spent on wars, and wars fought for preeminence, not profit. In such gallantry, one hears distant echoes of Achilles' refusal of ransom; Achilles was Alexander's greatest hero. Thus, even though plunder and profit may have in fact been considerations, they were rarely stressed as *determining* factors. From Achilles to Alexander, the martial ethos is an explicitly idealistic one: hero, hoplite, and Hellenistic king fight for some good greater than mere profit, whether that good be individual glory, or the glory of protecting one's family, gods, and the noble example of one's forefathers.

Another theme of the praise of martial poverty also has its first seeds in the Homeric poems, this time in the *Odyssey*. Odysseus differs in many ways from other kings of the Trojan War. He did not want to fight or leave home. His appearance and stature are unheroic. He brought a mere twelve ships from Ithaca, a small and unimportant kingdom on the fringes of the Greek world. Yet he redeems all by his own native intelligence, cunning, and eloquence, speaking with more insight than any other. This eloquence will unwittingly provide the kernel for later paradoxical arguments: Ithaca, he says to Alcinous, is my home, "a rough island, but a nurse of good men."[30]

The note of primitivism is only rarely sounded in the *Iliad* and *Odyssey*,[31] but this particular Homeric tag would be taken up in the fifth century by at least one sophist. Arcesilaus allegorized Odysseus' phrase, writing that "hard poverty is like Ithaca, a good nurse of men, habituating one to simplicity and perseverance, and in general, a gymnasium that produces *aretê*."[32] Arcesilaus was not alone in explicitly linking valor and geographical poverty. The Hippocratic writer of *Airs, Waters, Places* would also give a naturalistic justification for the assertion that inhabitants of the European continent are more courageous, energetic, and self-assertive than their Asian neighbors.[33] Indeed, the writer goes so far as to formulate a general law of how environment determines character:

> For in general, you will find assimilated to the nature of the land both the physique and the characteristics of the inhabitants. For where the land is rich, soft, and well-watered, and the water is very near the surface, so as to be hot in summer and cold in winter, and if the situation be favorable as regards the seasons, there the inhabitants are fleshy, articulated, moist, lazy, and generally cowardly in character. Slackness and sleepiness can be observed in them, and as far as the arts are concerned they are thick-witted, and neither subtle nor sharp. But where the land is bare, waterless,

rough, oppressed by winter's storms and burnt by the sun, there you will see men who are hard, lean, well-articulated, well-braced, and hairy; such natures will be found energetic, vigilant, stubborn and independent in character and in temper, wild rather than tame, of more than average sharpness and intelligence in the arts, and in war of more than average courage.[34]

Such thoughts appear in Xenophon, Aristotle, and Herodotus, whose concluding "soft lands make soft men" is a leitmotif that pervades his *Histories*.[35] This diversity of authors suggests that attitudes were in general quite susceptible to a deterministic view that also tended, happily, to celebrate Greek machismo and love of liberty.

But if poverty is the "gymnasium of virtue," wealth is commonly seen as incompatible with warlike prowess, for markets, shops, and counting-tables do not make fighters. Herodotus' stories are, again, as colorful as they are revealing. He writes, for instance, that before the defeat of Croesus, "in all Asia there was not . . . a braver or more warlike people"[36] than the Lydians. But when they revolted from Cyrus a second time, Croesus could dissuade Cyrus from exterminating them only by taking extreme measures. Let Cyrus spare the Lydians by transforming them into a "nation of shopkeepers":

> While forgiving the Lydians, give them the following orders so that they will never revolt or prove formidable again: send a message to forbid them to own weapons, and order them to wear tunics under their cloaks and soft boots on their feet. Command them to teach their sons to play the cithara and lyre, and to become retail traders (*kapêleuein*). Soon you will see that they have become women instead of men, so that they will never threaten you with rebellion again.[37]

Similar, but more surprising, is Herodotus' indirect criticism of Greek mercantilism—directed by Cyrus at the Spartans, of all people. After conquering the Lydians, Cyrus marched down to the Ionian coast and was met at Phocaea by a Spartan herald who sternly forbade him to attack any of the Greek cities, as "the Lacedaimonians will not allow it." Cyrus' answer is equally proud and disdainful:

> When Cyrus heard the messenger's speech, he is said to have asked those present what kind of people these Lacedaimonians were, and how

numerous were they that they dared to address him in this manner. When he was told, he said to the Spartan herald, "I never yet feared men who keep a place marked out in the middle of their city where they gather to swear oaths and deceive each other. If I remain healthy, the Spartans will not need to heed the sufferings of Ionians—only their own." These words Cyrus flung at all the Greeks, because they have market-places where they buy and sell. For the Persians themselves have no tradition of frequenting markets, and there is not one market-place anywhere in their country.[38]

Cyrus' (and Herodotus') comments are more directed at contemporary Athenian or Corinthian businessmen and their critics than at the Spartans themselves. Similar antieconomic attitudes may account for the reputation that plagued the mercantilist Ionians, who were major trade-carriers in the Aegean and beyond, but who rarely distinguished themselves in war. Hence, the popular view attributed the Persian conquest of coastal Asia Minor to the luxurious living of the Ionians; the proverb "once long ago, even the Milesians were valorous" contrasts an almost forgotten glory with Miletus' present ignominy.[39]

Clearly, this aspect of the praise of poverty relies heavily on national stereotypes: the relative poverty and valor of mainland Greece are contrasted with their opposites elsewhere. But there are also instances within individual states in which the poor classes are contrasted favorably with the rich. Aristophanes pokes fun at overweight Athenians who cannot carry a torch in a festival, let alone the seventy pounds that constituted the hoplite's gear. In the *Laws*, Plato names the insatiable love of money as "one of the causes which prevents states from pursuing in an efficient manner the art of war, or any other noble aim, but makes the orderly and temperate part of mankind into merchants, and captains of ships, and servants, and converts the valiant sort into thieves and burglars, and robbers of temples, and violent tyrannical persons." In the *Republic*, pale and fat oligarchs are no match for lean, sun-burnt democrats: the poor are like stinging wasps to the plutocratic drones. Aristophanes plays upon the same view in depicting his chorus of the *Wasps*: these Marathon-men of old, tough from hard living, ensure that nothing "is more manly than the Attic wasp." Most uncompromising is a passage in the *Laws*: those lovers of wealth and pleasure who live "battening like beasts . . . deserve to be torn in pieces by some other valiant beast whose fatness is worn down by brave deeds and toil."[40]

THE TESTIMONY OF HISTORY: POVERTY'S UNAIDED VICTORY OVER TYRANNICAL WEALTH

The Persian Wars of 499–479 haunted Greek attitudes towards war throughout the classical period, and quickly became a ready source of inspiration for reformers, military thinkers, patriots, and moralists. In particular, patriotic memory, love of drama, and indifference to historical detail all ensured that by the end of the fourth century, two lessons that might be drawn from the Persian and other wars were that martial virtue generally prevails over material advantages and that such virtue is most demonstrated by those who have been hardened by the conditions of poverty. For had not the valiant Greeks repulsed the glittering hordes of Asia? Had not the Peloponnesians marched out of their valleys and mountain villages to chastise the Athenian tyrants and liberate the Greeks? What of Epaminondas' near conquest of a Sparta ruined by greed? Or Timoleon's victories in Sicily? Thus, experience—or a selective view of experience—might seem to corroborate the view that poverty is the training ground of heroism while wealth often ruins soldiers and nations alike. *Aretê*, fostered by hard poverty, is sufficient for victory. Although Herodotus and Thucydides are the primary sources for information on the Persian and Peloponnesian wars, less historically precise writers— orators, poets, and philosophers—are a better gauge of average reactions to these formative events. For the great historians are rare specimens, and their fidelity to historical detail was not widespread. In two uncharacteristically exasperated asides, Thucydides pauses to complain of the ignorance and laziness of his contemporaries.[41] Given that most of these would have preferred a good story or an edifying discourse to dispassionate analysis, we can speculate that the praise of martial poverty was a popular, if implicit, aspect of interpretations of famous wars of Greek history.

The Persian Wars

"Then divine Justice will quench powerful Excess, the fierce raging son of Hubris."[42] So spoke the prophet Bacis concerning Xerxes' invasion of Greece, and Herodotus treats the utterance with highest reverence, for it proved true. Herodotus' *Histories* are permeated with moral considerations, two of which are relevant for the eventual emergence of Cynicism. First, individual virtue (courage, strength, temperance) are of greater importance than material resources, as demonstrated by the repeated defeat of Persia's millions by a relatively few disciplined Greeks. Second, Herodotus assumes a variant of the geographic determinism popular (as we have seen) among contemporary scientific writers and uses it to underpin a quasi-economic philosophy of history.

First, Herodotus hints at the notion that *aretê*, not material resources, determines the outcome of wars. Namely, the strength, courage, and discipline of individual Greek soldiers—not numbers, organization, strategy, tactics, or superior weapons—flung back the Persians' multitudes. The stage for this morality play is set when, in some forty impressive chapters, Herodotus catalogues Xerxes' army and fleet, giving his Greek audiences a panorama of soldiers and sailors from exotic places, their marvelous dress and ingenious weapons.[43] Most impressive of all are the ten thousand Immortals, the elite Persian guard, who were "adorned with the greatest magnificence. Besides their arms, they glittered all over with gold, vast quantities of which they wore about their persons."[44] Xerxes, king of kings, reviews this magnificent force and in premature triumph turns to his advisor Demaratus, the exiled Spartan king. Who would dare to contend with such overwhelming force? he asks rhetorically.[45] Demaratus' unyielding reply must have raised a cheer from the audiences who listened to Herodotus' stories at Olympia or Athens:

> King, since you order me to employ the truth in all things and not tell lies that will prove damning to me later—King, poverty has always been the companion of Greece, while *aretê* has been acquired through wisdom (*sophia*) and steadfast law (*nomos ischuros*). With these, Greece wards off both poverty and tyranny. . . . But concerning the numbers of the Greeks, do not ask how many they would have to be before they could fight against you. For if they happen to march with a thousand men, these thousand will fight you, and if with fewer, these too, no matter how few, will fight you?[46]

Demaratus' proud words implicitly contrast Greek poverty, valor, and love of liberty with Xerxes' numbers and wealth. Furthermore, there is an ominous hint in his speech that the *aretê*, *sophia*, and lawfulness that poverty forces the Greeks to adopt will overcome Xerxes' material superiority. Wild words!—the Persian tyrant dismisses Demaratus with a laugh, but the audience recognizes the dramatic irony. The Persians' hubristic display of power and wealth at Abydos is juxtaposed vividly with their catastrophic reception at Thermopylae. For when they venture into the pass there, Leonidas and his tiny army rout them repeatedly. Illustrating the virtues of Greek poverty, as outlined by Demaratus, Leonidas' soldiers show both skill (*sophia*) and discipline (*nomos ischuros*) by charging and retreating in tight formation. As he watches, Xerxes leaps up in fear for his army, and cries out in rage and dismay that he has "many men, but few fighters."[47] The Greeks of course lost at Thermopylae, due ostensibly to the bribe-taking of Ephialtes, but nevertheless it was long seen by many as a moral triumph.[48]

Herodotus admires the Greek victories as a vindication of the power of freedom, but he is at the same time too sensitive to the intricate interplay of conditions to attribute Xerxes' defeat to a single cause. In addition to the *aretê* praised by Demaratus, Herodotus offers tactical, technological, strategic, and geographical reasons for the Greek victories. At Thermopylae and Salamis, the Persians could not capitalize on their numbers. Thermopylae was too narrow to use their archers and cavalry effectively. The Greeks had better armor and longer spears. The Persians themselves (as opposed to their allies and subjects) were "in daring and courage not at all inferior to the Greeks" at Marathon, Plataea, and elsewhere. At a larger level, Xerxes' strategy had various shortcomings: he did not, for example, follow Demaratus' advice to use the island of Cythera to launch raids into Sparta. He also failed to heed Artabanus' warning that the land and sea would fight against him: the Greek landscape, with its mountains, bad roads, poor harbors, and small harvests, was too poor to support the great Persian army on the march.[49] Thus, for Herodotus at least, Greek heroism was only one cause of the Persian defeat.

Herodotus' historical sensitivity, however, was rare, and very quickly the Persian Wars became the stuff of legend. The mythologizing of the Persian Wars that began immediately, and continued through the fourth century, crystallizes, in Athens at least, around the battle at Marathon. For comedians, orators, and others composing for popular audiences, Marathon became a mighty contest between Europe and Asia, democracy and tyranny—and implicitly between poverty and wealth. Standing alone at Marathon, a few heroic Athenians would not yield, but repulsed the allied tyrants and defended free Greece against the barbarian hordes. In this popular rendition, it would ruin the effect to include the fact that the whole Plataean force fought alongside the Athenians.[50] Already Herodotus depicts how official rhetoric omitted the Plataeans: "There [at Marathon] we alone of the Greeks stood and fought single-handedly against the Persians; such was our daring, and we proved victorious and defeated forty-six nations!"[51] This is the first example of selective memory, and of mixed memories. The "forty-six nations" refer not to Darius' force of Persians and Medes, but to Xerxes' polyglot juggernaut, as detailed in Herodotus' catalogue. The same mythologizing can be followed through scattered passages in Aristophanes, in many of the speeches that Thucydides attributes to Athenian diplomats, in Isocrates, and in surviving funeral speeches.[52] To take just one example: eventually, the writer of the Demosthenic funeral speech makes Marathon a double Athenian victory over the entire land and sea forces of Asia; Marathon, Plataea, Artemisium, and Salamis have become compressed in popular rhetoric into a single struggle.[53] In the conclusion of Thomas, conflation and selective memory ensured that for the average Athenian the battle at Marathon "came to epitomize the whole" of the Persian Wars.[54]

But it is a philosophic text, the Platonic *Menexenus*, that first articulates the abstract moral lesson implicit in Marathon and the Persian Wars. Here Aspasia's speech differs from other *epitaphioi logoi* in its close attention to historical detail and chronology. Yet, at the same time, the author makes explicit the intuition that had inspired a century of stories, epitaphs, and speeches: Marathon and Salamis are proof of the general truth that military success is a matter not of material superiority but of courage and *aretê*:

> If one were there, he might recognize how heroic those men at Marathon were, when they withstood the power of the barbarians, punished the arrogance of all Asia and were the first to raise a trophy of victory over the foreigners, proving themselves to be leaders of others, teaching them that the power of the Persians is not irresistible, and that, on the contrary, *every multitude and all wealth yield to virtue*.[55]

According to Cicero at least, the speech was read aloud publicly every year in Athens,[56] a powerful testament to how popular this praise of *aretê* became in Athens from the mid-fourth century. Indeed, Aspasia's piece in the Platonic *Menexenus* is not the only funeral speech to celebrate the "invincibility" of virtue, as we will examine later.

We turn now to the second theme of Herodotus' *Histories* and popular attitudes towards the Persian Wars—geographical determinism and a quasi-economic philosophy of history. Most succinctly, Herodotus writes that "soft lands breed soft men."[57] As an ethnological writer, Herodotus must have been influenced by the same matrix of ideas that produced contemporary works like *Airs, Waters, Places*. But Herodotus does not merely adopt fashionable theories for display. He goes further to adapt deterministic ideas to one of his own purposes—the explanation of national development. Here the association of geographical poverty with military valor looms large: imperial nations progress from an initial, virile poverty to military victories, to dominion, wealth, and eventually to a luxury and arrogance that undo the pristine virtues of the race. The conquerors become tyrannical and complacent, and are in turn overthrown by new, uncorrupted peoples. There is a latent religious dimension to this pattern (similar to the "archaic law of wealth" in chapter 2), for wealth tempts the successful to scorn and transgress divinely established boundaries in their mania for acquisition. Most notably, the Persians transgress divine limits to attack poor and therefore formidable neighbors. After the Persian defeat at Plataea, Herodotus ends his *Histories* with an almost melancholy glance back at the simplicity of old Persia, at Cyrus and the wisdom that went unheeded, and that may have further application in the Peloponnesian Wars.

Herodotus' quasi-economic philosophy of history is first illustrated by the fate of Croesus. It would be folly, Croesus is advised, to attack the Persians, a poor and tough people from whom the Lydians could wrest no reward.[58] But confident in the Delphic oracle, in his soldiers and unsinkable fortune,[59] Croesus crosses the Halys River and is defeated. In his fall from king to "slave" of Cyrus, Croesus learns a tragic wisdom and comes to understand the insight of Solon, that lasting happiness is not dependent on external possessions. Yet, despite his eloquence, Croesus cannot enlighten Cyrus, whose own downfall repeats the same pattern of success, arrogance, and catastrophe. Recalling the advice once given to him, Croesus warns Cyrus that the Massagetae are very valiant, but too poor to enjoy the luxuries of the Persian lifestyle. Victory would gain Cyrus nothing. But still buoyed by an impious confidence, Cyrus ignores Croesus.[60] He crosses the Araxes river at the eastern edge of the world, attacks the Massagetae, and is defeated and brutally killed.

Successor to Cyrus' throne and destructive arrogance, Cambyses marches to the southern limits of the world, into the land of the Ethiopians, also poor and warlike. First, however, he sends spies whose encounter with the Ethiopians juxtaposes primitive and "civilized" man.[61] The Ethiopians are nomads who live solely from boiled meat and milk; they are amazed by the Persians' diet of bread and wine. They are even more perplexed by Cambyses' gifts of a purple robe, myrrh, and gold necklace and bracelets. The purple and myrrh are evil and deceitful inventions (their king says), for they conceal a person's real appearance and smell. As for gold, the Ethiopians have too much of it to consider it precious: they use it to make fetters for their prisoners. In a comic exchange, the ambassadors produce their gifts of gold jewelry, and the Ethiopian king laughs aloud, informing the astonished Persians that they have much stronger chains than these. But these poor Ethiopians can fight. In return for Cambyses' decadent presents, the Ethiopian king gives the ambassadors a bow and a warning: "When the Persians can pull a bow of this strength thus easily, then let him come with an army of superior strength against the long-lived Ethiopians—till then, let him thank the gods that they have not put it into the hearts of the sons of the Ethiops to covet countries which do not belong to them."[62] The Persians were famed archers, but back in Susa none of Cambyses' men can bend the bow, except Smerdis who manages to pull it by a feeble two finger-lengths.[63] Thus, the expedition against Ethiopia seems doomed from the start, but Cambyses' arrogant confidence[64] ensures that he does not even reach his target. His army sets off without proper preparations, attacks Zeus' oracle at Ammon on the way, and eventually founders in the desert.

Cambyses' successor Darius, confident in the wealth and manpower of his empire,[65] launches a pointless invasion in the extreme north against the nomadic Scythians, so different from the rest of mankind in their savage customs and their lack of settled communities, farms, and roads. Yet these primitives are, again, excellent soldiers. The Pontic Greeks spoke of them as descendants of a hero no less than Heracles—a genealogy that Diogenes of Sinope may well have heard. But again, the Scythians are poor. They have no cities or ploughed land, and Darius is reminded that subduing them would be fruitless.[66] But true to Herodotus' pattern (wealth → hubris → transgression → defeat at the hands of the valiant poor), Darius ignores all sound advice, invades, and narrowly escapes with his army.

One last boundary remained to be transgressed: across the Hellespont to Greece in the west. Ignoring Artabanus' recollection of the fates of Cyrus, Cambyses, and Darius,[67] Xerxes, in an act of supreme hubris, bridged the divine Hellespont to invade a poor but warlike Greece. The words of Pausanias in the rich tent left by Mardonius after the battle at Plataea echo the advice once ignored by Croesus, Cyrus, Cambyses, and Darius:

> Men of Greece, I have assembled you because I wanted to show you the idiocy of the leader of the Medes, who despite a life so luxurious as this, marched against us to rob us of our wretched poverty.[68]

Like his predecessors, wealth and power so infatuated Xerxes that he transgressed all boundaries—not only the physical boundaries separating Asia and Europe, but also the boundaries of reason itself, for Pausanias' phrase, "to rob others of their poverty," is a paradox akin to madness.

The final defeat of Xerxes is followed by the haunting conclusion of the *Histories*. Here, Herodotus' parting anecdote leaves the reader to ponder the lessons of time, which has seen so many nations progress from warlike poverty through conquest, wealth, and hubris, to corruption, excess, and eventual submission to a new conqueror. Herodotus' anecdote recalls the reader to the beginnings of Persian power and suggests that a new cycle is beginning, with ambiguous consequences for Athens. In Herodotus' story, Artayctes' impiety in robbing the tomb of Protesilaus reveals how godless Xerxes' generation has become in its pursuit of wealth and power. In retribution, Xanthippus (father of Pericles) and his soldiers nail Artayctes to a plank. As he is dying, they stone his son before his eyes. Herodotus juxtaposes this terrible death with Artayctes' grandfather Artembares, who so humbly submitted to the wisdom of Cyrus. Fired by the amazing Persian victories, Artembares once advocated that the Persians leave their rocky mountains and take rich land from their subjects. Renouncing such a plan, Cyrus recommended instead a kind of voluntary poverty: the Persians should remain inhabitants of their hard country, for poverty alone has made them capable of rule. The passage is worth quoting in full, given its seamless mingling of the praise of martial poverty, geographical determinism, and the quasi-economic philosophy of history:

> This Artayctes was the grandson of the Artembares who authored a plan that the Persians brought before Cyrus. It went as follows: "Since Zeus by striking Astyages down has given pre-eminence to the Persians and especially to you Cyrus, let us leave this cramped and rough country of ours to possess some better one. There are many either nearby or far away the possession of which would make us even more impressive to others. It is right that races that rule should do this. For when will it be more opportune than now, when we rule many people and all Asia?" Cyrus listened and was not surprised by their proposal. He ordered them to carry it through, but in so doing to prepare to rule no longer, but to be ruled. For soft people tend to arise from soft lands, and the same country cannot produce both marvelous fruits and warlike men. The Persians left in agreement, and chose empire, preferring to inhabit a hard country rather than sow their crops in the plains, and be the slaves of others.[69]

Thus ends Herodotus' account of why the Greeks and Persians fought. The conclusion is a somber one, recalling the reader to the wasted greatness of Persia. Melancholy also are the implications for contemporary Greece as it embarks upon the Peloponnesian Wars. By the time of Xerxes' invasion, the Persians have forgotten Cyrus' wise recommendation to retain voluntarily the poverty that geography had initially forced upon them.[70] Xerxes marches with his minions into Greece. At Salamis he sits at the foot of Mt. Aegaleus on a golden throne, while his slaves hold a golden umbrella over his head.[71] He is defeated. The lesson that Herodotus suggests is clear. When poor, the Persians were virtuous. Now their empire has grown evil and excessively wealthy, as symbolized in the person and character of Xerxes himself. They are bettered by the Greeks, a poor and still valiant race. The toil and poverty that once toughened the Persians now thrusts the Greeks to military supremacy everywhere from Himera to Mycale. One suspects that such ideas were not far from the consciousness of many in Herodotus' patriotic Greek audiences. Furthermore, Herodotus' conclusion is potentially chilling in its implications. Herodotus completed his work after the outbreak of the Peloponnesian War. Impaling—the death that Pericles' father Xanthippus dealt out to Artayctes—was a Persian form of punishment. Is Herodotus quietly cautioning Pericles and the Athenians that they must learn from the patterns of history? Is the Athenian empire acting like the Persian one did? Have the Athenians, poor and virtuous at Marathon, become the new tyrants of Greece?[72]

The Peloponnesian and Other Wars

Herodotus' own opinions cannot be definitively ascertained. If anything, he was sympathetic to Athens for her leadership, self-sacrifice, and courage in the Persian wars, and for the spirit of freedom that animated her people.[73] But when he was composing his *Histories* in the years prior to and after 431, the Athenian empire was becoming increasingly unpopular.[74] Moreover, the very nature of the conflict—between a commercial, maritime superpower and an agricultural defensive league—could accommodate dichotomies similar to those that gave the Persian Wars its epic quality: the war between Athens and Sparta also could be viewed as one between wealth and poverty, technology and individual virtue, aggressive imperialism and love of liberty. Spartan propaganda had traditionally emphasized that the descendants of the sons of Heracles were unrelenting enemies of tyrants.[75] Now the tyrant was Athens, impelled by the ambition, greed, and limitless will-to-power of the "imperialist work-ethic." Indeed, according to Athens' denigrators, she was a new Persia, bent upon the enslavement of the Hellenes. Thucydides would, famously, root out myth (τὸ μυθῶδες) for a more objective presentation of essential facts. Yet even his abstract prose has echoes of a moralistic rhetoric similar to that used in mythologizing the Persian Wars. Thucydides' emotional detachment was rare, but many others felt subconsciously that the war reinforced the lessons of Xerxes' invasion: in the guise of Athens, the "Mede" had descended on free Greece again, but once again the martial virtues of the poor Dorians had humbled him.

Many, on both sides, spoke of the Athenian empire as a tyranny, but the strongest language is that which explicitly compares the Athenians with the Persians. The Corinthians, as we have seen, speak of the violent restlessness of the Athenian character. Sthenelaidas fears their aggression; Pericles and Cleon say unequivocally that the empire is a tyranny.[76] The unnamed officers at Melos employ the language of *machtpolitik* with such brutality that Dionysius of Halicarnassus discredited the whole dialogue, speculating that the Melian dialogue was Thucydides' secret vengeance on the Athenians for exiling him: Thucydides deliberately depicted their officers as "barbarian kings"—that is, as Persian despots.[77] Dionysius was not the first to make the comparison. In appealing to the Lacedaemonians, the Mytilenian ambassadors play cunningly upon the parallel.[78] Even more frank is the speech of the Thebans to the Spartans. In order to stir latent fears that the Athenians were playing the role of Persian despots, Thucydides' Thebans coin the new word "Atticism" (*attikismos*), in imitation of the pejorative "Medism" (*mêdismos*) with all its connotations of a betrayal of fundamental Greek values.

> Next, when the barbarian invaded Hellas, they say that they (the Plataeans) were the only Boeotians who did not Medize (*ou mêdisai*); and this is where they most glorify themselves and abuse us. We say that if they did not Medize, it was because the Athenians did not do so either; just as afterwards when the Athenians attacked the Hellenes they, the Plataeans, were again the only Boeotians who Atticized (*attikisai*). . . . Who then merit the detestation of the Hellenes more justly than you, you who sought their ruin under the mask of honour? The former virtues that you allege you now show not to be proper to your character; the real bent of your nature has been at length damningly proved: when the Athenians took the path of injustice, you followed them. Of our unwilling Medism (*mêdismos*) and your wilful Atticizing (*attikismos*) this then is our explanation.[79]

Later in the war and Thucydides' *History*, Hermocrates vilifies the Athenians in similar terms before the Camarineans:

> In fine, in the struggle against the Medes, the Athenians did not fight for the liberty of the Hellenes, or the Hellenes for their own liberty, but the

former to make their countrymen serve them instead of him, the latter
to change one master for another, wiser indeed than the first, but wiser
for evil. . . . [We should blame ourselves, because we] do not stand together and resolutely show them [the Athenians] that here are no Ionians, or Hellespontines, or islanders, who change continually, but always
serve a master, sometimes the Mede and sometimes some other [i.e.,
Athenian], but free Dorians from independent Peloponnese, dwell-
ing in Sicily.[80]

But if Athens represented a new Xerxes for men like Hermocrates and the
Thebans, then the very nature of the Peloponnesian War would encourage
dichotomies similar to those attending popular reactions to the Persian wars.
Now, the *aretê* of the individual Dorian citizens is contrasted with Athenian
state-power, based on wealth and naval technology. To the traditional mind,
military power rising from individual strength of arms is more readily
intelligible—because it is more tangible and familiar—than the power of
money. Thus, the Corinthians can tempt the Spartans with the prospect of an
easy victory, because "Athenian power is bought rather than native to themselves."[81] An extra obol a day might induce Athens' foreign rowers and mercenaries to leave one paymaster for another, but, to adopt the Cynic phrase,
Lacedaemonian valor is a weapon that cannot be thrown away or lost
(*anapoblêton*). The Spartan hoplite will fight for the common good until
death; no threat or bribe can deter him from his duty. This same implied
dichotomy between *aretê* and *ploutos* appears in the speech of the Spartan
ephor Sthenelaidas—a short speech, but one crucial for understanding a
typical assessment of the nature of the war. Before Sthenelaidas, Archidamus
the Spartan king had spoken at length about the great material resources of
the Athenian empire, and admonished his countrymen to remember the
economic basis of warfare. An army marches on its stomach, and war "is a
matter not so much of arms as of money, which makes arms of use."[82]
Thucydides praises Archidamus as "intelligent," but Thucydides' recognition
that funds are the *sine qua non* of prolonged combat was not widespread, for
does hoplite-fighting require much more than the strength to push forward,
the bravery not to flee or break formation? Sthenelaidas scorns the claims of
ploutos: "Others have much money and ships and horses, but we have good
allies, whom we must not give up to the Athenians. . . . [W]ith the gods, let us
advance against the aggressors." [83] Thus Sthenelaidas appeals passionately to
the idealistic tradition that solidarity, loyalty, honor, and divine favor are
more formidable than money, horses, and ships. Fired by such sentiments,

the Spartan assembly followed Sthenelaidas' counsel, rejecting a respected king's vehement recommendation of delay—a decision that may have been unique in Spartan history.[84]

Sthenelaidas represents the traditional hoplite-ethos, with its focus on the martial virtues over logistics, tactics, and technological innovation. Men steeped in this ethos found it difficult to recognize the new importance of seapower, and hence of the money that was needed to build and maintain ships, and train and pay crews. Thucydides and his favored politicians, on the other hand, stress the centrality of money to this new form of warfare.[85] Pericles often reckons up the material resources at Athens' command as the surest indication of Athenian superiority. Victory is ours, Pericles predicts, if only we preserve the *status quo*, for the empire's wealth is the source of Athenian power.[86] On the other hand, the relative poverty of the Peloponnesian farmers will make them bungling enemies.[87] Financial arguments like these—so similar to the unheeded axiom of Archidamus that money is of more military importance than arms or virtue—were "usual" ones for Pericles to make.[88] Thucydides himself shares Pericles' optimism: he agrees that if Athens had followed a Fabian policy, she would have won, "so superfluously abundant were the resources from which the genius of Pericles foresaw an easy triumph in the war over the unaided forces of the Peloponnesians."[89]

But according to the ageless "law," wealth breeds *hubris* and *atê*: it would not be surprising if the average Greek interpreted the Athenian defeat at Syracuse in the light of this hallowed association. Even the ultra-rational Thucydides shows some inclination for this interpretation. He speaks of post-Periclean leaders like Cleon and Alcibiades as violent, grasping men, whose desire for private gain ruined the public good.[90] They, unlike Pericles, were not "superior to wealth."[91] Nor was the Athenian *dêmos*: Thucydides writes that the prospect of conquering Sicily fired the vast majority of the Athenians with a lust for profit.[92] His juxtaposition of the Melian dialogue and the Sicilian expedition positively invite the interpretation that "pride precedeth the fall." This is, indeed, the gist of one aside in which he himself writes that the Sicilian expedition is the kind of disaster that tends to plague "great and powerful cities" that have fallen under bad leadership.[93] Thucydides' own views are, of course, often extremely difficult to pinpoint, but if he can at times incline toward the view that the excessive desire for wealth was an underlying cause of Athens' defeat, all the more plausible is it that less intellectually demanding Greeks would have fallen back upon stock formulas and edifying polarities to interpret the events of the war: Athens the Mede vs. Sparta the liberator, Ionian wealth vs. Doric virtue, tyrannical riches vs. heroic idealism, the *hubris* of the former vs. the divinely sanctioned triumph of the latter.

Furthermore, that Sparta's eventual victory represented a triumph of unaided virtue over tyrannical wealth is illustrated partly by the fame of the Athenian armada and Sparta's understated response. Thucydides describes the long-lived impression that the fleet of 415 made on all those who lined the shores to watch it pull away. Among them were Athenians, slaves, metics, and other foreigners:

> Indeed this armament that first sailed out was by far the most costly and splendid Hellenic force that had ever been sent out by a single city up to that time. . . . [There follows a long description of the ships' ornaments, trappings, soldiers' pay, ship-captains' expenditure, and how much the fleet cost.] From this resulted . . . an idea among the rest of the Hellenes that it was more a display of power and resources than an armament against an enemy. . . . Indeed the expedition became not less famous for its wonderful boldness and for the splendour of its appearance, than for its overwhelming strength.[94]

If the flashy spectacle of the armada became famous among Athenians and others, equally celebrated must have been the "laconic" response of the Spartans: one officer (Gylippus), and one ship of soldiers, who did their own rowing.[95] And yet, under this indomitable Spartiate, the Syracusans annihilated the Athenian army and navy.

Only the historian must remember details: others are impressed more by the broad outline of events, and the useful or inspiring lessons they instill. Thus, while Thucydides refrains from explicitly dramatizing the Peloponnesian War as a victory of virtue over wealth and material means, his dispassionate stance was rare. Far more representative of popular interpretations of the war is a speech that Xenophon gave to the Ten Thousand barely five years after Lysander tore down the Long Walls to the music of flutes, and "restored the freedom of the Greeks."[96] At one point, the soldiers clamored for Xenophon to resume leadership. But the omens were unfavorable, and Xenophon reluctant. In the first speech he gives to dissuade the men, his assumptions concerning their views of the significance of Athens' defeat are revealing:

I am happy, soldiers, since I am a human being, to be honoured by you, and I am grateful also, and I pray that the gods may grant me opportunity to be the means of bringing you some benefit; still, I think that for me to be preferred by you as commander when a Lacedaemonian is at hand, is not expedient for you—for you would be less likely on this account to obtain any favour you might desire from the Lacedaemonians—and for myself, on the other hand, I believe it is not altogether safe. For I see that the Lacedaemonians did not cease waging war upon my native state until they made all her citizens acknowledge that the Lacedaemonians were their leaders also. But just as soon as this acknowledgement had been made, they straightway ceased waging war and no longer continued to besiege the city. Now if I, being aware of these things, should seem to be trying to make their authority null and void wherever I could, I suspect that I might very speedily be brought back to reason (*sophrosunê*) on that point.[97]

Abstracting from the speech's other considerations, we can see that Xenophon appeals to two prejudices. First, one notes the idealistic ethos of hoplite warfare, that Xenophon purportedly invoked even before an audience of mercenaries: the Spartans fought not for gain, but *solely* for the honor of being acknowledged the best, the leaders of the Greeks. Second, Sparta's victory has definitively proved the superiority of the Spartan soldier. Xenophon should not be leader when there are Spartan officers at hand, for as an Athenian, he is one of the defeated, and they automatically have a better claim, as if leadership were their birthright. To usurp their place would show lack of *sophrosunê*—self-restraint and obedience to one's superiors. Xenophon's appeal to such latent prejudices fails to convince the army, and he resorts to other tactics. Yet his initial expectation was that this interpretation of the war would be a persuasive one for the Panhellenic audience of the Ten Thousand. A speculative conclusion that one might draw, therefore, is that the Spartan victory inspired a populist interpretation of the war similar to that of the Persian wars: once again, individual valor, solidarity, and love of freedom had triumphed over the fleets, silver mines, mercenaries, and allies of a wealthy tyranny.

In the generations after the Peloponnesian War, many other wars could have reinforced the habitual, though subconscious, association of poverty and military prowess: the Athenian civil conflict of 404 and numerous other wars could all contribute to an emerging praise of martial poverty. First, the triumph of Thrasybulus' democrats over Critias and the "men of the city" lent itself to proto-Cynic ideas, for the Thirty were defeated by the democratic poor, despite being supported by the Spartan superpower and by many rich oligarchs. The speech in praise of the virtues of the Athenian *dêmos* that Xenophon attributes to Thrasybulus, is probably authentic in substance:

> There Thrasybulus spoke as follows: "I advise you," he said, "men of the city, to 'know yourselves.' And you would best learn to know yourselves were you to consider what grounds you have for arrogance, that you should undertake to rule over us. Are you more just (*dikaioteroi*)? But the commons, though poorer than you, never did any wrong for the sake of money; while you, though richer than any of them, have done many disgraceful things for the sake of gain. But since you can lay no claim to justice, consider then whether it is courage (*andreia*) that you have a right to pride yourselves upon. And what better test could there be of this than the way we made war upon one another? Well then, would you say that you are superior in intelligence (*gnomê*), *you who having a wall, arms, money, and the Peloponnesians as allies, have been worsted by men who had none of these*?"[98]

In subsequent generations, wars between Spartans and Persians, Thebans and Spartans, Greeks and Carthaginians, Macedonians and Persians might bolster the association of poverty and valor. First, the forceful character of that military ascetic Agesilaus was celebrated by many ordinary Ionians, who delighted to see their Persian overlords humbled by this simple Spartan:

> Another year of the war being spent, Agesilaus' fame still increased, insomuch that the Persian king received daily information concerning his many virtues, and the great esteem the world had of his temperance, his plain living, and his moderation. When he made any journey, he would usually take up his lodging in a temple, and there make the gods witnesses of his most private actions, which others would scarce permit men to be acquainted with. In so great an army you should scarce find a common soldier lie on a coarser mattress than Agesilaus: he was so indifferent to the varieties of heat and cold that all the seasons, as the gods sent them, seemed natural to him. The Greeks that inhabited Asia were much pleased to see the great lords and governors of Persia, with all the pride, cruelty, and luxury in which they lived, trembling and bowing before a man in a poor threadbare cloak, and, at one laconic word out of his mouth, obsequiously deferring and changing their wishes and purposes.[99]

This contrast between Greek/Spartan virtue and Eastern decadence should not be roundly dismissed as the result of later moralizing interpolation; the dichotomy pervades literature after the Persian Wars and becomes an almost indelible feature of the Greek language. One example is representative of many: with the experience of all his 100 years, and active engagement with fourth-century politics, Isocrates can in 337 write to Philip that their military history has caused the Greeks to "look upon [the barbarians] as effeminate and unversed in war and utterly degenerate through luxurious living."[100]

Given this widespread view, it would be surprising if the incredible Macedonian conquest of the Persian empire did not provide much material for any *laudatores inopiae Graecae*. In Arrian at least, Alexander reminds his troops of how Philip brought them down from their rugged mountains to become the masters of Greece, how under his leadership they had crossed the Hellespont with no monetary resources—and now behold! they are the masters of the world, undefeated and invincible (*anikêtoi*).[101] In the accounts of Diodorus and Curtius, on the other hand, the cyclical "law of history" overtakes Alexander also, as he succumbs to the arrogance and luxury typical of Oriental despots: "Persian vices conquered him whom Persian arms could not."[102]

But when Isocrates generalized about Greek valor, he might have had in mind the impressive exploits of Timoleon only a few years earlier. Timoleon's life and character could lend much inspiration to a Cynic encomium of poverty. For according to rumor, here was a man whose justice, courage, and native kindness would not yield to self-interest, wealth, or any weakness for pleasure; his wars to liberate Sicily from tyrants and Carthaginians seemed to provide one sustained proof of the "invincibility" of unaided virtue. In 344, at the summons of certain Sicilian cities, Timoleon was dispatched from Corinth with a ragtag fleet of ten ships. When he landed in Sicilian Tauromenia, he commanded (according to Plutarch's *Life*) a mere thousand soldiers and had "no more provisions, either of corn or money, than were just necessary for the maintenance and the pay of that inconsiderable number." Nor did he receive significant aid from other Sicilian cities.[103]

And yet resolution, courage, and the favor of Fortune eventually brought him to triumph over the Carthaginian-backed Leviathan. The conclusive battle at the Crimisus river (339) in western Sicily presents the familiar dichotomies: against the Carthaginian-led force of seventy thousand, Timoleon had twelve thousand men, with the gods (and weather) intervening crucially on the Greek side. Plutarch's description of the slow march of the Carthaginians themselves, with their white shields and splendid arms, echoes the poignancy of Herodotus' description of Xerxes' army and the Persian

Immortals as they marched to their first setback in Thermopylae. But on this occasion, the barbarians' defeat was utter. Fighting "few against many," the Greeks won a stunning victory, and Timoleon's subsequent relaying of the news to Corinth would contrast the justice and courage of his freedom-fighters with the rich Carthaginian spoils.[104] Thus, to people like Timoleon at least, the essential facts of a battle like Crimisus might corroborate moral expectations of the superiority of Greek virtue to barbarian wealth.

That this dichotomy was not framed only in Hellenic or xenophobic terms is illustrated by the common explanation of Sparta's decline and loss of hegemony to the Thebans. According to this view, empire brought an influx of money (and hence inflation) into Sparta. Economic inequalities appeared among the Spartiates to such an extent that a large proportion of its citizens could no longer make the requisite contributions to their *sussitia*. Demoted from their status as "equals" (*homoioi*), these individuals were hence categorized as "inferiors" (*hupomeiones*), and could no longer serve as heavily armed hoplites in the Spartan army. Prosperity thus led, surprisingly, to the weakening of the Spartan military. Demaratus had numbered the Spartan hoplites at eight thousand before Thermopylae in 480; only fifteen hundred such hoplites fought the Thebans at Leuctra in 371. Aristotle accepts this economic explanation of Spartan decline.[105] Plato reshapes it in his description of the timarchic character and state: modeled on the venal Spartan harmosts and generals, the timarchic man harbors a "secret lust for gold" that ultimately transforms him into the unfit, cowardly oligarch.[106] In this matter, historians and philosophers alike would seem to give their assent to the ancient prophecy, that "the love of money will ruin Sparta."[107] Yet, when Sparta tottered, Thebes rose. In contrast to the self-aggrandizing Spartan elite was the social and military asceticism of Epaminondas, the Theban general in the 370s and 360s. Epaminondas had close relations with the Pythagorean Lysis of Tarentum and Aristotle records the saying that Thebes flourished when led by "philosophers."[108] A eulogist of military poverty might look for inspiration to this Epaminondas and his astonishing victory at Leuctra. Not only did his tactics on the left-wing break with immemorial tradition, and not only was it the *Spartiates* who were decisively routed, their king Cleombrotus killed: less noticed by historians, but equally important for our purpose here was the fact that the Theban victory was won almost single-handedly, against a numerically superior army. Thebes' subsequent wars of liberation in the Peloponnese might support the familiar dichotomies—freedom vs. tyranny, the heroic poor (Arcadians, Messenians, and Epaminondas himself who led personally and even fought as a common soldier in 367) vs. a complacent Spartan elite.

Such reactions may not be reflected explicitly in existing sources, yet certainly Epaminondas in his dual role as "philosopher" and soldier brings us to the figure that immediately precedes the Cynic ascetics. This is the literary figure of the philosopher-king, the indigent war-leader whose poverty is, surprisingly and even paradoxically, seen as necessary to his martial preeminence.

FOURTH-CENTURY POLITICAL THINKERS

The philosopher-king comes to the fore of political theory when Xenophon and Plato would educate their ideal rulers as military ascetics. In this, they draw upon familiar aspects of the praise of martial poverty but also upon their early memories of a man who seemed to embody the virtues of such a poverty.

To his admirers, Socrates had many merits, and as a result he could be lionized as a paragon of virtue—intelligent, honest, insightful, kind, self-controlled. But Socrates' excellences were not just intellectual and moral. Plato, Xenophon, and even Aristophanes give their emphatic testimony to Socrates' courage and physical stamina. Plato draws particular attention to how levelheaded Socrates remained amidst the general panic at Delium when the Athenian army was routed, and to his almost superhuman endurance of hunger and cold that astonished the other soldiers at the siege of Potidaea.[109] Ambitious men like Critias, Alcibiades, and Charmides sought to emulate Socrates' fortitude in their own bid for political preeminence.[110]

Plato is perhaps most impressed by Socrates' dual capacity as both intellectual and soldier. This combination was not, of course, unprecedented. Compare, *mutatis mutandis*, Odysseus the many-minded sacker of cities; Archilochus, servant of the Muses and Enyalios; Aeschylus, veteran of Marathon and writer of the *Seven Against Thebes*, a play "full of Ares"; and Melissus of Samos, Eleatic devotee of the One and patriot who defeated the Athenian fleet in 440. Socrates himself seems not to have made much of his service to Athens. At the opening of the *Charmides*, for instance, he appears uniquely indifferent to news from the front and seems impatient to begin to talk philosophy.[111] In the *Symposium*, he endures Alcibiades' torrent of praise in silence.

Plato, however, elaborates upon the Socratic example in his construction of the ideal ruler. The philosopher-kings of the *Republic* will live in a poverty more austere than that of Socrates himself. They will own nothing—no gold or silver, no private property, and not even a spouse, children, or parents.

This complete communism among the ruling elite is justified partly as a response to the difficulties of reconciling military and civilian life. According to the principle "one person, one job," the guardian must devote himself utterly to the practice of war. Plato thus rejects the old system by which citizens fought the state's battles: professional mercenaries reemerged in abundance after the Peloponnesian War and impressed many leaders (Iphicrates, Epaminondas, Jason of Pherae, Philip, etc.) that the days of the amateur citizen-soldier were over. And yet, the mercenary typically has no state, no home, and hence no loyalties. He fights for the highest bidder. What will prevent a class of professional soldiers from plundering and oppressing the unwarlike citizens who hire them?[112] *Quis custodiet ipsos custodes?* War and peace are separate worlds, and the virtues appropriate to each seem incompatible, for how can the same person be both violent and gentle at once, a killer yet also a citizen, who can live on a level of equality with others? Socrates raises such questions as if they were paradoxes or insoluble dilemmas, but detects a solution in an unexpected source—dogs.[113] If sheepdogs are aggressive towards predators and protective of flocks, then surely (Socrates reasons) it is at least possible that a person could combine a specialization in violence with the citizen's patriotism. Socrates' guardians, then, are hybrid creatures—citizen-mercenaries whose specializations are philosophy and war. Yet these professional soldiers fight for no pay. Their voluntary poverty is grounded in a philosophic love of the transcendent. For this they fight, and for the state that alone of human communities nurtures and honors the philosophic calling. In addition, Plato justifies his kings' asceticism by appealing to what are by now common notions of the praise of martial poverty: frugality and a spare lifestyle inure the guardians to heat, cold, and hunger. As a result, the *kallipolis* can defeat an alliance of rich states as easily as a trained boxer beats two fat oligarchs.[114]

Similar themes return in the *Timaeus*, where Socrates expresses the desire to see his state proving its worth in a great enterprise, like a war.[115] Conveniently, Critias is at hand to retell a relevant story that he heard as a young boy. The epic war between Atlantis and ancient Athens will, he thinks, fulfill Socrates' desire, for this prediluvian Athens was very like Socrates' utopia. Critias' Athens has artisans, farmers, and good farmland. But its real "wealth" consists in its marvelous elite of twenty thousand philosopher-rulers, renowned through Greece for their physical beauty and many virtues. Their external lives are simple. They winter on the northern, summer on the southern side of the Acropolis. Their houses are neither ostentatious nor servile, and they share all possessions. They have, emphatically (*oudamose*), no use for gold or silver, either in their homes or temples. They take only necessary food from the working population, and do not abuse their power over them. Nor are they motivated by any imperial work-ethic. They concentrate on the intellectual studies of Socrates' ideal guardians—gymnastics, arithmetic, geometry, dialectic. It is striking that Critias does not mention the Laurium silver-mines, the sumptuous Periclean temples on the Acropolis, the Themistoclean walls, or the Piraeus. Mythical Athens is not an expansive naval power, and her gods are Athena and Hephaestus: Poseidon, who according to traditional myth vied with Athena for patronage of Athens, is associated in the *Critias* only with Atlantis.[116]

Contrasted with the inscrutable calm of "owl-eyed Athena," Poseidon is typically a furious god, and correspondingly Atlantis differs radically from Critias' Athens. While Critias' Athens is self-sufficient for its simple material needs, Atlantis is superlatively rich, in land, wildlife, forests, and mines. As a result of its wealth, it becomes a center of trade and industry, its twin harbors stuffed with ships, its markets loud with merchants shouting out their wares. Moreover, wealth makes the inhabitants of Atlantis luxurious. Baths they love, to such an extent that they build them for their horses and cattle to enjoy.[117]

But the luxury of this mythic Sybaris is fatally attended by violence. Ringing the pleasure-spots of Atlantis are hired *doruphoroi*, spear-bearing bodyguards—a recognized harbinger of tyranny.[118] Soon the kings of Atlantis do indeed become despotic. Initially their greatness of soul ensured that they found wealth more a burden than a blessing.[119] But gradually their self-control and high-mindedness fade away. The kings become prey to envy and *pleonexia*. Zeus decides to punish them for their betterment. Calling together the gods, he addresses them thus—

The *Critias* breaks off tantalizingly, just when the plot thickens. Yet one knows the general outlines of what follows, for Critias has told us already. Launching an unprovoked attack on Europe and Asia, Atlantis will at first sweep all in its path. Athens' allies will all abandon her. Yet she will persevere, fighting "few against many" until the final victory and liberation of the Mediterranean from the tyrants' hordes. *Timaeus* 25, as well as the whole *Critias*-fragment, is saturated with the ethos of the mythologized Persian Wars. The Leviathan of Atlantis is another Persia, whose arrogant wealth the gods punish through the agency of a poor but virtuous Athens. After her sublime victory, Critias' Athens will not succumb to the temptations of power and lord it over her neighbors—as Aristides, Cimon, and the conservative Athenian leaders of the Delian League sought not to tyrannize weaker allies.

Indeed, Plato's wording in one passage echoes the rhythms of Herodotus' majestic prooemium: both histories will record the great and wondrous deeds that time threatens to rub away.[120] The echo is not coincidental or unimportant: both Herodotus and the *Critias* play upon the popular expectation that valor triumphs unaided over wealth.

Plato draws not only on the Herodotean narrative, but also on the widespread association of voluntary poverty with military prowess. The legends of Sybaris may have been one of his models for his epic of Atlantis and "Athens." According to the story, the war of Sybaris and Croton featured the familiar polarities. Sybaris is wealthy, luxurious, and decadent to the point that its late-sleeping inhabitants ban blacksmiths from working and roosters from crowing in their city. If the citizens of Atlantis pamper their animals with warm baths, the Sybarites were said to have taught their horses to dance to the flute. And according to rumor, the luxurious Sybarites were useless soldiers. A Sybarite once found himself in Sparta and was so appalled by the Lycurgan barracks-regime that he swore he would prefer to die a coward's death than live such a life—thus comically inverting the hero's choice of a brave death over a dishonorable surrender. In this regard, Plato would differ from the legendary model: he gives his Athenians a formidable opponent, for the Atlanteans bring innumerable mercenaries and allies with them to battle. But Sybarites and Atlanteans do share the same motivation. In the story, wealth made the Sybarites grasping and they provoked neighboring Croton to war. Milo the Pythagorean led the Crotoniates to victory over vastly superior numbers (three to one, according to the ancient sources), and they proceeded to divert the river Crathis over Sybaris, washing away the city and its memory as effectively as Plato's tidal wave did Atlantis.[121]

Fantasy blends with historical fact also when we turn to that other great work advocating a military asceticism, Xenophon's *Cyropaedia*. The life of the actual Cyrus the Great could again, from the simplifying lens of selective memory, provide material for proto-Cynic views. Under Cyrus, the Persians burst from their barren mountains, and within twenty years conquered much of the Middle East from Afghanistan to Turkey. Herodotus notes the transformation of the Persians, or at least of the Persian nobles: Cyrus' generation, with its leather clothes, plain diet, and thorny fields, ceded to the Persians of Xerxes' time, who dined off gold plate even on campaign.[122] But if he points to the seeming causes of Persian decline, Herodotus also hints at a cure. The virtues of a geographical poverty may not last, yet a voluntary asceticism may continue to train the ruling class to the physical and mental toughness that distinguished their predecessors. Thus, in his final anecdote, Herodotus'

Cyrus delivers his counsel: let the Persians remain a mountain-race capable of empire, rather than live in the plains as slaves to others.

Herodotus' passage is characteristically succinct and evocative. Xenophon's *Cyropaedia* expands Herodotus' insight into eight laborious books. Cyrus' conquests of Medes, Assyrians, Lydians, and others bring the Persians wealth and freedom from hard labor. Yet empire might have endangered the virtues of the Persian soldier if Xenophon's Cyrus had not recognized the frugality and unselfish morality of traditional Persian culture as the basis of their power.[123] So when the ruling Persians need no longer remain poor due to geographical accident, Xenophon's Cyrus would make them deliberately so. Military asceticism becomes the primary means of maintaining the ethos proper for a ruling nobility, and thus, through his vision of a reformed Persia, Xenophon presents a veiled praise of Sparta before hegemony ruined it.[124] Five passages from the *Cyropaedia* might be selected as particularly illustrative of the transition from ancestral simplicity to voluntary temperance, from a geographic to a legislated poverty: the contrast of the disciplined Persians and the drunken Medes after Cyrus' defeat of the Assyrians (4.1.14); the Assyrian Gobryas' amazement at the self-restraint and incorruptibility of the victorious Persian nobles (5.2.16–18); Cyrus' imperial legislation, according to which noble Persian youths will undergo a systematic training in *ponos* (heat, cold, hunger, thirst, lack of sleep), will not engage in trade or any money-making activities, and will associate only in the "free (i.e. political, non-commercial) agora";[125] the competition between the generous Cyrus and the miserly Croesus to see who is richer, which Cyrus wins easily by asking his numerous friends for a small gift, thus proving that even in purely monetary terms, good-will and loyalty are more profitable than an obsession with quantitative wealth (8.2.13–23); and finally the partnership of Pheraulas and the Sacian soldier.

From early in the work, this Pheraulas appears almost as an advocate of all the virtues of poverty. Pheraulas was born a farmer, who rose by means of his intelligence to become one of Cyrus' closest advisors (8.3.5; cf. 2.3.7). But first he appears rising in the army assembly to praise the common man and his martial poverty. Cyrus had proposed that all the soldiers, even the rank and file, be rewarded in proportion to their merit. Pheraulas applauds the proposal, but warns that the nobles may thereby be superseded, for, he says, the poor are trained by necessity, the hardest teacher of all, to endure hunger, thirst, and cold (2.3.13). Swords, spears, and shields are light to them who must always dig and cut with heavier tools (2.3.12–14). The Persian nobles, then, might well fear a true meritocracy in which they might not in fact be "the best."

Pheraulas' own trajectory mirrors that of the Persians. Once a farmer, Pheraulas grows rich under the empire of Cyrus—alas too rich! Wealth is more a burden than a blessing, and, like Cyrus, Pheraulas longs to free himself of all its worries (8.3.39–40). To become rich is delightful but to remain so is disaster. The rich do not enjoy their food, drink, or sleep any more than the poor (8.3.40). Though he need not now dig in the fields, Pheraulas finds worse the thousand petty details of daily management (8.3.41). Indeed, wealth actually increases one's misery, for the rich constantly fear the loss of their property, and are devastated when they do lose it or must use it for the state or the gods (8.3.43–44). "Take my fortune and keep me as a guest-friend!" exclaims the hapless Pheraulas at the end of a litany that might read like a Cynic praise of poverty. The Sacian soldier is happy to oblige, since for him happiness is being able to possess and spend freely (8.3.45–46). And so the two strike up a partnership: the soldier will become permanent steward to Pheraulas' wealth, while Pheraulas himself will devote himself to the army, politics, and Cyrus' court (8.3.47). Yet, this friendship is not between equals. Pheraulas has chosen the better, more manly half to suit his sociable, gregarious nature (8.3.49). The materialistic Sacian, on the other hand, is impressed by coverlets, furniture, and armies of servants. He stays inside, contentedly managing the household—"like a woman," a chauvinist Greek reader might have added.

CYNIC MILITARY ASCETICISM

A Greek praise of martial poverty, then, involves a complex of interrelated ideas that surface in different combinations through various authors and periods. All are reunited in the Cynics' rhetoric of virtue. If for an Odysseus, Arcesilaus, Herodotus or Xenophon, geographical poverty is the "gymnasium of virtue," then the Cynic adopts a *pithos*, ignominy, indigence, or even Nature itself as his "fatherland" and source of strength. Most clever, perhaps, in this vein is Crates' pun in his poem *Pêra*. Here, Crates' impregnable island Pêra ("Leather Bag") brings forth only healthy, hardy plants like figs and thyme. The pun on *thúmos* (thyme) and *thumós* (courage, high spirits) plays wittily on the Cynics' link of poverty and the martial spirit: eaters of wild thyme are naturally vigorous and tough.[126] In fact, the witticisms may continue with the next word: Pêra also bears garlic. It was a classical practice to rile cocks for a fight by rubbing them with garlic; in later antiquity, Lucian speaks of "garlic-fighters"; and gladiators were sometimes fed it, in the belief that it increased aggression. If Crates has similar notions in mind, then it were as if soft plants and soft people have no more place in the Cynics' world than they do in Odysseus' rough Ithaca or the mountains of Herodotus' Persia.

The Cynics also supplement their "geographical" poverty with some self-legislated asceticism. Diogenes rolls in hot sands and embraces snowy statues, for the Cynic "soldier" must be able to endure winter cold and summer heat as unflinchingly as any soldier of Xenophon or Agesilaus.[127] In this regard, the "dog" harbors some respect for Lycurgan Sparta. Returning from Sparta to Athens, Diogenes said that he was moving from the men's quarters to the women's.[128] On the other hand, wealth ruins the martial virtues. Aristotle quotes one of Diogenes' metaphors: "taverns are the mess-rooms (*phiditia*) of Attica," implying that the Athenians are to indolence as the Spartans are to military discipline.[129] And as Dorians might taunt Ionians, or Greeks would stereotype Lydians, Babylonians, Persians, and other Asians, Diogenes would ridicule wealthy peers for effeminacy, obesity, and lack of fitness. Thus, for the Cynics also, Wealth is a cowardly god, incompatible with their brand of "valor."

Furthermore, the rhetorical trope well established by epinician poetry and the Athenian funeral oration—that the heroic patriots fought "few against many" and triumphed despite tremendous inferiority in material resources—filters also into the Cynics' self-celebration. For Antisthenes, it is better to fight with a few good men against all the bad than vice versa.[130] Indeed, the Cynic improves upon the traditional hyperbole: the solitary, unaided Cynic can beat all the world; true virtue is invincible (*anikêtos*) vis-a-vis *Tuchê*. Therefore, the arrows of Fortune never hit the true Cynic.[131] His virtue is a weapon that cannot be taken away by any contingencies.[132] His virtue alone saves cities and lives.[133] One should therefore defend oneself with walls of virtue and unassailable syllogisms.[134] The invincible "fatherland" of Crates was not Thebes, which Alexander razed in 336, but "Poverty unsacked by Fortune."[135] Or, alternatively, it was Pêra and the traveling bag that gave the Cynic perfect self-sufficiency: "You do not know what great power there is in the *pêra*, in a quart of lupins and in caring for nothing."[136]

Furthermore, the Cynics celebrate heroes who triumph single-handedly against enemies and adversity. Heracles' myths provide abundant matter for a panegyric of unaided valor: he killed the Nemean lion with his bare hands and subsequently wandered through the world armed only with a club and lionskin, ridding the earth of monsters and tyrants; he defeated the Amazons and sacked Troy with little help; he single-handedly routed the Eleans when they ambushed him. Little wonder that the Cynics sought to emulate his endurance, simplicity, and courageous solitude.[137] The heroism of Odysseus could be allegorized along similar lines. For though Odysseus was king of insignificant Ithaca, he distinguished himself by sheer talent above all the other Greeks except Achilles: due to his intelligence and bravery, Achilles was detected in his hideout in Scyros, the Trojan Palladium was stolen, Heracles' bow recovered, the Trojan horse built, and hence Troy taken. In the contest over Achilles' arms (*hoplôn krisis*), Odysseus was honored over Ajax: wisdom triumphs over physical strength. Later, with Athena's aid or without, he overcame Polyphemus and numerous other dangers. When he returned to Ithaca, he came almost like a beggar, yet could still defeat a veritable army of suitors, even though he was an older man helped only by a shepherd and his adolescent son; an Athenian like Antisthenes might be reminded of Myronides' famous exploits. Certainty is impossible, yet some remaining evidence at least suggests that the Cynics gave such a slant to their chosen myths: in Antisthenes' set-piece, Odysseus slipped into Troy unarmed (*aoplos*) and, by stealing the Palladium, effectively sacked Troy unaided (*monos*); this same hero was always able to harm his enemies, even when he had only the weapons and rags of a slave.[138]

Finally, some sense of historical decline may have troubled Diogenes and his followers. Most Greek cities now relied upon mercenaries to do their fighting, and during the generation in which Demosthenes repeatedly urged the Athenians to leave their seats in the theater or assembly, one hears stories of Diogenes berating the Athenian youths to train for war.[139] Perhaps it is in this context that he remembered with admiration the spirit of a former generation, which had produced an Agesilaus or Epaminondas. If he did in fact require Xeniades' sons to read about those military ascetics, then, in this respect at least, he might be placed among the many *laudatores temporis acti* of the Greek tradition. The old perennially exhort the young to remember their ancestors and forefathers, and to be ashamed before their glorious legacy.[140] Demosthenes longs for the simpler, more heroic days of Miltiades and Aristides; Herodotus, Xenophon, and Plato look back to the virtues of a hardier era. It is impossible to say that such pessimism was dominant or even widespread. But, fears of decline were certainly present, and the Cynic message must have spoken to them: easy living has ruined Greece; Cynic *askêsis* can recapture the heroic ethos of Heracles, Odysseus, Agesilaus, and the Spartans of old.

Yet the Cynics' delight in militaristic rhetoric seems puzzlingly paradoxical, even inconsistent. For the first Cynics probably did not fight in any battles, and they certainly condemned war as another instance of the idiocy of custom (*nomos*).[141] Critiques of war surface as early as Homer's Achilles; there is a strong deprecation of war in both Herodotus and intellectual communities like the Academy and Lyceum.[142] In their idealism, the Cynics made such critiques far more radical. For, according to them, why would one fight a war? If it were for the sake of wealth or honor, then what are wealth and honor? True wealth is self-sufficiency, not the coin and plunder that contemporary mercenaries covet. Honor is but a word, a "mere scutcheon," and the Cynics will have none of it. The feckless wars of the late fifth and fourth centuries could only deepen this sense of disillusion: now Athens, now Sparta, now Thebes, now Jason of Pherae, now Philip, now Antigonus, now Seleucus, now some other king is in the ascendant, each contending furiously for the hegemony and spot of distinction. Yet, in the end, all this ambition comes to nothing, for all its objects are subject to the caprices of *Tuchê*; in the end, even Alexander is just a wanderer with his shadow. It is more honest to reject the false absolutes of wealth, honor, and fatherland. Wisdom is seeing through such false notions and freeing oneself from the tyranny of customary language and thought-patterns. The true absolute is the self and in the self, all other values are recovered.

Therefore, the Cynic readapts old rhetorical tropes for his own purposes. Courage, hardiness, and "manliness" (*aretê*) remain essential virtues, and with them the Cynic will fight his metaphorical "wars" to defend his Pêra or to assert the superiority of poverty over a myriad of barbaric opponents—luxury, complacency, greed, violence. In this internalization of values, the Cynics were not unprecedented. Most noteworthy is the idealism prevalent in the Athenian funeral orations. Here, a plethora of dichotomies—most notably soul vs. body, inner goodness vs. external circumstances—looks forward to the central Cynic dichotomy between the self and Fortune. So too, the power of virtue is lauded even to the point of paradox. When an army suffers a calamitous defeat, the speaker will often still praise the fallen for their victory: the soldiers who fell were "conquered in body, but remain undefeated in their souls," and thus the failure is transformed into a moral triumph. Variations on this theme appear in Lysias and Isocrates, in reference to the Corinthian War of the 390s or the Spartan defeat at Leuctra, respectively.[143] Diodorus later invokes it to describe the Spartans who "won" at Thermopylae. In responding to the disaster at Chaeronea, the Demosthenic funeral speech again affirms that the dead remain "unbeaten in their souls." Blame should be assigned to the Theban generals, some malign divine power, or to *Tuchê*.[144] Lycurgus similarly writes that the Greeks who resisted the phalanxes of Philip were in fact conquerors:

[I]f one must speak the truth, even if it seems extremely paradoxical (*paradoxotaton*), then one must affirm that they [the Greeks at Chaeronea] died victorious (*nikôntes apethanon*). For good men, the prizes of war are freedom and *aretê*, and both of these belong to those that died there. Therefore it is impossible to say that these men, who in their minds did not yield to terror of their attackers, were defeated.[145]

All of these passages (with the exception of Lycurgus) use some variation of the adjective *aêttêtos*, to describe the "undefeated" soldiers. The term would become a regular epithet of the Cynic-Stoic sage, who was "invincible" with regard to all pleasures and pains. To this supreme idealist, poverty, disease, dishonor, and death are not evils, for he knows that the true self is an absolute, unmoved by external contingencies, and therefore indomitable.

War brings with it the greatest tragedies, and if the Cynics could demonstrate their imperturbability in the midst of war, they might appear impressive indeed to some contemporaries. But it was not the force of sheer personality that contributed to the appeal of the Cynics' militaristic asceticism. The Cynics also drew upon the common associations of poverty and valor, wealth and degeneracy. Their words and conceits echo the hallowed rhetoric of funerary literature, with its praise of the few who for freedom's sake fought so valiantly against so many. They appealed to the grand traditions of Greek heroism, from recent times back to the most distant myths—Timoleon, Epaminondas, Agesilaus, Cyrus, Socrates, Gylippus, Leonidas and the Spartans of old, the men of Marathon, Milo, Odysseus, Heracles, and no doubt others. Thus history seems to prove that *aretê* is sufficient for victory: the seemingly powerless are in fact supremely powerful. Many figures and wars of the past could become precedents for the invincible Cynic "soldier," who by invoking the spirit of an idealized past could boldly compare himself with contemporary kings and appropriate for himself the epithet that was once used of Heracles and the Spartans, and was now being applied to the great Alexander himself—the appellation *anikêtos*.[146] Indeed, the Cynic-king surpasses all others, for while the huge reversals at Aegospotami, Leuctra, Mantinea, Chaeronea, and Gaugamela demonstrate the frailty of empire, the wise man's kingdom remains untouched by all external calamities.

Much of this is rhetorical cleverness, old martial rally-cries being modified for a radical pacifism. Yet the Cynics' claim to be invincible vis-à-vis *Tuchê* is not merely a rhetorical one, nor one inspired solely by selective adaptation of history. Nor does the juxtaposition of the self and external world depend simply on narrow city-state patriotism, or the dichotomy erected between virtuous Greeks and decadent barbarians. Rather, the Cynics' insistence on the invincibility and absolute freedom of the inner self has deeper roots in some of the most important tenets of Greek philosophy— a theme to which we now turn.

CHAPTER FOUR

Praise of Poverty and Philosophical Wisdom

πόλλ᾽ οἶδ᾽ ἀλώπηξ, ἀλλ᾽ ἐχῖνος ἓν μέγα.
The fox knows many things, but the hedgehog one big thing.

—Archilochus, fr. 201 (West)

πολυμαθία νόον οὐ διδάσκει.
Much learning does not teach insight.

—Heraclitus, DK 22 B 40

And therefore it is just that the mind of the philosopher only has wings, for he is always, so far as he is able, in communion through memory with those things the communion with which causes God to be divine. Now a man who employs such memories rightly is always being initiated into perfect mysteries and he alone becomes truly perfect; but since he separates himself from human interests and turns his attention toward the divine, he is rebuked by the vulgar, who consider him mad and do not know that he is inspired.

—Plato, *Phaedrus*, 248c4–d3

"The fool is wise": our final paradox may not seem at all characteristic of the Greek philosophers. A St. Paul may reject the wisdom of the world for the folly of Christ. Or a Tertullian might praise the wisdom of an irrational faith: "I believe because it is absurd." The prophet may seem mad, but speak true; in truth the blind seer sees. Shakespeare's jesters speak a crazy sense. So too, Nietzsche's Zarathustra is greeted with laughter or silence: mankind is not yet ready for him, and to others he appears a fool. Such paradoxomania and deliberate flouting of expectations can seem alien to the great ideals of Greek thought—coherence, consistency, clarity of conception and expression, form. And yet, the whole Cynic lifestyle is pervaded by the conviction that one who is truly wise will dismiss the burdens of prudence and knowledge. Why worry about tomorrow? Why study, conduct research, or formulate complex theories about experience? No scholar or scientist, the Cynic dismisses the ambition to know many things. For only one "big thing" can be known: Fortune rules all externals, and the self alone may be understood and mastered. Consequently, while all around is so much "smoke," the self may be self-contained, self-sufficient, "rich," and thus "powerful" enough to be invulnerable to Fortune. These Cynic conceits of "wealth" and "invincibility" are not simply a rhetorical ploy, however. Rather, they are grounded in a deep sense of what is real: the Cynic paradoxes are inspired ultimately by a full ontology.

Too easily seduced by the Cynics' rhetoric of otherness, major historians of Greek philosophy have tended (as we saw in chapter 1) to deny or downplay continuities, not only between the Cynics and Greek culture generally, but even between the Cynics and the philosophical tradition. To this end, the saying of Diogenes Laertius is commonly brought forth as a *locus classicus* for later scholarly opinion: Cynicism is a way of life, but not a philosophy.[1] Or again, many repeat the saying attributed to Plato, that Diogenes was "a Socrates gone mad;"[2] stress here is laid on the madness of Diogenes, rather than his resemblance to Socrates. Such phrases, therefore, only lead to further questions: What is a philosophy? Was Socrates himself "mad"? The post-Socratic stress upon ethics as the inner core of philosophy should make one hesitate to dismiss Cynicism simply as a series of ethical prejudices; not all philosophies need be complete Hegelian systems. Furthermore, Socrates is, at least in Plato's depiction, an odd creature both physically and psychologically: though Athenian born and bred, he is out of place, and his *atopia* is a personal reflection of his otherworldly philosophy. That is, Socrates is inspired by a divine madness, and in general Plato speaks of the philosopher as a fool to the world.

With these caveats in mind, one returns to the question of the Cynics' Greekness. That Greekness has not always been denied. Höistad, for instance, argues that the Cynics transform the political ideal of *homonoia* (harmony between the classes) into the more purely ethical goal of self-consistency (*homonoia heautôi*).[3] But the Cynic precedents that Höistad offers are Lycophron and Antiphon, relatively minor figures. Far more suggestive on this point is Zeller, who writes that Diogenes was "the most typical figure of ancient Greece," and that "the Cynic, like the Megarian School, arose from a fusion of the teaching of Socrates with the doctrines of the Eleatics and Sophists."[4] Such a pedigree would place the Cynics firmly within the intellectual framework of the Greek tradition. But Zeller does not fully explicate his conclusions. This chapter will seek to bolster Zeller's approach, though with a contention that Zeller himself does not make. Namely, the Cynics should be seen as ethical Eleaticists. That is, Cynicism is not so much a fusion of disparate elements like Socrates' voluntary poverty and the Sophistic dichotomy of nature-custom. Rather, Cynicism represents one possible ethical interpretation of Parmenides' ontology. As such, Cynicism is further proof of the immense influence that that metaphysic had over the entire tradition of Greek thought. Parmenides' vision of the One and of true Being gave powerful impetus to Democritus' atom, Empedocles' elements, Plato's Forms, Aristotle's doctrine of potentiality and actuality, as well as concepts like self-sufficiency. To this list should be added the most typical Hellenistic conception of the sage: the Cynic is the Parmenidean One personified.

In comparing Parmenides' One to Diogenes in the tub, one can hardly argue that the Cynics *were* Eleatics or even that they were *directly* influenced by Eleaticism. Far from it: the Cynics' espousal of a wise foolishness is loudly hostile to the type of intellectualism that Eleaticism represents. Thus Diogenes is said to have refuted Zeno's arguments against motion by getting up to walk: the Cynic brushes through all complex subtleties as so many cobwebs of the mind. Similarly, a strictly historical progression from Parmenides to Diogenes would be unhelpful. Yet, surprisingly, this has been attempted, for according to the traditional "succession of philosophers" (*diadochê philosophôn*), Parmenides taught Zeno, Zeno taught Gorgias, Gorgias taught Antisthenes, and Antisthenes taught Diogenes "the Dog." There are difficulties in the Zeno-Gorgias and Antisthenes-Diogenes links, as well as in what constitutes "teaching." But although external ties between the Eleatics and first Cynics are scanty, the conceptual resemblances are striking. Again, one must not read literally, and must bear in mind that the tenets of Eleaticism were so compelling that they essentially created the philosophical atmosphere breathed by the Cynics: these tenets determined a general orientation that the Cynics unconsciously adopted, despite the fact that their explicit rhetoric was to reject the convoluted "wisdom" of Eleatics, Academics, Peripatetics, and other schools.

In order to trace the intellectual asceticism of the Cynics back to Eleatic ontology, we will first describe Parmenides' vision of the One and the attributes of reality itself. These attributes had immense influence especially over subsequent physics and epistemology. Moreover, they give the Greek praise of poverty a philosophical aspect: the truth is so beautiful and absorbing that to glimpse it transforms a person, turns him in a different direction, and wrenches him away from his previous devotion to conventional goods.

Philosophy is a solitary activity that pulls the thinker away from work, marriage, family, citizenship, away even from sensual pleasure and the distractions of sense-experience. Indeed, the physical world as a whole loses its hold over the "wise," who knows something far more real and compelling. That is, the Eleatic elevation of the absolute over the relative—of the singular, eternal, and unchanging over the heterogeneous, temporal, and shifting—introduces a lasting dualism into much Greek thought. This dualism culminates eventually in a variety of types of philosophical poverty. The Platonic philosopher becomes an intellectual and even religious ascetic who devotes himself to the pursuit of divine Ideas. The Cynic, on the other hand, dismisses such talk of eternity simply to contrast mundane Fortune and the self. While the external world is filled with "smoke" (*tuphos*), and is as undesirable as it is unintelligible, the Cynic unconsciously emulates the attributes of the Eleatic One, and so proclaims his self-sufficiency, unity, consistency, and inner purity from contaminating desires and relations.

PARMENIDES AND ELEATIC ONTOLOGY

In further explication of the Eleatic background to Cynicism, let us begin with Parmenides of Elea. The fragmentary poem "On Nature" is a difficult and controversial one, yet clearly in its contrast of the "Way of Truth" and the "Way of Seeming," it inaugurates a set of influential dichotomies. These Eleatic dualisms occur at three interrelated levels. Ontologically, the real is separated from the unreal or less real. Epistemologically, reason is privileged over the physical senses. And socially, the philosopher removes himself from "the many." Latent then in these dualisms is the sense that the philosopher's thoughts are distant from those of his contemporaries.

Many see Parmenides as the father of idealism, others as the first logician. The claims are correct to the extent that Parmenides seems to assert that reality is known by the mind, not the senses, and to the extent that he seems to be struggling to articulate the laws of contradiction, identity, and the excluded middle. By the law of noncontradiction, what is cannot be said not to be, and what is not cannot be said to be: it is impossible that both P and not-P. According to the law of identity, P is P: what is is and cannot not be. By the law of the excluded middle, being must either be or not be: either P or not-P must be true. In conjunction, these laws yield Parmenides' fervid declaration that Being is one, eternal, alone, simple, homogeneous, and changeless. For instance, the eternity of Being derives from the consideration that

Being did not come into existence and will not cease to exist. For if Being came to be, then there was a time when it did not exist. Thus there would have been a time when non-Being preceded Being, in other words, when nothing existed and Being did not exist—a contradiction. By similar reasoning, Being cannot die, move, or change. But that to which time and change do not apply is timeless or eternal.[5] Thus, by a few simple arguments, Parmenides transforms the quasi-divine material substance of previous Pre-Socratics into something less obviously tangible.[6] Thales' primordial water, Anaximenes' air, Pythagoras' numbers have parallels in sense-experience, but Parmenides' Being is colorless, intangible, and cannot be seen.

The ethical implications of this epistemological and ontological discovery are not wholly passed over by Parmenides. Wandering on the Path of Seeming, the multitude is ignorant of true reality: "they are both deaf and blind, a stunned, undiscerning crowd, who think that Being and non-Being are the same, and yet not the same."[7] One need not interpret this line as a pointed refutation of Heraclitus. Instead, this is a general criticism of the unenlightened: their minds remain tied to the multiplicities of sense-experience; without a fixed measure of reality, they cannot distinguish the real from the false.

This critique is in harmony with the religious enthusiasm of the poem. Parmenides' "On Nature" is not simply a theoretical argument with propositional conclusions. More, it is a hymn about a revelation, the testament of a man transformed by logical insight. The religious dimension to Parmenides' logical deductions is apparent from a variety of perspectives. Just as many other Pre-Socratics spoke of their material substance in religious terms, so too Parmenides' supratemporal, undying *esti* is akin to the divine. Hence, Parmenides writes in the elevated verse of epic and oracular responses, as the solemn hexameter is fitting for the higher dignity of the divine. Modern idealists may see in Parmenides the seeds of the ontological argument: "it is" is a necessary statement that cannot be denied. Or (using other terminology) the essence of Being is itself, existence; the more usual term for this necessary thought is "God." But most of all, the fragments themselves convey the personal excitement of extraordinary revelation. The Daughters of the Sun have pushed away the veils from their radiant faces; the mortal crosses the threshold of Night and Day, from darkness into light. This language of enlightenment has led some to describe Parmenides as a mystic who experienced the fundamental oneness of all things, or as a shaman-like figure who tells of the soul's wanderings far from the body. Parmenides as shaman might be a successor of other, more obscure figures—Epimenides, Abaris, Aristeas, Aithalides, Hermotimus, and Pythagoras—about whom similar out-of-body experiences are told.[8] On the same note, one might make him spiritual brother of the Platonic Socrates, with his strange contemplative trances.[9]

What kind of mystic Parmenides was may be impossible to determine given the relative lack of evidence. A surer conclusion that one can draw from the poem is that it highlights and recommends the solitude of the philosopher. As the poem begins, the horses and divine charioteers speed the lone Parmenides, "the knowing man, above all cities."[10] The relentless speed of the divine chariot (fr. 1.1–10) is in contrast with the aimless wandering of two-headed mortals—that blind, dazed, undiscerning tribe (fr. 6). For they drift about enslaved to the senses: they believe that things come into being and perish, change place, have color (fr. 8.39–41). But in order to learn the astonishing truth, the goddess urges the mortal "boy" (fr. 1.24) to attend to her words: "if now I speak, you attend and listen to my word" (fr. 2.1; cf. 6.2). Protreptic language is strong as the goddess exhorts him to keep his mind clear of normal ways of thinking (fr. 2.2, 6.3, 7), and not to let the "the habits formed by much experience" force him back into the haze of sense-experience (fr. 7.3–6). Such exhortation is necessary, because it is a long and difficult road from darkness to light.[11] The truth lies far indeed from the paths of men (fr. 1.24–28); few fly free of the nets of sense-experience and social tradition. But the mind is its own place and has its own distinctive realm ("path") and object. That is, thinking is for the Eleatics itself nonempirical. Not for them the doctrine that "whatever is in the mind was first in the senses," and that the ears and eyes lend the brain all its concepts. For in truth, there are no things, no becoming, death, motion, color, multiplicity. What is seen does not truly exist. The sole reality is Being, ever-living, motionless, one. An individual cannot experience this Being like some object, and yet it is more present to the mind than any thing is present to the eye or ear. This idea cannot be denied or avoided. It haunts the mind. Those who explore its depths will be transformed by it.

Parmenides may be difficult to understand, and even harder to appreciate, but we must keep one thing in mind—his enthusiasm for an unadorned idea. Hegel, who shares Parmenides' idealism, recognizes this "pure enthusiasm of thought" as characteristic of the philosopher:

> It was the Eleatics, above all Parmenides, who first enunciated the simple thought of pure being as the absolute and sole truth: only being is, and nothing absolutely is not, and in the surviving fragments of Parmenides this is enunciated with the pure enthusiasm of thought which has for the first time apprehended itself in its absolute abstraction.[12]

In particular, Hegel has Parmenides' sublime intellectualism in mind when he ridicules Kant's critique of the ontological argument. Kant argues in the *Critique of Pure Reason* that the idea of 100 thalers (dollars) does not make any difference to one's wallet, and so, analogously, the mere idea of a perfect God does not prove His existence. For Hegel, however, as for Parmenides, pure reason is not sterile: there are ideas that are not *mere* thoughts, are not the shadows of sense-impressions fluttering briefly through the brain.[13] Rather, certain ideas are simply themselves, existing in their own right and not merely as representations of things. The thinker who is impressed by the necessity of such ideas may make them the foundation of ethical life, even when those ideas have no "cash-value" and are not recognizably useful within whatever cultural conventions he happens to find himself. This is essential for appreciating the radical independence of some of the Greek thinkers.

This philosophical freedom from conventional notions might be traced back to Parmenides himself. Later sources hint at this when they record the dichotomy between Parmenides' background and his philosophical schooling. Parmenides hailed from a rich and noble family. He must have been a respected member of his community, as he is said to have written a constitution for Elea. But on the other hand, Diogenes Laertius also writes that he was the student of the Pythagorean Ameinias, "a poor man."[14] Whether true or not, the story shows how quick Hellenistic writers are to assume any philosopher to be indifferent, if not openly hostile to material concerns; the philosopher is poor, unless enriched by a Fortune for which he does not care. One cannot make much of Diogenes Laertius' testimony here. Yet the separation of the philosopher from conventional norms and ideals is abundantly clear in the case of Parmenides' pupil, Zeno. In his famous paradoxes, Zeno argued plausibly that the very notion of plurality, change, and motion are unintelligible. If for instance a flying arrow moves, then it must do so either where it is or where it is not. But the latter is impossible, since then the arrow would be and not be in the same place. And in the former case, the arrow moves in its place. But as long as it is in the same place, it does not move. In both cases, therefore, the arrow cannot move. For Zeno then, the only rationally defensible view is that the arrow be stationary, just as Parmenides' arguments demand that the One be full, pure, and unmoving. If sense-experience seems to contradict such reasoned conclusions, then so much the worse for the authority of the senses, and so much the worse for motion and variety: all these are illusory and unacceptable. Thus, a severe rationalism drives the Eleatic to part ways with common sense: a thinker should have the courage of his convictions, and cling to what seems truest no matter how mad or foolish his wisdom may seem to the "many."

The Pluralists Empedocles, Democritus, and Anaxagoras afford another glimpse of how the Eleatic ontology lies behind the expectation that wisdom transform the thinker into something different and strange. First, it has often been noted that the Pluralists transferred the Eleatic conception of Being to the material elements. The Eleatic axiom that nothing comes from nothing rules out the possibility of any radical becoming: something cannot come from nothing. All events and things must have prior causes; but to avoid an infinite regress in explanation, one must posit some first, ultimate causes that lie behind all changes. These causes are described in various ways. Empedocles posits four elements. Anaxagoras thought that elemental matter must be infinitely diverse, containing an aspect of all things that are. Democritus coins a new word, "atom." In all three cases, the elements, like Being, do not themselves come into or out of being. They may be subject to physical motion and enter into *external* relations with each other, but in themselves they remain unaffected by these relations. They remain simple, homogeneous, internally the same; they are eternal. Democritus is perhaps the most explicit in acknowledging his Eleatic assumptions when he draws a parallel between Being and the "full" atom or between non-Being and the Void (i.e., whatever is not-atom).

The concept of an atom or element is so familiar now that we may not appreciate either its ontological underpinnings or the unconventional conclusions it may inspire. One such conclusion is the denial of those phenomena that dominate ordinary life. That is, there is no motion, growth, birth, or death. Certainly, things animate and inanimate appear to the senses to move; the young are born, grow big, and die. But for the thinker, such phenomena have a derivative reality, because all change is simply the recombination of elements that themselves do not change. There is a worldly renunciation here that may surface briefly among some of the Pluralists. Anaxagoras for instance vociferously differentiates himself from the "Hellenes," who do not know that birth and death do not really exist.[15] Democritus' injunction to tranquillity of mind may, similarly, be inspired by the conviction that phenomenal change is less than fully real. For by convention (*nomos*), there is the sweet, sour, adazzle, dim; to the senses, there is hurry and annihilation; but "in reality, there is only atom and the void." Therefore, "the wise" who have reached this truth by pure thought no longer fret about appearances, and maintain a noble serenity throughout life's vicissitudes.[16]

Even more aristocratic in his philosophical pride is Empedocles: "Fools! They expect indeed that what was not formerly can come into being or that things die and perish utterly."[17] For these foolish "many," life and death are the greatest realities. These creatures of a day (*ephêmeroi*) confuse the particulars of which they have experience with the whole itself.[18] In this vast ignorance, they inhabit a "darkly covered cave,"[19] clamoring for superstitions and medicines for their various ailments. In contrast is the wise man who can offer them "purifications" for their sickness. Thus, Empedocles begins his *Purifications* (*Katharmoi*) by proclaiming to the citizens of Acragas that he returns to them now as a god, no longer a man.[20] Cosmic knowledge has elevated him above daily trivialities to consciousness of the whole.[21] This whole is a transtemporal one, and one begins to rise to knowledge of it when one realizes that change is just a reshuffling of eternal elements according to the perennial competition of Love and Strife. Bodily existence too is just a reshuffling, but to know this is to transcend it.

Empedocles has transcended it, and proclaims to his hearers how his life as a god was disrupted when the "ancient law of necessity" flung him from the divine aether into disparate multiplicity. An "exile from the gods and a wanderer,"[22] Empedocles was buffeted through all the elements. He was a bush, a fish leaping from the sea, a boy, a girl.[23] But now, he returns a god to his mortal birthplace, bringing the "healing word" to the Acragantines. Moreover, he comes announcing the great "wealth" that his wisdom would afford. Twice in the fragments Empedocles speaks of the "wealth of wisdom," which distinguishes the seer from the conventional person:

> Blessed is he who possesses the wealth of divine intelligence.
> Miserable he who cultivates hazy notions about the gods.[24]

Pythagoras also possessed this "wealth of intelligence," for he was able to remember up to thirty previous lifetimes.[25] Like him, Empedocles remembers that the fall from the divine to the elemental realm is a fall from "such great honor and such magnitude of happy wealth"[26] into their opposites. Sensual reality is necessarily limited and poor in contrast.

But Empedocles' ostentatious promises of healing and riches are not broadcast indiscriminately. He proclaims his superiority loudly, but he also focusses his attention and hopes upon one hearer: "Pausanias, son of wisehearted Achites, you listen!" Empedocles' protreptic language was insistent and regular, judging from its prevalence in the fragments: Pausanias should turn aside from the paths of the masses, and "[h]arken unto my words, for learning will increase your mind. . . . Look at this with your mind, and do not sit gaping wide-eyed."[27] Such exhortations to philosophy are also calls to renounce the testimony of the senses, which give access to a merely derivative reality. "And I will tell you another thing": there is no birth and death, but only a mixing and separation of the mixed. The "many" live by their senses, suffering in life as in death; only the philosopher thinks his way to a higher, happier reality. Indeed, his wisdom brings material rewards, and if Pausanias learns right, he too will become something of a powerful wizard: he will be able to cure diseases, calm storms, heal old age, and revive the dead (fr. 111). Crowds will flock to him, seeking medicines, oracles, and "the way to profit" (fr. 112.9–10).

Thus, Empedocles offers rewards of wealth both material and spiritual, unlike a Diogenes who would later promise a purely nonmaterial "wealth." Indeed, one should note that Empedocles' knowledge of the cosmic life of the elements, the alternating reigns of Love and Strife—his knowledge that the eternal whole is more real than temporal events—does not seem to inspire him to embrace poverty as a means to enlightenment. Tradition has it that Empedocles himself enjoyed the trappings of wealth. He grew up in a wealthy family; his father "raised horses." When grown, he delighted in his purple robes and flowing luxuriant hair. As his *Katharmoi* opens, he appears stepping through fawning crowds, crowned with garlands, honored by all.[28] Though Pythagorean and mystical elements of his philosophy might have moved him closer to an intellectual or religious asceticism, his self-portrait suggests a man who robustly enjoyed his fame and perhaps even the *dolce vita* (*bios eudaimon*) that became proverbial of prosperous Sicilian cities like fifth-century Acragas.[29]

Before turning from the Eleatics and Empedocles to the Sophists, let us step aside for a moment to examine how similar dichotomies—between the wise man and fools, truth and opinion, reason and sense-experience—also characterize the fragments of a thinker who probably stood outside the Eleatic sphere of influence. Heraclitus is an enigmatic figure, and later anecdotes probably only dramatize the enigma and alienation of a writer whose nickname was "the shadowy." Thus, according to one source, Heraclitus was so disgusted with his peers that he retired to the temple of Artemis to spend his days playing knuckle-bones with little boys.[30] In another story, the exile of Hermodorus so enraged Heraclitus that he retired from political life and refused to make laws for the city (cf. DK 22 B 121). But foreigners recognized his greatness, at least in the fictional Hellenistic letters that purport to be the correspondence between Heraclitus and Darius. Here, the King of Kings invites Heraclitus to Susa to instruct him in philosophy and Greek culture. The sage's reply is appropriately pithy: Heraclitus is too pleased with his "little fortune" to exchange it for the luxury, jealousies, and arrogance of a tyrant's court.[31] Even more dramatic stories depict Heraclitus as a misanthrope who so hated mankind that he fled into the mountains to live on grass and herbs.[32]

Such anecdotes probably reflect the Hellenistic expectation that the philosopher be a man apart, stern and uncompromising in his love of truth. But whether or not the historical Heraclitus actually fled to the mountains, his surviving fragments do ring with a profound scorn for his more conventional contemporaries. Thus, from what may be the very beginning of his work, Heraclitus writes that of the ever-living Logos, men are always ignorant, even when they hear it spoken (DK 22 B 1). They stumble on, like sleepwalkers, as if they had never heard the Logos; they do not know how to hear or speak (fr. 19). Heraclitus regularly contrasts himself and the few good men with these stupid "many" (fr. 104): the best choose everlasting fame before all else, but the many glut themselves like cattle (fr. 29); if happiness were bodily pleasure, we would call cows happy when they find cud to chew (fr. 4); the many pray in front of lifeless statues and houses, and try to purify themselves with blood (fr. 5; cf. 128); they piously bury or burn their dead, not knowing that bodies should be thrown out even more quickly than dung (fr. 96). The commoner may rest content with the celebrated wisdom of Homer, Hesiod, Xenophanes, or Pythagoras, but Heraclitus would have Homer flung from the musical contents and whipped (fr. 42). All their learning has not taught Hesiod, Xenophanes, or Pythagoras insight (fr. 40); Hesiod, for instance, despite all the details in his almanac of daily tasks, was such a fool that he did not know that day is night (fr. 57). Hence, much learning does not teach wisdom (fr. 40), and fools flutter excitedly at every word (fr. 87). In contrast to all these are the wise who, like Parmenides and Empedocles, recognize the inner unity of the seemingly disparate. "The wise is one thing—to know the mind (*gnomê*) that governs all through all" (fr. 41). The one unity of things is called by many names: it is God, Zeus, *logos*, mind (*gnomê*), fire, the thunderbolt, war (fr. 30, 32, 53, 64, 66, 80, 90). "God is day, night, winter, summer, war, peace, feasting, famine" (fr. 67). Seeming disharmony is inner harmony (fr. 8, 10, 54); unity is multiplicity (fr. 10, 50); the way up and the way down are one and the same (fr. 60); the path of the screw is both straight and twisted (fr. 59); sea-water is both pure and foul (fr. 61); the beginning and end are the same, as on a circle (fr. 103); mortals are immortals and vice versa (fr. 62, 77); life and death, Dionysus and Hades are the same (fr. 15; cf. 48); into the same river we step and do not step, we are and we are not (fr. 49a). Thus wisdom confounds the normal categories of experience, for the wise recognize that *all* things are one and good (fr. 89, 102). Few appreciate this wisdom, and therefore, few recognize the wise: "of all the words I have heard, none has come to the point of realizing that the wise is separate from all" (fr. 108).

Sophistic Wealth and Socrates

Heraclitus' tone is aloof, and the language of superiority remains almost as emphatic with the appearance of the professional "wise man," the *sophistês*, in approximately the middle of the fifth century. The strengthening of important democracies, notably in Sicily and Athens, created a new demand for oratorical skills and the ability to persuade large crowds with arguments. Appearing largely to fulfill this need, the sophists taught first and foremost the "art of words." There was no set curriculum of course, and different teachers brought their own approach. Some demanded a broad study of a range of ancillary topics, from geometry to the theory of language. Others dismissed general studies as unnecessary. Often the sophistic art was tied to the older aristocratic equation of virtue and political ability. Thus, the sophist promotes himself as a teacher of *aretê*, as when Protagoras encourages Hippocrates to hire him: "Young man, if you associate with me, on the very first day you will return home a better man than you came, and better on the second day than on the first, and better every day than you were on the day before."[33] Despite Protagoras' calm dignity, his *epangelma* is essentially a sales-pitch: the student-teacher relationship becomes a contract with a view to virtue. Yet, in the end, this "virtue" is not moral goodness but the older aristocratic ability to help one's friends and harm one's enemies. Sophistic-taught rhetoric and "virtue" are means to wealth and power.

Thus the sophist could potentially be described either idealistically, as a trainer of the "best" (*aristoi*), or more cynically, as a self-interested peddler of intellectual goods. Depending on sensibilities, stress could be placed in different ways. A common reaction from approximately the 420s was to denounce sophistry as a shameless form of money-making. For though in reality most sophists probably made a modest living,[34] all eyes are drawn to the spectacle of success. The great sophists became relatively rich, and so rumors multiplied. Extravagant prices are said to have been paid for individual speeches and lesson-plans: Evenus of Paros, for instance, charged five minas for a course in morals, a sum that represents five hundred days' labor for the average skilled laborer in Athens.[35] But this was cheap compared to the one hundred minas that Protagoras is said to have charged. Here, the conveniently round sum is probably an exaggeration; rumor has it that the Eleatic

Zeno and Gorgias also demanded one hundred minas. Whatever the exact figures, fees for these intellectual superstars must have been quite high, for Plato depicts the young Hippocrates despairing of ever being able to hire Protagoras: all Hippocrates' money and all the money of all his friends would not cover the fees.[36] Such prices made some sophists rich beyond belief.[37] Protagoras, it is said, was once a wood-carrier, but is now richer than Phidias and ten other sculptors combined.[38] Not to be outdone, Hippias loudly proclaims that he was the wealthiest of all Sophists, richer than any two together.[39] Others give the title of wealthiest sophist to Gorgias: was not the famous golden statue of him at Delphi erected by none other than Gorgias himself? Here indeed was the king of sophists; it is rumored that Gorgias assumed the garb of royalty and, like his teacher Empedocles, marched around in robes of flowing purple.[40]

Such stereotypes about Sophistic extravagance helped to bring a reaction against their craft, as if here were another instance of the evils of the profit-motive. The typical Sophist, it is said, cares nothing for his student, truth, tradition, or the gods. Nothing is sacred to him as he hunts profits by clever words. Indeed, his trade is a strange one: there seems something suspect in the notion of "selling wisdom" or exchanging virtue for money, as if understanding and goodness could be traded as callously as any commodity.[41] Thus, the term "sophist" was pejorative as early as Aristophanes' *Clouds*; Plato depicts Hippocrates embarrassed and Anytus enraged by the mere mention of the word.[42] The authority of the fourth-century schools succeeded in giving the term a decidedly negative connotation. Plato may speak highly of individual Sophists like Protagoras, but when treating the group as a whole, he condemns them as avaricious "prostitutes" of the truth, mercenary hunters of rich youths, merchants or hucksters of soul-merchandise, promoters of their own knowledge-products, and argumentative profiteers.[43] Aristotle continues this critique and caricature of the movement when he basically defines the Sophist as a pseudo-philosopher: the Sophist practices the art of making money by appearing wise.[44] Isocrates too expresses his reservations, and prefers at times to call himself a *philosophos* rather than a *sophistês*; on the other hand, the sophist's "best and greatest reward" should be the prudence and good reputation of his students.[45]

Among the first to satirize this aspect of the Sophistic movement was Socrates. In comparison with the great Sophists, Socrates was a poor man. He cannot afford to hear Evenus, and jokes that he might be able to pay for Prodicus' one-drachma course, but not the fifty-drachma executive version. He describes himself as a "peasant-farmer of philosophy" (*autourgos tês philosophias*), as if he were like a typical countryman, who works his own land for a subsistence living and rarely goes to the market.[46] The personal poverty of Socrates has sometimes been doubted: in one source, his total possessions (including house) are estimated at five minas—not an impressive sum, but not nothing either. In addition, he had wealthy friends, including Callias, Crito, Cephalus, Alcibiades, and Plato and his brothers. If he fought as a hoplite at Potidaea, Delium, and elsewhere, he surely owned a panoply and belonged to the class of the *zeugitae*, not the *thetes*. Certainly, therefore, he was not among the poorest of the poor. Yet poverty is a relative term, and Socrates' poverty cannot be dismissed as a mere trope. His house and his panoply were probably inherited; again, Aristotle implies that the *zeugitae* are poor, for "the ox is the poor man's slave."[47] Socrates wife, wife's family, and others may have seen to the household's needs, which Socrates himself undutifully neglected as he spent his time outdoors philosophizing: in his case, he had little to spend and the sources never depict him buying anything. Even at his trial, it was with the utmost reluctance that he offered to buy his life with a single mina.[48]

In further contrast to the tycoon Sophists, Socrates was a decidedly plebeian and democratic figure. For he often asks, why should anyone *pay* for conversation?[49] Talking is free. Again and again, Socrates prides himself on his willingness to talk with rich and poor alike, and with anyone who might help him answer a question. Like Hippias, he is also a "philosopher in the marketplace," but one who does not demand payment for his talk.[50] He satirizes those who will talk only for money, like Prodicus who teaches nothing for free, and has a habit of quoting Epicharmus' phrase "Hand washes hand: give something and take something." But if in fact self-interested reciprocity is the right course, then soul-merchandise should be rewarded in kind: learning and enlightenment should be repaid with the same coin, or else with praise and gratitude, as Socrates tries to "pay" Thrasymachus.[51] Thus Socrates would transform the sophistic relationship of seller-client into the more intimate bond of friendship. Friends share all things in common, and intellectual exchange becomes a form of barter. In such relationships, what is of paramount importance is goodwill and generosity towards the other.

Thus the "profits" of a philosophical friendship become wholly noneconomic in character, as Socrates competes with Sophistic and commercial language by praising the "wealth of wisdom." Socrates teases Euthyphro for "luxuriating" idly in his "wealth of wisdom." In the same ironic vein, he flatters Meno: the Thessalians were famous for their horsemanship and wealth, but now their wisdom is equally illustrious; Athena has fled north, impoverishing her native city to such an extent that Socrates does not know even what virtue is, let alone whether it can be taught. Thus the Socrates who will soon quote Pindar and speak of spiritual recollection (*anamnêsis*) is contrasted with a man of brutal worldly ambitions. The *Gorgias* depicts an even sharper clash of principles and personalities. For Callicles, Socrates' style of philosophy will bring only poverty and adversity. In response, Socrates says, "If my soul were golden, Callicles, you would prove a perfect touchstone"; Callicles' violent materialism becomes the foil to Socrates' "golden" idealism. In a different context, Phaedrus promises that he will dedicate golden statues at Delphi if Socrates speaks better than Lysias. Socrates responds by praising Phaedrus himself as truly golden: generosity is better than gold. In the *Symposium*, Alcibiades extols Socrates' golden soul, hidden beneath the ugly satyr's exterior. Golden too are the souls of the philosopher-kings. Externally poor, they possess "true wealth" in virtue and knowledge, and indeed this is their highest prayer. All such golden souls deal with each other directly, rather than through a cash medium: in dialogues and symposia, they entertain each other with "feasts of arguments" and "gifts of speeches." Their souls are "enriched" by virtue, or by the books that are the "treasure-troves of ancient sages." As cicadas are nourished by purest dew, so the thinkers are sustained by thought alone, and true Being is ambrosia for the soul. On the other hand, one should beware of being poisoned by the sophists' rotten soul-food. The Socrates of Plato and Xenophon uses such metaphors so frequently that one suspects that the man actually did talk like this.[52] If so, then the historical Socrates spiritualized the rewards of Sophistic *epangelmata*, exhorting his interlocutors to abandon conventional ideals as primary and cultivate their souls as the source of all value. Socratic "riches" consists solely in wisdom, and so Antisthenes can pay the debt of gratitude to Socrates for making him "wealthier" and more fun-loving than their more conventional peers.[53]

Socrates, then, is something of a creature of paradoxes: a voluntarily poor man, yet preoccupied with the "wealth of wisdom;" a critic of the Sophists who yet taught his own "art of words," stressing essential definitions as the basis of an ordered and methodical speech; one who questioned the teachability of virtue, yet in his own person impressed many with a sense of the worth of honesty, self-restraint, generosity, and intelligence. The man's oddness (*atopia*) most impressed Plato, and perhaps gave Plato his initial sense of what a philosopher and even a human being generally should aspire to be. Life should be oriented towards spiritual values, and so Plato offers many images of how his idealized Socrates constantly treads the "upper road" of philosophical inquiry, whether he is at a drinking-party (*Symposium*), just home from war (*Charmides*), alone with a beautiful boy (*Phaedrus*), defending himself before an angry crowd (*Apology*), or preparing to die (*Phaedo*). Ironic, irreverent, sometimes even aggressively critical of the opinions and customs of the "Way of Seeming," Plato's Socrates adheres to the "Way of Truth" regardless of practical consequences. In the sequence of dialogues leading from his trial to execution (*Meno, Euthyphro, Apology, Crito, Phaedo*) he literally philosophizes unto death; at each stage, his contempt for conventional men like Anytus becomes more pronounced, until in the end he defines philosophy itself as a practice of death, a voluntary renunciation of the world as primary. Unawed by death itself, a fortiori such a man will not be deterred from philosophy by fear of poverty or worries about what to wear. That is, Socrates is an intellectual ascetic, who sacrifices all for the life of the mind. In the *Apology*, Socrates says this explicitly: philosophy, the service of Apollo— god of light, music, medicine, and reason—has made him poor.[54]

In the same vein, the Platonic Socrates is able to inspire a "pure enthusiasm of thought" in hearers of all backgrounds and abilities. Some of Socrates' conversations could be described as bacchanalia of reason: as if possessed by the spirit of a divine argument, the thinker leaves the ruts of conventional thought, runs riot in his speculative frenzy, praising death or some Idea, abolishing private property and the family, exiling the poets and banning religion—a veritable *sparagmos* of normality. Alcibiades recognizes this bacchic fury in Socrates: Socrates is a Marsyas who charms with unadorned words, a Silenus hubristic in his intellectual strength.[55] Hardly understanding the nature of his passion for Socrates, Alcibiades both loves and hates this satyr, so enthralling and repulsive, so ugly and beautiful at once. Socrates is a gadfly and a god; philosophy a snake's bite, venom, and species of madness.[56] In another image, Meno likens Socrates to the torpedo-fish, for at a touch he numbs to perplexity all with whom he speaks.[57] Socrates influenced a generation of Greeks of various abilities and dispositions—Plato, Xenophon, Charmides, Alcibiades. Lesser names are his manic followers Apollodorus and Aristodemus: Aristodemus appears as Socrates' comic sidekick in the *Symposium*, always barefoot and eager to follow the master everywhere, even uninvited to Agathon's victory party; Apollodorus was forever praising Socrates and berating everyone else for their comparative worthlessness. At the opening of the *Symposium*, he is at it again, barking at a rich businessman for thinking about everything except philosophy.[58] Indeed, Socratic folly took hold of Plato too, if one credits the anecdote that upon first hearing Socrates he rushed home to burn his tragedies and other poems[59]—an irrevocable break with a conventional career. Antisthenes too is said to have left his first teacher Gorgias to become an enthusiastic "hearer" of Socrates, forsaking rhetoric for Socratic "wealth" and friendship.[60]

PLATONIC POVERTY

As often noted, it is difficult to separate the ideas of Socrates and Plato, given that Socrates wrote nothing, while most of Plato's dialogues have Socrates as the main interlocutor. But one possible view is that Plato was the more ardent soul of the two, and that he fastened upon those otherworldly aspects of the actual Socrates as the basis of his own more spiritual philosophy: Socrates' incessant philosophizing, his carelessness about practical affairs, and consequent poverty develop into the systematic intellectual and religious asceticism of Plato's philosopher-kings; Socrates' search for essential definitions as the basis of ethical life becomes the Platonic claim that Ideas, moral and mathematical, structure temporal reality itself; and finally, Socrates' personal idiosyncrasies are reinterpreted as philosophical folly and divine madness.

Again, it is difficult if not impossible to generalize about Plato's "philosophy," given that his thoughts are scattered over dozens of dialogues, with their many different themes, characters, and dramatic situations. Nevertheless, for much of his life, Plato was interested in a theory of Forms or Ideas, and these provide a central theme especially for "middle" dialogues like the *Symposium, Phaedrus, Republic,* and *Phaedo.* One interpretation runs as follows. Plato's is a mystical doctrine in the sense that the Forms are non-empirical, absolute entities that lend unity to thought, experience, and the material world. Platonic enlightenment may come with years of mental training, if at all. Such training and the content of the philosophical vision of the Beautiful in itself, or the Good beyond *ousia,* remove the thinker from concern for physical reality. Therefore, the Platonic philosopher is poor for and because of wisdom. The search for and intuition of a higher reality makes him a fool in the world's sight, for because of his deeper vision, he is bleary-eyed amid the shadows of the cave.

The conviction that the intuition of the Forms will bring a radical transformation of the inner person is most apparent in certain "middle" dialogues, and it is on these that we focus here for Plato's variation on the Eleatic doctrine of Being. In the *Symposium,* Socrates speaks of all types of beauty and desire as manifestations of a single desire for an absolute Beauty. As absolute, this Beauty is unchanging, perfect, simple, homogeneous, self-contained, and not relative to anything other than itself.[61] As noted so very often, these attributes clearly imitate Parmenides' language of Being.[62] Moreover, Beauty in itself is an Eleatic postulate of thought, for where Parmenides insists that the truest statement is that "what is, is," the Platonic thinker finds safety in the tautology that "the beautiful is beautiful." A slight variation of this is that "Beauty is beautiful," and thus it seems that the hypostatized Idea of Beauty is an a priori thought, logically necessary to discuss or even to recognize beautiful particulars. Any skeptic who discusses beauty thus automatically has some intuition of Beauty itself, even if this intuition be dim and ill-developed. Yet, this Idea of Beauty is not merely a logical construction, a postulate necessary for discursive thought and physical experience. Like the Eleatic One, Beauty is an end in itself, almost like a living god. To see this god is to be transformed utterly:

> If you should ever see the Beautiful itself, it will not seem to you to be like bits of gold or clothes or beautiful boys and young men. When you and many others see these, you are astonished and are ready to gaze upon them and be with them forever; if it were somehow possible, you would not eat or drink, but would gaze only and be with them. What then would it be like ([Diotima] asked), if someone could see Beauty itself, simple, pure, unmixed and not full of human flesh and colors and all other mortal nonsense, but if one could look upon divine beauty itself in its singleness?[63]

Genuine philosophical erôs then, drives the thinker "mad." All lovers are proverbially mad, and neglect family, friends, duty, property, health—everything in their enthusiasm for the beloved. A fortiori, the lover of an Absolute disregards temporal reality itself and its affairs as of paltry significance: they are "as straw," compared to what he has seen, or longs to see. The Phaedrus moves from conventional notions of love and the lover's infatuation to the fever-pitch of philosophical erôs. Indeed, Socrates ranks the different types of desire as so many approximations to the philosopher's divine mania to see "the things that are truly real," the colorless, formless, intangible essences seen only by pure mind.[64] Many fail even to recognize what they truly want, and in the confused traffic of ascent and descent, many souls are crippled, many wings broken. But those souls that do not fail in their quest come to overlook, even despise the lower grades of reality. Nourished on the divine, they become themselves godlike, solitary, self-sufficient, and forgetful of normal human things: the many consider them mad, not knowing them to be inspired.[65] Philosophical wisdom is worldly folly.

Plato reserves his most uncompromisingly dualistic language for the *Phaedo* and *Theaetetus*. In the *Phaedo*, a dying Socrates defines philosophical thinking as a "practice of death" and exhorts his hearers to flee sensual particulars. For the body is the locus of evil, passions, war. What we truly desire is not here. What is perfect is not here. We must fly free of the bodily prison, and to do so the soul must curl and contract itself wholly within itself.[66] This voluntary separation of the self from externals is analogous to the moment when soul and body are finally separated in death. Therefore, to philosophize is almost literally to die to the world. Death is not at all to be feared. Rather, one should search every land and pay any sum of money to procure the argument or rational incantation that would banish the fear of death.[67] The urgency of world-flight is expressed even more concisely in the *Theaetetus*. "It is not possible, Theodorus, that evil will vanish from this world, for there must always be something opposed to the good. . . . Therefore one must try to flee from here to there as quickly as possible. To flee is to become like God as much as possible." This flight is total: the god-seeking philosopher despises wealth, pedigree, honors. A king appears to him as little more than a shepherd, tending a human flock; when he hears of someone's landed estates, he thinks them a trivial possession, for he is accustomed to thinking of Being as a whole. The philosopher is present in his city only bodily, but his real self—his soul—is elsewhere, lost in the eternal thoughts of mathematics, astronomy, dialectic, and the like. But not knowing "what is before his feet," the wise man appears ridiculous to the Thracian maid and her ilk. They mock him as a fool.[68]

The *Republic*, again, finds an almost unbridgeable chasm between the otherworldly philosopher and the sensual "many." To be a philosopher is to love eternal ideas, and therefore, though they may have other social virtues, common people are not and cannot be philosophers. Consequently the thinker is a lonely and misunderstood figure. Carpenters, tanners, and the like cannot appreciate what the thinker does: "your business, Socrates, what is it?"[69] The "wise" is to "the many" as the near-sighted captain is to his ignorant crew—a useless talker, a stargazer who does no useful work. Worse, if caught among a corrupt people, the true philosopher is like a man among wild beasts, a traveler caught out in a violent storm. He is persecuted, even unto death.[70] But when he is "alone with the alone," the contemplative becomes so absorbed in thought that he cares little for all this. He recognizes the human race as a small thing; their wealth, honors, and magistracies are small things. The small-minded pursue these goods with relentless fury, incapable of recognizing them as mere shadows of a Good beyond determination in time and place. Plato knows well that the vision of this Good may be ruinous: those who are unchained too early, or improperly educated, will be lamed or blinded for life. Furthermore, the philosopher is the least political animal, a fact that will paradoxically make him supremely qualified for political leadership. But on the other hand, philosophical enlightenment will remove him from the *polis*. He is present there only physically. The Homeric image of the Sirens was easily adapted to a Platonic context, even though Plato does not explicitly use it in this way in the *Republic*. In the *Odyssey*, the Sirens lure Odysseus and all travelers to their shore, where they idle until death overtakes them, enthralled by the song of the goddesses, who "know all that has happened on the much-nourishing earth." In the *Symposium*, Alcibiades has fears that he might grow old sitting by Socrates, seduced by his Siren-voice. Archimedes also was so ensnared by the Sirens of geometry that he would forget to eat and bathe. So too in the final vision of the *Republic*, Socrates depicts the Sirens and Fates singing together of what was, is now, and will be in time to come. Surely, the truly philosophical soul will someday hear that cosmic music: if so, then he will always keep to the "upper path" of philosophy and justice, scorning the sensualism of those whose ears are blocked with wax.[71]

Thus in the *Symposium*, *Phaedrus*, *Phaedo*, *Theaetetus*, and *Republic*, one finds central statements of an idealistic philosophy that would orient the best life towards a realm of quasi-Eleatic absolutes. Many considerations contribute to this segregation of the "wise": a reaction against the profit-motive of the Sophists and the desire to make the philosopher an unbiased lover of the truth; Plato's dualistic conviction that the temporal and sensual are less than fully real and rational; and his consequent stress upon a noetic "Way of Truth" and an intellectual "care for the soul." On the other hand, from the "many" comes the perennial mockery of the intellectual as an oddity and bumbler. The comic poets play to these common prejudices with many funny exaggerations: in the *Clouds*, Socrates is a "spaced-out sophist" (*meteôrosophistês*) who rides in a basket contemplating the sun and conducting silly thought-experiments; Phrynichus mocks the poet Lamprus as a "water-drinker, twittering arch-sophist, skeleton of the Muses, ague of nightingales, hymn to death"; and Aristophanes often jokes that the souls of Euripides, dithyrambists, and other literary aesthetes can be found fluttering on high, searching for their brightly colored but meaningless phrases.[72]

Yet, what the comic poets mock as idiocy, Plato takes as a potential sign of wisdom. Indeed, he gives one-sided emphasis to the previously latent possibility that philosophy is incompatible with worldly prudence. Most famous in this regard is Socrates' fable of Thales and the Thracian slave-girl, which occurs first in the *Theaetetus*. If the girl did laugh at Thales for falling stupidly into a well, the event was hardly typical of the historical Thales himself. In Herodotus, Thales is no absent-minded astronomer but an advisor to kings and cities; he engineers a way for Croesus' army to cross the Halys river.[73] Yet, Plato uses the name of the great man to promote his new vision of the otherness of philosophy. Similar is the reappropriation of the name of Anaxagoras in the *Hippias Minor*. Ironically impressed by Hippias' many talents, Socrates is surprised to realize how foolish the "ancient" philosophers were by comparison. For like Anaxagoras, "they" were so foolish that they avoided politics, made no money, and dedicated themselves so purely to their studies that they often lost everything. Unlike Hippias they did not realize that "the wise" should be clever in his own interests, and that true wisdom is the ability to make the most money.[74] Once again, Socrates' fluent manner (and Plato's art) disguises the fact that the Seven Sages and the Pre-Socratics did not divorce contemplation and action in so strict or explicit a fashion. If anything, sages like Bias and Pittacus were famed more for their political acumen than for any theoretical speculations, while some significant political activity is ascribed to Parmenides, Zeno, Melissus, Heraclitus, Empedocles, and other Pre-Socratics. Anaxagoras may partially foreshadow the emerging contemplative ideal, for according to him, mind (*nous*) is unmixed with the lower world; yet Anaxagoras himself was a close enough associate of Pericles to be targeted by his political enemies. Socrates, on the other hand, made a point of his avoidance of political life. This may have been one of Plato's inspirations both for seeing the philosopher per se as apolitical and for emphasizing the unworldly aspects of Pre-Socratic speculative wisdom; this unworldliness is what makes the notion of a "philosopher-king," for instance, so paradoxical for Plato.

All the dichotomies that inform the Platonic figure of the "foolish" sage lie behind the suggestive allegory of Diotima in the *Symposium*. In the story, Eros is the bastard son of Wealth (*Poros*) and Poverty (*Penia*). Accordingly, he has a double, schizophrenic nature. As child of Poverty, he is ugly, leather-skinned, barefoot, and homeless. But as son of the father he never knew, he is cunning, courageous, energetic, unflagging in his schemes, and a magician, sophist, and philosopher all his days.[75] Here is a transparent allegory about the human condition: man exists in an intermediate position between plenty and poverty, wisdom and utter ignorance, divinity and animality. The perpetual serenity of the gods is not granted to him. They do not philosophize, because they have no lack to overcome. Animals, on the other hand, have no questions and doubts because they are absorbed in momentary pleasures and pains. But man is a divine animal, or a god in exile. Tormented by a sense of emptiness and some unlearned instinct for the eternal, he is *erôs* personified, a perpetual restlessness for something beyond change. He rises or sinks, sometimes feasting, sometimes suffering hunger and despair. Many forget their father and divine ancestry; these rarely escape the poverty of sensation and mere habit. But those who resolutely seek an Olympian "wealth" become strangers even to their peers with whom they have spent their entire lives. Socrates left his city only on a few occasions when the army went on campaign; he spent his life talking on the streets of Athens, and yet for all this, "none of you knows this man."[76]

Cynic Poverty

Thus Plato offers one version of a philosophical poverty, by which wisdom alienates one from conventional ideals and makes one indifferent to worldly concerns. The Cynics philosophized in the same general rubric, though obviously details differ significantly. One notable difference between the two is the value placed upon learning and science. Unlike his Platonic counterpart, the Cynic rejects arithmetic, geometry, dialectic, and the rest as superfluous distractions from the "one big" requirement of self-knowledge. So in the famous anecdote, when Plato and his followers have defined man as the "featherless biped," Diogenes rushes into the Academy with a plucked chicken, crying, "Here is Plato's human being!" For the Cynic, logical exercises, definition-making, and the like are not preparatory to the vision of some Good or intuition of eternity. All such talk is a form of pride, a strategy to overawe others, and contributes less to the good life than does a healthy skepticism.[77]

Yet, like Plato, the Cynics also travel along the Eleatic Way of Truth and shun what they ridicule as the Way of Seeming. For what can be said truly? In short, the Cynics are profoundly skeptical about the possibility of almost all knowledge. This becomes apparent first in a more theoretical fashion as Antisthenes adheres to some form of the doctrine that predication is impossible. Sources for this doctrine are few, but the most important is the following passage by Aristotle:

> Antisthenes was too simple-minded when he claimed that *nothing could be described except by the account proper to it,—one predicate to one subject;* from which the conclusion used to be drawn that there could be no contradiction, and almost that there could be no error. But it is possible

to describe each thing not only by the account of itself, but also by that of something else. This may be done altogether falsely indeed, but there is also a way in which it may be done truly; e.g. eight may be described as a double number by the use of the definition of two.[78]

What Aristotle seems to imply in this controversial passage is that according to Antisthenes, one may legitimately say "A is A" but not "A is B." For if A and B are different, then A is not B. But if A and B are not different, then they are the same, and one should call them by the same name, for example, A; that is, one should say "A is A." Thus, for instance, one can call an apple an apple, but not red, since only red is red; one can say "eight is eight," but not "eight is two times four." In such arguments, the assumption of a rigid dichotomy between sameness and difference, Being and non-Being, are wholly Eleatic. Eleatic also is the intransigent insistence on the absolute status of Being or a being: A is A, complete in itself, and not related to anything else.

One ethical consequence that Navia detects in Antisthenes' denial of predication is the Cynic practice of *parrhêsia*, speaking the truth.[79] Another may have been the demand to live spontaneously in the moment. For the parallel to accepting only tautologies is to privilege only the present as psychologically compelling. If one can say only "A is A," then analogously, one can point only to "this object or situation here." One cannot rightly assert that "this A is similar to that A yesterday," for either they are the same or they are not. As a result, comparison of entities, metaphors, and the formation of universal and complex concepts are impossible; relations other than the identity relation are deceptive. Hence traditional concepts like community, work, and war—which assert the individual to be a father or wife, farmer, artisan, or soldier, Sinopean or Theban—are false: the individual is just himself and nothing else. Capable only of knowing the immediate, the individual can only live in the moment, here and now.

This in turn leads on to the Cynic's rigid dichotomy of self and Fortune. The Cynic is himself, and all else is "smoke" (*tuphos*), the realm of unknowable Fortune, or (in Eleatic terms), a dark Way of Seeming. There, one cannot see very far, and therefore should not try, for what cannot be known should not be desired. Amidst the turbulations of *Tuchê*, one should not worry about tomorrow, but live minimally, spontaneously. For Nature will provide as long as one has the physical and psychological toughness really to be able to live in the moment. But this is in truth quite difficult: not only is the Cynics' physical life demanding, but also the *ponos* of renunciation is embarrassing and hard to maintain. Nevertheless, those who do succeed in freeing themselves from the convoluted webs of conventional thought will come to know and master themselves. And his is the only possible knowledge and possession. For in contrast to the Way of Seeming is the Way of Truth: while Fortune is a swirl of vapors, the self alone is real and unchanging. Like Parmenides' Being that simply *is*, so too one just simply exists. One does not live for any group, cause, purpose, or abstract end. Mere life is enough and it is good, in all circumstances.

The Cynic renunciation of both nontautologous predication and otherness is, paradoxically, not in fact a renunciation of the philosophical tradition, but an almost direct ethical application of the Eleatic ontology. Again, for the Eleatics, Being is an absolute that admits of no degree. What is cannot not be, and therefore what is is always, immutable, simple, unaffected by externals, unmixed with otherness. Democritus transfers most of these qualities to the atom: the atom is eternal, self-contained, full, unmixed with void, hard, and internally unaffected by external relations. It may be joined with and separated from other atoms, but despite being buffeted eternally through the void, in itself it remains unchanged. The Cynics, on the other hand, transfer these qualities to the sage. The Cynic beggar is self-sufficient, internally full ("rich"), hard and tough, unaffected by external events and relations. Seemingly powerless vis-à-vis *Tuchê*—that great void of human meaning—the Cynic-beggar wanders, buffeted by chance, from city to city. And yet though he rejects possessions, home, family, friends, and city as alien to him, the wise man is nevertheless "everywhere at home." Indeed, he is everywhere a king, for he is sole citizen and king of himself and he carries his kingdom with him, like a snail its shell. He is "the Absolute Dog" as Antisthenes may have been known in his lifetime.[80] No external contingencies can ruffle his internal imperturbability. He does not fear poverty, exile, defeat, torture, or death, but remains unassailable by Fortune against whom he fights his verbal wars. Thus, Parmenides' indubitable "it is" becomes the Cynics' self-insistent "I am"—two "unshakeable" truths, which become in fact the *only* truths for the Eleatics and Cynics respectively. Zeno debunks belief in motion, multiplicity, and the senses; the Cynics debunk conventional notions of money, power, and honor as mere smoke.[81] Such wisdom seems folly to "the many," yet despite any incredulity, Eleatics and Cynics alike cling uncompromisingly to the "one big thing" that they know.

That the attributes of Eleatic Being could become the individual virtues of impassivity, self-sufficiency, self-consistency, and the like is borne out more explicitly with certain other thinkers. Horace speaks of the philosopher as "complete in himself, smooth and rounded, who prevents extraneous elements clinging to his polished surface."[82] In a similar vein, Empedocles hints that the enlightened one personifies the properties of the well-rounded whole.[83] So too, the common Socratic claim to be consistent and "always the same" has an Eleatic aura. Socrates' followers Aristodemus and Apollodorus are "always the same," just as Socrates himself is simple and unchanging: he is always talking about cobblers and tanners, saying the same things about the same things because this is how philosophy herself speaks to him.[84] In this context, consistency is one of the highest philosophical virtues because Being itself is unified and non-contradictory; the philosopher models his speech, his life, and his ideal state upon coherent definitions and Ideas. That is, the Socratic thinker strives to base his conduct upon first principles: ethical life should not be a haphazard mix of opinions and habits, but should be inspired by the highest truths.

It was Parmenides who essentially gave the Cynics (and Empedocles, Democritus, Plato, Aristotle, and others) their highest notions of truth. They may have ostensibly rejected the intellectuality of the Eleatics for a rough sensualism. Yet this latter too is an idea, something not given immediately, but elaborated into a many-sided morality. The vision of the sage—self-sufficient, whole, unaffected by any external relations—was their one big idea that informed a thousand other derivative assertions, maxims, actions, mores, and anecdotes. Ancient Cynicism is not, therefore, an ultimately nihilistic outlook; it is inspired by a unified, positive vision with strong resemblances to the Eleatic ontology.[85] It is clear that this ontology is an idealistic and remarkable affirming one. Hence, at its core, ancient Cynicism is not at all "cynical" in the modern sense: it affirms the dignity, power, and worth of the unadorned human animal that needs nothing but natural simplicity to be happy. Therefore, of the four paradoxes that have informed our discussion of the Cynic philosophy, it is the last that is really determinative. Cynic wisdom is worldly folly: therefore, the Cynic can dismiss *all* the seductions of Fortune—from specious wealth to specious shows of power to the specious knowledge offered by concepts, theories, and impressive words. Renouncing these, the Cynic turns enthusiastically to the simplicity of truth—"I am." One is now, and that is enough. Fully realizing this "one big" truth makes one "rich" in one's poverty, "powerful" in one's apparent weakness, and, despite one's seeming enslavement to Fortune, free and glad to follow whatever direction the road may take.

CHAPTER FIVE

The Persistence of Cynic Ideals

Early Cynicism in our analysis was a movement peculiar to Greek society at one moment in its history. In turn, the appearance of Cynics throughout the Greek world of the late classical period suggests that Greek society was to some degree already permeated with Cynic ideas: a Greek praise of poverty long preceded the Cynics themselves. Such a praise of poverty has three aspects, as we have seen. In economic attitudes, wealth is rarely seen as an unqualified good, nor is work an unmitigated evil. Instead, in the relatively undeveloped markets of classical Greece, the seeming benefits of wealth could be plausibly belittled: hence the Cynic view that true "wealth" is frugality, self-sufficiency, and "not needing much." Furthermore, work is not only economically necessary, but also morally beneficial. A praise of poverty can therefore attribute many virtues to the poor—industry, honesty, justice, temperance, piety, and the like. The rich, on the other hand, can be stereotyped as hubristic, unjust, and profligate. Work completes a person, but material rewards are necessarily finite, and so the most ambitious work for nonmaterial ends like honor or knowledge: so too, the Cynics "labor" for a kingdom of inner virtue.

The Classical Greeks excelled in war as in the arts of peace: "War is the father of all" riddled Heraclitus, the *Iliad* was perennially inspiring, and war ever remained the expected state of international relations. Yet communal poverty made the typical Greek experience of war very different from that of Assyrians or Persians. Because they were short, intense conflicts with a neighboring city over a border or political difference, Greek wars did not pay, and were regarded primarily as contests for honor, not wealth. The outcome of the Persian and Peloponnesian Wars might confirm in some minds the old feeling that material resources are antithetical to martial valor: poverty fosters the military virtues of endurance and courage whereas soft wealth ruins a man. Cynic asceticism develops such incipient ideas to an extreme. In turn, when the Cynics adopt the traditional vocabulary of valor to speak of the "weapons" of virtue or the self's inner "invincibility," they alert one to notions that had long been broached by literature like the Athenian funeral oration.

Finally, the Cynic insistence on self-sufficiency is not due wholly to psychological idiosyncrasies; it is neither just an exaggeration of Socrates' personal example, nor simply an individualist's version of old-fashioned political *autarkeia*. Rather, their idealistic vision of a self-contained, impassive self is the ethical aspect of the Eleatic ontology. For the Eleatics, to exist is to be one, unified, undifferentiated, unmoved, and impervious to outside influences. This axiom had long dominated Greek thought: Empedocles' elements, Democritus' atoms, or Plato's Forms provide for each thinker the makings of worlds. In the fourth century, this principle inspired Plato's vision of the divine philosopher, physically poor and dependent upon others, but spiritually "rich" and complete in intellectual insight. The Cynics, on the other hand, find wisdom in renunciation itself: for them, the self is the only reality, and to try to know or control external Fortune is simply a form of customary folly. Wisdom is worldly folly—a paradox that with suitable modifications would not be unworthy of a Parmenides, Zeno, Heraclitus, Socrates, or even Democritus.

If, then, ancient Cynicism was a product of classical conditions, classical society might in turn be described as a "Cynical" one, in the limited sense that it showed some sympathy for the Cynics' idealistic asceticism. In many arenas, the individual is felt capable of attaining the highest excellence with relatively few material aids. Indeed, such aids can often prove distracting or corrupting: the essential ingredient of personal advancement is heroic determination and an "industrious optimism." The traditional fixation upon an individual's *aretê* can, then, be seen as a precursor to the Cynic cult of virtue. The Greeks, for instance, exercised and competed in their games *naked:* so too, the Cynics would strip all away—wealth, status, titles—in order to judge a person wholly on their unadorned personal merits.

Such continuities between Cynicism and aspects of classical society are perhaps not surprising. At first, the radicalism of the "dogs" would seem wholly out of place in an intellectual and artistic culture that could so prize moderation, self-restraint, and harmony. But it is, paradoxically, the radical otherness of the Cynic movement that betrays its Greekness. For if the Greek "miracle" between 500 and 320 B.C. was crowded with triumphs in architecture, sculpture, poetry, rhetoric, history, medicine, mathematics, philosophy, and so forth, should one be surprised if "dog philosophers" also appeared on the scene? Tropical jungles throw forth many new and strange life-forms; it is not surprising that a culture with such diversity, creativity, and competitive energy would throw forth such willful individualists as the Cynics. Though new and seemingly strange, they nevertheless bear likenesses to many ancestors: Sophists delighting in paradox and the verbal *agôn*, democrats scornful of pretense, peasants proud of their frugality and fearful of ruinous luxury, Spartan and Socratic "craftsmen of *aretê*," Marathonian heroes fighting "few against many," and Eleatic rationalists yearning for an absolute. The plurivocity of Greek culture cannot be reduced to a single narrative; yet for a short period, the first Cynics successfully combined, in an uneasy tension, some previously disparate themes.

This combination did not last long. Yet, as the Hellenistic kingdoms were consolidated and the city-state grew politically and culturally less important, the blend of ideas, passions, and prejudices synthesized by the first Cynics would adapt to new conditions and find new resonances with new audiences. The Cynic ideal of self-sufficiency finds echoes in the Stoic and Skeptic *apatheia*, or Epicurean *ataraxia*. The *polis* lost its military autonomy, and war became a trade practised by mercenaries and distant monarchs. Hence, the Cynics' militaristic rhetoric lost some of its old force.[1] Yet, at the same time, the Cynic would maintain a rivalry with the fighting kings. For the years after Alexander were often ones of relentless energy and an imperial "work-ethic": witness Demetrius "Stormer of Cities"; Pyrrhus; the unsleeping Seleucid kings; warships and war-engines of astounding size; armored war-elephants; the massive colonization of the East; the heroic labors of men like Chrysippus, Callimachus, Eratosthenes, Poseidonius, or Didymus "Chalkenteros";[2] and the tempestuous sculptures of the Altar of Zeus at Pergamum.[3] The image of Alexander might well preside over such an age—restless and stormy, as if filled with longing (*pothos*) for some infinite end. But one extreme mirrors another: Alexander and Diogenes were said to have died on the same day, and a third-century B.C. statue of Antisthenes depicts the Cynic with the peculiar hairstyle (*anastolê*) associated with Alexander and later kings.[4] Furthermore, new appreciation of the world's vastness is balanced by the self-contained literary miniatures of the epigram and idyll. Fluctuating empires and treacherous allegiances are contrasted with loyal bands of Epicurean friends or Theocritus' peaceful shepherds. Material power stands juxtaposed with the inner resources of the unaided mind, not only when Alexander faces Diogenes, or Pyrrhus Cineas, but also in offhand remarks, as when Archimedes boasted, "Give me a place to stand and I will move the earth." The occasion of the celebrated saying was the inauguration of Hiero's titanic new warship, the *Syracosia*, which the tyrant's men struggled to launch—once again, the one "good" man proves superior to myriads.

But most of all, the Hellenistic period was one of unprecedented wealth and economic opportunity. The gulf between rich and poor widened. Yet, the old theme that wealth is not worth the trouble was renewed and adapted, not only by philosophers, but by poets like Leonidas of Tarentum. In one story of Hellenistic origin, "much-golden" Gyges, tyrant of Lydia, once consulted the Delphic oracle. "Who is the happiest person alive?" Gyges asked the god, just as Herodotus' Croesus had once asked Solon. Apollo's response to Gyges was equally unflattering: Aglaos of Psophis is happiest, because he is content to farm his small plot of land and has never seen the sea.[5] Psophis was in deepest Arcadia, tranquil and unchanging, while the fickle sea lured thousands to their fortune or death. In the Hellenistic period especially, when the Greek world expanded enormously, the sea was the highway for all discontents: upon it wandered generations of kings, mercenary-captains, pirates, scholars, exiles, colonists, traders—"the dreams of men, the seed of commonwealths, the germs of empires." Yet amidst such manifold ambitions, Apollo's oracle speaks to a continued longing for some Arcadian, or Cynic, simplicity.

In and beyond the Hellenistic era, the Cynics had a surprisingly varied influence for a relatively minor philosophical "school." A short survey of authors and topics in antiquity shows how widely the Cynic praise of poverty resonated through different intellectual circles, literary genres, and social classes. Founder of Stoicism, Zeno was the "student" of Crates. Subsequently, Stoic ethics never formally abandoned its "indifference" to externals, no matter how accommodating particular Stoics might have been to the "preferred indifferents" (*adiaphora proêgmena*) of Fortune. Epictetus the slave, as well as Marcus Aurelius the emperor, explicitly admired Antisthenes and the first Cynics. Many Hellenistic and imperial accounts of the good king's qualities—philanthropy, kindness, generosity, transcendence of self-interest, valor—owe much indirectly to the Cynic "kings." The satirical genre named after the Cynic Menippus includes such disparate authors as Varro, Petronius, Seneca (*Apocolocyntosis*), and Boethius (*De consolatione philosophiae*). Other miscellaneous figures testify to the wide and long appeal of the Cynics' idealistic asceticism. Dio Chrysostom, once a Cynic wanderer, gained the ear of Trajan. Julian the Apostate admired Cynicism as the true philosophy. Christians also might admire the first Cynics: Justin Martyr wore the Cynic's rough cloak even after his baptism; St. Basil compared Christian poverty with that of Diogenes.[6] Some scholars have detected Cynic rhetoric in other Church Fathers, early Christian monasticism, even Jesus himself.[7]

If, as it seems, there were people who called themselves Cynics at the beginning of the Byzantine period in 500 A.D., then the "movement" lasted for approximately 900 years. But even with the passing of pagan antiquity, some Cynic themes, particularly the economic ones, have resurfaced time and again. Dudley in concluding his *History of Cynicism* finds latter-day Cynicism among medieval monks and anchorites, the Albigenses or Catharists, Dominicans, Franciscans, Anabaptists, anarchists, and the figure of the pioneer, whether "in the woods of America, on the African veldt, [or] in the bush of Australia."[8] One could add a wide variety of literary works that echo Cynic sentiments. In his *Critique of Judgment*, Kant praises the sublimity of the soldier and Stoic, unmoved by personal fears, desires, and all the contingencies of the phenomenal world (i.e., *Tuchê*): would a Kantian Kingdom of Ends be populated by "invincible" Cynic "kings"? Nietzsche celebrates the Cynics' self-overcoming and scorn for conventional happiness, so much more impressive than the pettiness of the "last men." So too Sloterdijk hopes for a revival of the *fröhliche Wissenschaft* of a Diogenes.

One could multiply quotations and authors almost indefinitely, but let a few references from Shakespeare suffice to demonstrate the perennial appeal of certain Cynic ideas. In particular, great wealth is a dangerous and dubious blessing: many will kill for what they covet, and so Shakespeare's monarchs often long for the relatively carefree oblivion of the lowly.

Uneasy lies the head that wears a crown. (*Henry IV*, Part II, III.i.31)

Poor and content is rich and rich enough
But riches fineless is as poor as winter;
To him that ever fears he shall be poor. (*Othello*, III.iii)

My crown is in my heart, not on my head;
Not deck'd with diamonds and Indian stones,
Nor to be seen: my crown is called content:
A crown it is that seldom kings enjoy. (*Henry VI*, Part III, III.i.62–65)

Or the soliloquy of Henry VI when he wishes for the leisure and peace of a shepherd's life:

Ah what a life were this! How sweet! How lovely!
Gives not the hawthorn-bush a sweeter shade
To shepherds looking on their silly sheep
Than doth a rich embroider'd canopy
To kings that fear their subjects' treachery? (*Henry VI*, Part III, II.v.41–45)

Prophecies of the "end of history" have not allayed the continuing appeal of ideas reminiscent of ancient Cynicism. The present focus on economic productivity has produced its opposite, a reaction against "affluenza" that emphasizes how one can live well on less, provided one enjoys what money cannot buy—time, friends, inner strength, calm. Similarly, the speed of an information-society inspires calls for slowness, "quality time," more genuine human interaction. On a different note, admiration in some quarters of the Muslim world for the *mujahideen* in Afghanistan, Chechnya, and elsewhere may replay one aspect of the classical praise of martial poverty: a few, ill-equipped heroes hold out against wealthy empires.

Yet, these different ways of praising poverty are never united into a single vision or way of life identical with that of the ancient Cynics. If there is recurrence in history, there is no exact repetition. Each event and person is a unique occurrence, never to be reiterated precisely: when Socrates dies, there is no other. The ideas of the ancient Cynics have been modified in varieties of Stoicism, Christianity, and postmodernism. But that peculiar growth of individualism, class prejudice, patriotism, asceticism, satirical intelligence, rationalism, paradoxomania, and carefree humor has not been, and perhaps will never be, fully transplanted out of its original soil in the culture of classical Greece.

Preface

1. Sloterdijk, *Critique of Cynical Reason*. See also Navia's remarks in *Classical Cynicism:* "It is difficult not to agree with Sloterdijk's assessment of the human condition in the twentieth century. Cynicism appears to have permeated every niche of human activity," 2–3. The following is a short catalogue of books (and authors) directed to audiences that enjoy a cynical humor, or are leery of its cultural effects: *Everybody Knows: Cynicism in America* (W. Chaloupka); *A Return to Innocence: Philosophical Guidance in an Age of Cynicism* (J. Schwartz, A. Gottlieb, and P. Buckley); *Beyond Cynicism: The Practice of Hope* (D. Woodyard); *The Culture of Cynicism: American Morality in Decline* (R. Stivers); *Spiral of Cynicism: The Press and the Common Good* (J. Capella and K. Jamieson); *Dialogic Civility in a Cynical Age* (R. Arnett et al); *Cynicism and Postmodernity* (T. Bewes); *The Politics of Meaning: Restoring Hope and Possibility in an Age of Cynicism* (M. Lerner); *Cynic's Guide to Coping with Life* (P. Chichinskas); *Public Spaces, Private Lives: Beyond the Culture of Cynicism* (H. Giroux); *Cynic's Dictionary* (A. Malone); *The Cynic's Dictionary: Disgruntled Definitions for Our Times* (R. Bayan); *Business Babble: A Cynic's Dictionary of Corporate Jargon* (D. Olive); *Canadian Political Babble: A Cynic's Dictionary of Political Jargon* (D. Olive); *The Cynic's Lexicon* (J. Green); *How to be Happy, Dammit: A Cynic's Guide to Spiritual Happiness* (K. Salmansohn); *A Cynic's Guide to an Absurd World* (D. Morsey); *My Goodness: A Cynic's Short-lived Search for Sainthood* (J. Queenan); *Today I Will Nourish My Inner Martyr: Affirmations for Cynics* (A. Thornhill); *Today I Will Indulge My Inner Glutton: Health-Free Affirmations for Cynics* (A. Thornhill).

2. Some one hundred Cynics are mentioned as "Cynics" in ancient literature (*CC*, viii). Goulet-Cazé discusses eighty-two historical figures as Cynics in *L'Ascèse cynique*. Some Cynics or quasi-Cynics that I will discuss or quote later are Antisthenes, Diogenes, Crates, Hipparchia, Metrocles, Monimus, Onesicritus, Bion, Cercidas, Menippus, Bion, Lucian, Dio Chrysostom, and Epictetus.

CHAPTER ONE
APPROACHES TO ANCIENT CYNICISM

1. All dates, unless otherwise indicated, are B.C.

2. Explicit references to the poverty of Greece are Hdt. 8.102.1 (Demaratus), 8.111.3 (Andrians); Men. *Dys.* 603–6 (Cnemon); Diod. Sic. 9.37.2 (Pisistratus); Ar. *Pl.* 436ff. Cf. Alcman, fr. 64 (Campbell), Xen. *An.* 3.26, Pl. *Criti.* 111b4–7.

3. For Demaratus quoted, see *EAG*, 352; *GC*, 217, 222; Andreades, *A History of Greek Public Finance*, 363; De Ste. Croix, *Class Struggle in the Ancient Greek World*, 117, 294.

4. Artist. *Pol.* 1253b33–1254a1. For Hephaestus' tripods, see Hom. *Il.* 18.373–77. Another poetic fancy is the marvelous self-cleaning kitchen of Crates the comedian—pots and plates jumping up to wipe themselves clean (Ath. 267e–268a).

5. *MT*, 4n.10.

6. For the formalist position, see Trever, *A History of Greek Economic Thought*. A primitivist approach is now more readily accepted: see Weber, *Economy and Society*; Hasebroek, *Staat und Handel im alten Griechenland*; Polanyi, Aremsberg, and Pearson, *Trade and Market in the Early Empires*; M. I. Finley, *The Ancient Economy* and *Economy and Society in Ancient Greece*; Cartledge, Millett, and Todd, *Nomos*; *MT*; Morris, "The Athenian Economy Twenty Years after *The Ancient Economy*," and "Foreword" to M. I. Finley, *The Ancient Economy*; and *AET*. Foxhall ("Cargoes of the Heart's Desire," 295–96) and Meikle (*AET*, 147–79) have useful overviews of the literature. Meikle summarizes his own approach in these terms: "Antiquity was predominantly a system of use value, not of exchange value" (171). Also to be mentioned with honor in the primitivist bibliography is Zimmern's *Greek Commonwealth*, a book that masterfully assimilates the facts of Greek material poverty with the rich idealism of its "higher" culture.

7. Sol. fr. 1.71–73; Thgn. 232–37, 1157–60 (Campbell); Pl. *Leg.* 869e10–870a6; Arist. *Pol.* 1.9 *passim*, esp. 1257b22–34, and 1267a21–b5.

8. See Xen. *Symp.* 4.36; Arist. *Pol.* 1267a2–16 (tyranny and the cold), 1271a16–18, 1295b9–11; cf. Dem. 21.182, 51.11; and *GPM*, 109–10 (for the association of poverty with *petty* crime).

9. For Phaleas and Plato, see Pl. *Resp.* and Arist. *Pol.* 2.1–7.

10. Wool: Ar. *Nub.* 54–55. Lamp-oil: *Vesp.* 251–53. Love of drink: *Vesp.* 78–80. Cf. *Pax*, 120–21, 253–54 (do not use Attic honey; it costs four obols!); *Ran.* 404–7; Xen. *Mem* 1.3.5 (incredible frugality of Socrates). The extremely frugal are called "cumin-splitters" (Sophron, 110; Arist. *Eth. Nic.* 1121b27; Men. 1025; Theoc. 10.55), or in Aristophanes' comic coinage, cumin-splitting-cress-scrapers (κυμινοπριστοκαρδαμόγλυφος, *Vesp.* 1357).

11. Pericles: Thuc. 2.40.1. Antiphon, 164.1.

12. Pl. *Grg.* 491e2.

13. For example, Diog. Laert. 6.58; Crates *Pêra* (fr. 6); Teles fr. 4 (Hense); cf. Sayre, *Diogenes of Sinope*, 8–9 and *infra*, chapter 2, n.268.

14. On the staff, see Voss, "Die Keule der Kyniker."

15. Diogenes named "the Dog": Arist. *Rh.* 1411a24. Monimus: Diog. Laert. 6.82. Metrocles: Diog. Laert. 6.94. Onesicritus: Strabo, 15.1.63–66; cf. Brown, *Onesicritus*, 38–46. Philiscus, Menander, Hegesias: Diog. Laert. 6.76, 6.84.

16. "Absolute Dog" (ἁπλοκύων): Diog. Laert. 6.13. On the Cynosarges, see Diog. Laert. 6.13 and Billot, "Antisthène et le Cynosarges."

17. Hegel, Zeller, Ueberweg, Grote, Gomperz, Windelband, Dümmler, Höistad, Guthrie, and Kesters favor Antisthenes as the founder of Cynicism, while Diogenes finds champions in Wilamowitz-Moellendorff, Schwartz, Joël, Dudley, Sayre, Rankin, and Giannantoni. See Guthrie, *The Sophists,* 307n.1 and *CC,* 17–20 for detailed references; cf. Rankin, *Sophists, Socratics, and Cynics* 227. Navia's conclusion is sensible: "Cynicism was never a 'school' in a formal sense. Hence, it could not have been 'founded' either by a philosopher or in a given place. It was a movement, or rather an attitude of amorphous contours and characteristics, accompanied by a set of convictions, for which reason it is futile to assign a beginning date or a single originator" (*CC,* 20).

18. For example, *CC,* 92.

19. *HC,* 39. Dudley explicates some of the vicissitudes of Fortune: "Our civilization admittedly has the disadvantage that it may be completely shattered by war: but in other respects we have far greater security than was known to the Hellenistic world. Slavery, in particular, is so remote from us that it is hard to comprehend how real a terror it was to the Greeks of that period. Yet one has only to consider how powerful were the pirates in the Mediterranean until their suppression by Pompeius, to see that any traveller by ship was running a real risk of being captured and sold into slavery. Exile has only recently been the lot of thousands of citizens of European States; in the Hellenistic world it existed not only as a common form of punishment, but also as one of the normal risks attendant on a high position in politics. Again, during this period several cities were completely destroyed, as Thebes by Alexander, Lebedos and Kolophon by Lysimachus, and most notable of all such catastrophes in the Greek world, Corinth by the Romans" (x).

20. See, for example, the fates of tyrant Dionysius II (Plut. *Tim.* 14), and of Agesilaus, king of once indomitable Sparta, now mercenary for an Egyptian rebel (Plut. *Ages.* 31, 36).

21. Aesch. *Sept.* 321–68.

22. Xen. *Hell.* 2.2.3.

23. So Tarn: "Alexander, Demetrius, and Antigonus Gonatas . . . [introduced] a little chivalry into the business of war" (*Hellenistic Civilization,* 81).

24. Pl. *Resp.* 364b2–365a3.

25. See especially Goettling's "Diogenes der Cyniker" (reprinted in Billerbeck, *Die Kyniker in der Modernen Forschung,* 31–57), published in 1851, three years after the publication of the *Communist Manifesto;* cf. Nakhov, "Der Mensch in der Philosophie der Kyniker." Sloterdijk describes ancient Cynicism as the true form of "dialectical materialism" (*Critique of Cynical Reason,* 101). For archaic Greek thought on money as a universal standard of values, see passages like Heraclitus, DK 22 B 90.

26. Henne, "Cynique (Ecole)," 335.

27. K. O. Müller, "Antisthenes and the Cynics," 177.

28. McKirahan, for instance, makes this association in his "Cynicism." Nietzsche's "revaluation of all values" is partially inspired by Pl. *Grg.* 481b9–c4.

29. Sayre, *Diogenes of Sinope,* 42.

30. Sayre, *Diogenes of Sinope,* 16.

31. Lazy and a snob: Sayre, *Diogenes of Sinope,* 80, 94–98. Sayre is rarely so straightforward, but this is the drift of his argument, as Höistad has clearly articulated (see *CHCK,* esp. 123, 135–38).

32. Romm suggests a link between Cynicism and the "Dog Heads" (κυνο-κέφαλοι) and other savage tribes of fifth-century ethnography ("Dog Heads and Noble Savages: Cynicism before the Cynics," in Branham and Goulet-Cazé, *The Cynics,* 121–35). Martin looks north from Sinope, across the Black Sea to Scythia and the Scythian sage Anacharsis, in search of Diogenes' first inspiration ("Diogenes and Anacharsis" in Branham and Goulet-Cazé, *The Cynics,* 136–55). McEvilley finds conceptual similarities between Cynicism and Mahayana Buddhism, though he rejects the notion of Buddhist origins of Cynicism ("Early Greek Philosophy and Madhyamika").

33. Höistad: e.g., *CHCK,* 123, 135–38. Arnold: *Roman Stoicism,* 16.

34. Hastings, *Encyclopaedia of Religion and Ethics,* 11:860.

35. Hastings, *Encyclopaedia of Religion and Ethics,* 4:378.

36. See Robinson, *Ancient Sinope,* esp. 131–32, 151–53; cf. *CC,* 84–85.

37. Socrates and Aristippus: Xen. *Mem.* 2.1. Prodicus' Heracles: Xen. *Mem.* 2.1.21–34.

38. As Sayre argues in *Diogenes of Sinope* (117, 146).

39. *CHCK,* 34.

40. *CHCK,* 34 (Heracles as Willens-mensch), 37 (Cynics as supermen).

41. Livingstone, *The Mission of Greece,* 27.

42. Thomas Aquinas: *Summa Theologiae,* Second Part, II, Q.186, Art. 3, in the Reply to Objection 3. On Cynics as proto-Christian monks: e.g., Russell, *A History of Western Philosophy,* 228–39; Kidd "Cynics," 284–85; and Durant, *The Life of Greece,* 506–9 (Cynicism was "a religious order without a religion" and Diogenes "a Greek Franciscan without theology"). Note also that the early Dominicans sometimes punned on their name to call themselves *domini canes,* "the hounds of the Lord."

43. Diogenes Laertius and all ancient sources have Diogenes looking simply for "a person," not a "just person" (Diog. Laert. 6.41): thus *CC,* 103–4. On Nietzsche, see esp. Niehues-Pröbsting, "The Modern Reception of Cynicism: Diogenes in the Enlightenment," in Branham and Goulet-Cazé, *The Cynics,* 329–65. Foucault lionizes Diogenes as a *parrhesiast,* one who tells the truth regardless of consequence: see Flynn, "Foucault and the Politics of Postmodernity" and "Foucault as *Parrhesiast.*" For Sloterdijk's praise of Diogenes' "cheekiness," see *Critique of Cynical Reason,* esp. 101–33. According to Onfray, "the Cynics teach one how to live, to think, to exist, to act in face of the fragments of reality. . . . With them, one will discover an alternative to the spirit of gravity, to the peddlers of doom and to the theoreticians of nihilism" (*Cynismes,* 167). Finally, Branham and Goulet-Cazé invoke Cynicism as the champion of "liberty, autonomy, impassiveness" (*The Cynics,* v).

44. *King Lear,* III.iv, 103ff. See Butler, "Who are King Lear's Philosophers?" and Doloff, " 'Let Me Talk with this Philosopher.' "

45. Even Navia resorts ultimately to the "philosophical" generality: "[W]e must conclude that before there were Greek Cynics, there were indeed other 'Cynics,' both in Greece and elsewhere, Cynics who only lacked the name that would identify their

movement in classical times. This supposition would lead us to reassess the issue as to the origins of Cynicism, and would compel us to say that this movement has ultimately no known origins and has roots that are buried in times immemorial. . . . [C]lassical Cynicism is an expression of universal human tendencies that can claim neither a place nor a time as its own" (*CC*, 21–22).

46. Höistad draws attention to this at the end of his *Cynic Hero and Cynic King*: ". . . it is clear that the Cynic preaching also contained, among other things, a conception of kingship of a unique character—the solitary, poor, and suffering basileus. . . . The question of the origin of this Hellenic ideology has not been posed. Such a question demands an examination on a wider basis than has been here possible. One finds an answer in so far as the material of the Cynic-Stoic tradition provides it. Earlier we have the well-known Platonic passages concerning the completely just man who has to endure every hurt in order, at last, to be crucified, *Gorgias* 473c and *Repub*. II 363d. My study has tried to show, in any event, that the Cynic Heracles-allegory has played a decisive role in this connection" (221).

47. See the list in *CC*, 87.

48. *PRIA*, 118–19.

49. Lovejoy and Boas: "the Cynic ethics may be said to be reduced in its practical outcome, almost wholly to primitivism. . . . [It] was the first and most vigorous philosophic revolt against civilization in nearly all its essentials" (*PRIA*, 118–19).

50. *CC*, ix

51. The Delphic oracle's response to Diogenes (παραχαράττειν τὸ νόμισμα): Diog. Laert. 6.20. According to LSJ, νόμισμα has a double sense as (1) "anything sanctioned by current or established usage, custom" and (2) "current coin . . . coin money."

52. Arist. *Rh.* 2.16 (1390b32–1391a19).

53. The κυνογαμία ("dog-marriage") of Crates and Hipparchia was the sole exception, predicated on their primary acceptance of the Cynic lifestyle. That is, in a sense, they each married Lady Cynicism. It would be interesting to know how their three children fared.

54. Hom. *Od.* 11.488–91 (Achilles); Hes. *Op.* 638, 717 (οὐλομένην πενίην θυμοφθόρον); *Theog.* 593; Thgn. 155, 173–82, 351; Ar. *Vesp.* 564; Aeschin. 1.88; Thgn. 351–54, Ar. *Plut.* 415–37, Men. *Dys.* 208ff (the image of Poverty as an old hag in the house).

55. Ar. *Plut.* 535–45.

56. Finley, *The Ancient Economy*, 35. On this passage, Ober (and others) argue that "Finley tended to oversimplify the issue" (*ME*, 192n.1).

57. Silloi: Hom. *Il.* 16.233–5; cf. Janko, *The Iliad: A Commentary*, ad loc. Socrates: Pl. *Ap.* 23b7–c1.

58. Cicero lists Junius Brutus, Gaius Mucius, Coclites, the Decii, Gaius Fabricius, Manlius Curius, Gnaius and Publius Scipio, Scipio Africanus, Lucius Mummius, the two Catos, and "innumerable others" who welcomed hardship as the price of Rome's survival or glory (*Paradoxa Stoicorum*, 12–13, 38, 48). One might add Fabricius, "powerful in little" (*parvo potentem*: Verg. *Aen.* 6.843–44), or later leaders like Catiline (Cic. *Cat.* 1.26; Sall. *Cat.* 5.3), Julius Caesar, Mark Anthony (Plut. *Ant.* 17), Vespasian (Tac. *Hist.* 2.5), and Julian the Apostate. Cf. De Ste. Croix, *Class Struggle in the Ancient Greek*

World, 121–22, and Garnsey on "Peasant Power" ("Peasants in Ancient Roman Society," 222–24).

59. "In so great an army you should scarce find a common soldier lie on a coarser mattress than Agesilaus: he was so indifferent to the varieties of heat and cold that all the seasons, as the gods sent them, seemed natural to him. The Greeks that inhabited Asia were much pleased to see the great lords and governors of Persia, with all the pride, cruelty, and luxury in which they lived, trembling and bowing before a man in a poor threadbare cloak, and, at one laconic word out of his mouth, obsequiously deferring and changing their wishes and purposes. So that it brought to the minds of many the verses of Timotheus, 'Mars is the tyrant, gold Greece does not fear'" (Plut. *Ages.* 14); cf. the meeting of Agesilaus and the delicate Pharnabazus (Plut. *Ages.* 12), and Agesilaus among the pampered Egyptians (Plut. *Ages.* 36).

60. Epaminondas: "He, however, stepped down into his poverty, and took pleasure in the same poor attire, spare diet, unwearied endurance of hardships, and unshrinking boldness in war; like Capaneus in Euripides, who had 'Abundant wealth and in that wealth no pride'" (Plut. *Pel.* 3). Phocion: "Abroad, and in the camp, he [Phocion] was so hardy in going always thin clad and barefoot, except in a time of excessive and intolerable cold, that the soldiers used to say in merriment, that it was like to be a hard winter when Phocion wore his coat" (Plut. *Phoc.* 4). Alcibiades, Critias, and Xenophon admired Socrates' toughness, as did Grote who writes: "He [Socrates] is the semi-philosophical general; undervalued indeed as a hybrid by Plato—but by high-minded Romans like Cato, Agricola, Helvidius Priscus &c. likely to be esteemed higher than Plato himself" (*Plato and the Other Companions of Sokrates*, 206–7).

61. *Canterbury Tales*, Prologue, 293–96.

62. Democritus is said to have spent all his patrimony to travel to Egypt and other ancient centers of knowledge (Diog. Laert. 9.35); more reliable may be the saying attributed to him, "I would prefer to discover one causal law than be king of Persia" (DK 68 B 118). Similarly, Socrates would spend any sum of money to learn the truth about immortality (Pl. *Phd.* 78a3–9). Archimedes so lived for divine geometry that he would forget to eat or wash, and while servants carried him bodily to the bath, would continue to draw circles and triangles in the bathing-oil (Plut. *Marc.* 17). Aristotle tells the story about Thales and the olive-presses to make the general point that philosophers do not care about wealth but accept a relative poverty as the price of an intellectual life (*Pol.* 1259a5–21). So Spinoza the spectacle-grinder; Nietzsche, a "wanderer [with] his shadow" and his books; Wittgenstein giving away his inheritance, finding simplicity in an Austrian village, Norway, or the Irish Connemara. For Hipponax, see fr. 24a, 24b, 25, 29 (Campbell).

63. For example, *CC*, 70–71.

64. Diog. Laert. 6.71. On the Cynics as enemies of pleasure, cf. Lucian, *Vit. auct.* 10; Dio Chrys. 8.20, 9.12.

65. *37th Letter* of "Diogenes" (translated by Sayre, *Diogenes of Sinope*, 2).

66. See Max.Tyr. *Diss.* 3.9; cf. Dio Chrys. 6.9–12.

67. Cynic asceticism as an "end-in-itself": *HC*, 10. But contrast *HC*, 44, where Dudley contradicts himself: "asceticism, and even philosophy, are not ends in

themselves. They are means to the supreme end, which is of course, eudaimonia [i.e., happiness], or what is synonymous to the Cynic, *apatheia* [i.e., indifference or emotional invulnerability to external things]". Cf. *CHCK*, 9–10, 45, and 123 where a "strict" or "fundamental asceticism" is given an "oriental origin." On the other hand, Sayre claims that "a Cynic had no motive for asceticism; ascetics are always idealists and the Cynics were gross materialists" (*Diogenes of Sinope*, 80; cf. 4–5).

68. Arist. *Rh.* 1411a24.

69. Alcidamas: Men. Rhet. 346.9–19; cf. Meyer, *Laudes Inopiae*, 15. Polycrates: Quintilian 2.174 (Clytemnestra), Arist. *Rh.* 1401a13–14, 1401b15 (mice); Alex. 3.3.10 (pebbles, pots); cf. Gribble, *Alcibiades and Athens*, 226n.36. For speculation that Polycrates wrote a *laus inopiae*, see Meyer, *Laudes Inopiae*, esp. 8, 17–40. Zeller on Prodicus' allegory of Heracles: *Outlines of the History of Greek Philosophy*, 84. For other examples, see Pl. *Symp.* 177a5–c5 where Phaedrus is said to complain that there are encomia of salt, but not of *erôs;* Isoc. *Helen* 1 and Lucian's *Muscae Encomium.* Cf. Erasmus' *Praise of Folly* (esp. the introduction), or Russell's *In Praise of Idleness.*

70. Demetr. *Eloc.* 170.

71. Juv. *Sat.* 3.58–125, esp. 73–78. Verg. *Aen.* 2.49

72. On the impossibility of precise *Quellenforschung*, see Navia's monitory remarks: "The only facts about Diogenes that can be affirmed are these: (1) that his place of origin was Sinope, a Milesian colony on the southern coast of the Black Sea; (2) that he traveled to Athens and to Corinth, where he lived for a number of years; (3) that he was an older contemporary of Alexander the Great; and (4) that at some point he became known as 'the Dog'. Beyond these four facts it is unwise to affirm anything with certainty" (*CC*, 84). But in fact, there are *no* certain truths in history: one can doubt everything. To avoid the silence entailed by excessive doubt, I would add another general "fact" to Navia's list: Diogenes and the Cynics were ascetics, and criticized money and praised poverty in ways that can be related to themes of a pre-Cynic praise of poverty.

CHAPTER TWO
PRAISE OF POVERTY AND WORK

1. Diog. Laert. 6.37, 6.72.

2. Diog. Laert. 6.40.

3. Lucian, *Pisc.* 35; cf. Lucian, *Peregr.* 3, and the *7th Letter* of "Crates" to "the rich" ("having nothing we have everything, but you who have everything in fact have nothing due to your cantankerousness and jealousy and fear and empty desire for honor") (Malherbe).

4. Diog. Laert. 7.4–5. Cf. Sen. *Dial.* 9.14.3; Arnold, *Roman Stoicism*, 65.

5. Cic. *Fin.* 5.84. Cf. Sen. *Med.* 333 *(parvo dives)*, *Ep.* 14.17.

6. Diog. Laert. 7.1; cf. Diog. Laert. 7.27.

7. Plut. *Mor.* 1058d5.

8. 2 Cor. 6:10.

9. *Sent. Vat.* 25 (Arrighetti); cf. Diog. Laert. 10.11, 10.144, 10.146; Lucr. 5.1178–79.

10. For Antisthenes' fragment, see Diog. Laert. 6.2. Lovejoy and Boas postulate a Cynic "Gospel of Work" (*PRIA*, 131); cf. Schulz-Falkenthal, "Zum Arbeitethos der Kyniker" in Billerbeck, *Die Kyniker in der Modernen Forschung*, 287–302.

11. Chroust, *Socrates: Man and Myth*, 275.

12. Austin and Vidal-Naquet, *Economic and Social History of Ancient Greece*, 16, alluding to the conclusions of Hemelrijk (*Penia en Ploutos*, 140–50). These conclusions are often repeated; see, for example, De Ste. Croix, *Class Struggle in the Ancient Greek World*, 116–17, 122 ("The essential thing is that one should not need to work for one's daily bread") and JACT, *The World of Athens*, 147.

13. See for instance Xen. *Mem.* 2.8; Dem. 57.43 ("often poverty forces free men to do slavish things"). More examples can be found in *GPM*, 30–33; *ME*, 220–21, 272–77; and Wood, *Peasant-Citizen and Slave*, 126–45.

14. Many oligarchs and aristocrats view the mob as violent, stupid, and "incapable of virtue." To them, the poor become οἱ κακοί, οἱ μείονες, οἱ ἀχρεῖοι, or οἱ πονηροί, while the rich view themselves as οἱ καλοὶ καὶ ἀγαθοί, οἱ ἀγαθοί, οἱ εὐδαίμονες, οἱ χρηστοί, οἱ χαρίεντες, οἱ ἐπιεικεῖς, οἱ βελτίονες, οἱ ἄριστοι, οἱ γνώριμοι, and so forth.

15. In *De Corona* 252–62, Demosthenes satirizes "those things for which one might blame Aeschines' poverty" (263). Yet, he begins his tirade by acknowledging that poverty or wealth is a matter of Fortune, and that one should not blame another for their circumstances: "On the whole I consider him stupid who reproaches a fellow human being for his *tuchê* (252). This apology is important in a democratic context: see *infra*, n.17. Similarly, a passage like Plato's *Republic* 495c–496a is often cited as a prime instance of the Greek scorn for manual labor. Here Socrates ridicules the "bald little bronze-worker" who comes into a little money and therefore decides to take up philosophy. But he has spent his life bent over a bench: his soul is maimed and broken, incapable of a sublime thought. It is too easy to take this passage as proof of Plato's aristocratic priggishness or of a *general* Greek disdain for labor (Meikle's remarks about Aristotle are relevant here; see *AET*, 126–28). There is obviously scorn here, but this should be understood primarily in the specific context of the *kallipolis*: each must do one job well and no one can be both a geometer and an efficient carpenter. Furthermore, the Platonic utopia is envisioned as a pure meritocracy: Plato in fact would demand that *talented* "tinkers" and other seemingly "low" types in contemporary Athens be guardians in an ideal state. Socrates, that ugly, snub-nosed, pot-bellied sculptor, is one such unrecognized king.

16. See, for instance, words like ἐργάτης (e.g., Ar. *Ach.* 611, *Pax* 632; Xen. *Mem.* 1.2.57, 2.1.27; Pl. *Euthphr.* 218c6–8, *Resp.* 544a5; Dem. 59.50; Men. *Dys.* 527; Lucian, *Tim.* 34.2), ἐργτις, ἐργατικός (Pl. *Meno* 81e1), ἐνεργός, φιλόπονος (Soph. *Aj.* 879; Pl. *Resp.* 535c1, *Alc.* 1.122c7; Men. *Dys.* 528), φιλεργός (Dem. 36.44, 42.32) ἐθελόπονος, ἐθελουργός, ἀποχειροβίωτος ("living by one's hands," used of the virtuous poor man, Pheraulas, in Xen. *Cyr.* 8.3.37, as well as the fisherman who generously gives the prize-catch to ill-fated Polycrates, Hdt. 3.42), and αὐτουργός ("farmer, who does his own work," who in Eur. *Or.* 917–30 rarely goes to market and is praised for his intelligence, bravery, and blameless lifestyle). Poetic words δαιδάλλω, ποικίλλω express admiration for ornate handiwork. On the other hand, other words connote the pain

and hardship of toil and drudgery—λατρεύω, μοχθεύω, ταλαιπωρέω. For further discussion of positive attitudes to work, even among philosophers, see Guiraud, *La Main-d'Oeuvre Industrielle dan l'Ancienne Grèce*, 36–50; Trever, *A History of Greek Economic Thought*, 29–30; *GC*, 260–83; and Balme, "Attitudes to Work and Leisure in Ancient Greece." For the censure of laziness, *lalia*, and related notions, see Hes. *Op.* 302–5, *Theog.* 590–99; Democr. DK 68 B 212; Soph. *Ant.* 320; Eur. *HF*, 592, *Med.* 296, *Supp.* 462; Ar. *Ach.* 61–74, *Eq.* 348, 1381, *Ran.* 91, 1069–72, 1160–61, *Pax* 653, *Thesm.* 461, *Plut.* 517, et al.; Thuc. 3.38.4–7; Pl. *Grg.* 515e, *Resp.* 552b6–c5; Arist. *Pol.* 1277b23. Comedians lionize the common working man, and keep an armory stocked with terms scornful of the "talking classes" and their activities—λεπτολογεῖν, ἐγγλωττοτυπεῖν, κενολογεῖν, κομπολακεῖν, ματαιολογεῖν, μετεωρολογεῖν, στενολεσχεῖν, στωμυλλεῖσθαι, φλυαρεῖν. A mere talker is λαλιστικός, a μετεωρολέσχης, καταστωμυλλάδης, στωμυλιοσυλλεκτάδης filled with λαλία, λῆρος, φλήναφος, and τὸ φλαττοθραττοφλάττοθρατ of "Aeschylus" (Ar. *Ran.* 1286ff) or the smoky-boasts (ψολοκομπία) of the Paphlagonian tanner (Ar. *Eq.* 696); the last is close to the Cynics' mockery of customary norms or intellectual theorizing as so much "smoke" (τῦφος). One illuminating instance of the *logos/ergon* dichotomy is Plato's *Apology*, 32a4–5. The phrase λύειν λέσχας, "to break off gossiping" (Plato Com., fr. 223 [Kock]), was idiomatic for getting down to serious work.

17. Hesiod's ἔργον δ᾽ οὐδὲν ὄνειδος, ἀεργίη δέ τ᾽ ὄνειδος (*Op.* 312) is repeated by Socrates (Xen. *Mem.* 1.2.56), is echoed by Pericles (Thuc. 2.40.1), Demades (1.87.8) and Demosthenes (18.252; cf. *supra*, n.15). For the *graphê argias*, see Isae. 6.61, 7.38–9; Diog. Laert. 1.55, 8.32; Plut. *Sol.* 17, 22, 31.2; Harrison, *The Law of Athens*, 1:79–80; *CF*, 242 with n.27.

18. Xen. *Mem.* 3.9.15: "The best men and dearest to the gods are those who do their work well . . . He who does nothing well is . . . not dear to the gods."

19. Some pejorative words for "lazy" or "idle" are ἀργός, ἀεργός, κακόσχολος, κηφηνώδης, ῥάθυμος, and ἀδολέσχης.

20. See, for example, Hes. *Op.* 298–308, 381–82, 396–404.

21. Thuc. 2.36.3, 2.64.4 (wealth), 2.63.1 (work).

22. Pl. *Resp.* 552a7–b3, d3–10.

23. Hes. *Op.* 120 (golden age), 307, 374 (barns), 405–6 (house, slave), 228–37 (abundance).

24. Plut. *Sol.* 2. Cf. fr. 24 (West).

25. Hdt. 6.125.

26. Hdt. 7.27–30.

27. Hdt. 5.49.

27. Lys. 19.48.

29. Xen. *Symp.* 4.45.

30. Ar. *Plut.* 803–22.

31. See for example Thucydides' catalogues of the resources of Athens (2.13.3–6), of the Thracian Sitalces' realm (2.97.3), and of the armada sent to Sicily (6.31.1–5). Cf. Kallet-Marx, *Money, Expense, and Naval Power in Thucydides' History 1–5.24*, for Thucydides' heightened awareness of state finances.

32. Xen. *Vect.* 1.3–2.1, 3.1–2.

33. Pl. *Leg.* 3.679b5–7.

34. Arist. *Rh.* 1361a12–16. Cf. *Eth. Nic.* 1119b26–27 where Aristotle gives a pragmatic definition of wealth as "all things whose worth is measured by money (νόμισμα)."

35. Arist. *Rh.* 1361a23–24.

36. "Idealistic" in the technical sense that objects exist in necessary relation to a subject.

37. Alcaeus: fr. 112 (Lobel and Page). Sophocles: *OT* 565–67. Thucydides: 1.143.5, 7.77.7. Euripides: fr. 20 (Nauck). Concerning the Thucydidean passages, such assertions would, according to Runciman, make the *polis* a "citizen-state" rather than a city-state ("Doomed to Extinction," 348).

38. See, for instance, Ar. *Av.* 37, 1313; Xen. *An.* 1.2.6, 1.2.10–14, 1.4.1, 2.14.13, 3.4.7, *HG* 5.2.16; Arist. *Pol.* 326b20. In Thucydides' "Archaeology," the cause of poverty in early Homeric and Mycenean times was not so much ὀλιγανθρωπία as ἀχρηματία, lack of money that facilitates trade (1.11.1). But Thucydides' focus on money-matters was exceptional and revolutionary.

39. Stob. 4.1.88.

40. Pl. *Ap.* 29d2–30b4 (italics added).

41. Thuc. 6.24.3. For other pictures of vulgar materialism, see Ar. *Ach.* 27–36; Xen. *Mem.* 3.7.6–7.

42. Locke, "Second Treatise on Government," in Barker, *Greek Political Theory,* chap. 5.

43. Pl. *Leg.* 870a2–c1. This (as Plato stresses) is a central statement, and its tenets are repeatedly emphasized, as in *Leg.* 679a10–c3, 727c7–728a5, 743e1–8, 913b3–c1.

44. Pl. *Resp.* 8–9.

45. Pl. *Resp.* 572b10–580a8, esp. 577e5–578a3, 579e1–3.

46. Arist. *Pol.* 1323a36–b21 (italics added). Cf. *Pol.* 1271b6–10: "There is another error, equally great, into which they [the Spartans] have fallen. Although they truly think that the goods for which men contend are to be acquired by virtue rather than by vice, they err in supposing that these goods are to be preferred to the virtue which gains them"; and *Pol.* 1334b25–28: "Wherefore the care of the body ought to precede that of the soul [i.e., in time], and the training of the appetitive part should follow: none the less our care of it must be for the sake of the reason, and our care of the body for the sake of the soul."

47. In non-political works, however, Plato does treat the philosophical vocation as one of bodily transcendence—a theme for chapter 4.

48. Wealth of Antisthenes and Socrates: Xen. *Symp.* 4.34ff. Socrates as Antisthenes' benefactor: Xen. *Symp.* 4.43.

49. For example, Cic. *Paradoxa Stoicorum,* 49: "O immortal gods! People do not understand what a great source of revenue (*vectigal*) is thrift (*parsimonia*)!"

50. For example, Xen. *Oec.* 2.11, *Cyr.* 8.2.23; Pl. *Euthd.* 281b4–e2, 288d9–289b6, *Meno* 88d4–89a1, *Resp.* 505a1–506a2, *Erx.* 397e3–8; Arist. *Eth. Nic.* 1096a5–8. Cf. Democr. DK 68 B 77; and Monimus' saying, "how one conceives something is all" (πᾶν ὑπόληψις, M.Ant. *Meditations,* 2.15).

51. God is happy without material wealth: Arist. *Pol.* 1323b21–29. Divine contemplation and wisdom are self-sufficient: *Eth. Nic.* 10.7–9, esp. 1177a32–b1. The injunction

to be God: "as much as is possible, one must make oneself divine (*athanatizein*) and do everything in order to live in accordance with what is best within oneself" (*Eth. Nic.* 1177b31–3).

52. Arist. *Pol.* 1253a26–29.

53. Arist. *Eth. Nic.* 4.1.

54. See Arist. *Pol.* 1254a7–13 ("But life is action and not production, and therefore the slave is the minister of action. . . . The master is only the master of the slave; he does not belong to him, whereas the slave is not only the slave of his master, but wholly belongs to him"), *Pol.* 1328a34–37 ("And so states require property, but property, even though living beings are included in it, is no part of a state; for a state is not a community of living beings only, but a community of equals aiming at the best life possible"), and *Pol.* 1329a18–26 (slaves or barbarian Perioeci that work for the ideal state do not belong to it).

55. Hdt. 1.32.9.

56. Thuc. 2.36.3.

57. Xen. *Mem.* 1.6.10.

58. Antisthenes: Xen. *Symp.* 4.45. Diogenes: Diog. Laert. 6.104. Cf. *11th Letter* of "Crates" (Malherbe); Cic. *Tusc.* 5.92.

59. Self-sufficiency and the good: see esp. Pl. *Phlb.* 67a5–8. Self-sufficiency and the state: *Leg.* 704a1–705b6, 842c1–e3. The self-sufficiency of the Cretan city is bolstered by domestic legislation to discourage the profit-motive and consumption: "Let there be no retail trade for the sake of money-making" (*Leg.* 847d7–e1; cf. Ar. *Pol.* 1328b39–1329a2); citizens can buy necessary commodities wholesale on particular days of the month (19. *Leg.* 849b1–c1) but prices will be fixed and there can be no haggling (*Leg.* 915, 917).

60. *Eth. Nic.* 1097a28–b21.

61. Great-souled person is psychologically self-sufficient: Arist. *Eth. Nic.* 1125a12 (cf. Pl. *Resp.* 387d11–e1). Honor is "the greatest of external goods": Arist. *Eth. Nic.* 1124a5–20 and 1123b17–21. The great-souled man resembles the Stoic, whose motto is *nil admirandum:* "nothing is μέγα to him" (*Eth. Nic.* 1125a2–3; cf. 1125a14).

62. Arist. *Pol.* 7.5–6 *passim.* Cf. *PRIA*, 174–77.

63. DK 68 B 210, 283, 284, 219, 246.

64. See Stewart's "Democritus and the Cynics."

65. Cf. *PRIA*, 118–20.

66. Citizen of Diogenes: Diog. Laert. 6.93. At home in Pêra: Diog. Laert. 6.85. Sage at home everywhere: Diog. Laert. 6.98; Crates, fr. 15 (cf. Democr. DK 68 B 247).

67. Hesiod does not of course forget the productive role of capital—land, ploughs, oxen, barns, slaves—but what is essential for him is the farmer, the subjective factor.

68. Hes. *Op.* 20–24. Meyer argues that these lines give the first adumbration of a later Sophistic praise of poverty: "Juppiter etiam hoc effecit, ut Elpis et bona Eris hominem ad laborem incitent, labor autem est salutaris atque utilis. Quae sententia nondum est agonis Aristophanei cogitatio, sed eius quoddam fundamentum" (*Laudes Inopiae*, 18–19).

69. Hes. *Op.* 381–82. Admonitions to work: e.g., *Op.* 298–301, 396–97, 410–12. Contrast this with injunctions to avoid politics and "crooked judgments": *Op.* 27–29, 213, 248–49, 263–64, 274–75.

70. Ar. *Plut.* 507ff.

71. Hes. *Op.* 27–34 (*agora*), 39, 221, 264 (venal kings). On town vs. country in Hesiod, see Nelson, *God and the Land,* 34–36.

72. Hes. *Op.* 37–39.

73. Might is right: Hes. *Op.* 192, 220, 202–12 (the fable of the hawk and the nightingale). "Eating the bread of idleness": *Op.* 303–6.

74. Hes. *Op.* 320 (χρήματα δ' οὐχ ἁρπακτά, θεόσδοτα πολλόν ἀμείνω). Cf. Nelson: "It is 'god-given' because it is wealth won under the conditions that Zeus has intended for human beings, justice and toil" (*God and the Land,* 129).

75. Arist. *Pol.* 1258b4–8. Aristotle was not the first to use the pun. In *Clouds,* 1155–66, Aristophanes' Strepsiades solemnly curses moneylenders, their principal, and the interest of their interest (ἰώ, κλάετ' ὦ 'βολοστάται, αὐτοί τε καὶ τἀρχαῖα καὶ τόκοι τόκων), with phrasing that echoes traditional imprecations upon a person, his sons, and his sons' sons; see Dover, *Aristophanes' Clouds,* 234.

76. Aristotle does suggest in passing that certain metals have an intrinsic value (*Pol.* 1257a36–38), but does not dwell on the thought.

77. See instance, Meikle's discussion of Schumpeter (*AET,* 87–88).

78. Arist. *Eth. Nic.* 5.5 and esp. 1133a3–5; cf. Meikle, *AET,* 101–2, 153–57.

79. Millett, *Lending and Borrowing in Ancient Athens,* 73.

80. Reed (*MT,* 62–74) discusses various possibilities, but concludes that the fundamental distinction in the classical period lay between those amateurs and professionals who "relied for much (or probably most) of their livelihood on interstate trade." Amateurs might include farmers, craftsmen, soldiers, pirates, philosophers, and others. Reed cites Plutarch's story that Plato financed his travels to Egypt by selling olive oil (Plut. *Sol.* 2.8); cf. stories of the Stoic Zeno's trade-ventures and shipwreck (Diog. Laert. 7.4–5; cf. *supra,* n.4).

81. See *MT,* 23 and 66 with n. 31 citing Hesiod, Theognis, Solon, and others for merchants of the archaic period.

82. Cf. *GC,* 210–31; *EAG,* 231–33. For the fact that merchants gravitated to wherever rumor spoke of greatest profits, see, for instance, Xen. *Oec.* 20.27–28 (grain-merchants); Dem. 34.36–37, 56.8–10; Lycurg. *Leoc.* 14–15, 18–19; and *MT,* 11–12 with n. 20.

83. Concerning "the level of wealth of maritime traders" (*MT,* 34–42), Reed concludes that "those trading at classical Athens were mainly poor and foreign" (3). *Emporoi* and *nauklêroi* (ship-owners) did not rival aristocrats in wealth, or form "anything like a 'merchant aristocracy' in the classical period" (42).

84. See, for instance, Hom. *Od.* 7.158–64; Xen. *Mem.* 3.7.6; Pl. *Leg.* 918d4–8.

85. Hom. *Od.* 14.229–313; cf. Knorringa, *Emporos,* 9; *EAG,* 211.

86. Cobbler: *Eq.* 315–18. Grain-dealer: *Eq.* 1009. Bar-maid: *Plut.* 435–36. Fishmonger: Ath. 224c–25d. Furies: Ar. *Plut.* 422–28. For more instances of "commercial dishonesty," see Hopper, *Trade and Industry in Classical Greece,* 64–67: "[I]t would be a mistake to suppose that they [Plato, Aristotle] did not, though perhaps in an exaggerated manner, reflect common notions and prejudices relating to small-scale trading" (64–65).

87. Lys. 22.14–15. Cf. Xen. *Oec.* 20.27–28; *EAG,* 270–75.

88. Arist. *Eth. Nic.* 1122a2–3, 1158a21.

89. Pl. *Resp.* 371c5–d8.

90. Pl. *Resp.* 554a5–c2.

91. For the moneylender and oligarch, see esp. Pl. *Resp.* 552c1–4, 555c1–e4. Such passages give a notion of how relations between creditor and debtor might have felt "on the street." Actual interest rates could range from around 12 percent annually (Dem. 27.9, 27.19, 27.23, 28.13; Aeschin. 3.104) to 33.3 percent (Isae. fr. 23) to the 25 percent that one moneylender charged per day (Theophr. *Char.* 6.9). Cf. *EAG*, 342–43. Death as moneylender: Pl. *Ax.* 367b2–5.

92. Strepsiades, for instance, borrows from a fellow demesman (Ar. *Nub.* 1219); his refusal to repay makes enemies of both his creditors (1214–99). For *eranos*, see Millett, *Lending and Borrowing*, 71–72.

93. Alciphr. 1.26 (trans. *EAG*, 337) The phrase "take a mortgage and ruin is nigh" (ἐγγύα, παρὰ δ' ἄτη) of Thales or Chilon was proverbial from the sixth century.

94. Dicaeopolis in town: Ar. *Ach.* 27–36. I here paraphrase Ar. fr. 287 (Edmonds) and its dislike of τῶν κατ' ἀγορὰν πραγμάτων. For other praise of the countryside, see for instance Ar. *Pax*, 520–38, 566–600.

95. Pl. *Resp.* 373a3–54.

96. Thuc. 2.14.

97. See, e.g., Ar. *Eq.* 180–81, 217–18, 293.

98. Thus, Poverty argues (and Chremylus agrees) that only the poor orators do well by the city (Ar. *Plut.* 568–73).

99. Hdt. 8.4–5, Timocr. fr. 5 (West; from Plu. *Them.* 21).

100. Thuc. 3.38.2, 3.40.1, 3.42.3 (Cleon and Diodotus in 428). The mutual recriminations of Demosthenes and Aeschines are legion: compare Dem. *De Cor.* and Aeschin. *In Ctes.* For a long list from Demosthenes alone, see De Ste. Croix, *Class Struggle in the Ancient Greek World*, 298n.58. For more, see Chroust, "On Bribery; *ME*, 236–38, 331–32.

101. Hdt. 5.51 (Aristagoras, Cleomenes); Plut. *Ages.* 10, 19 (Agesilaus refusing Persian bribes, returning to Sparta as poor as he left).

102. Hdt. 6.72 (Leotychides); Plut. *Lys.* 16 (Gylippus found with a "stash of owls [i.e., Attic coins] under his roof"); Plut. *Per.* 22; Pl. *Resp.* 548a5–b2. Cf. the alleged "Medism" of Pausanias after Plataea (Thuc. 1.131–35).

103. See for instance Hdt. 7.213 (Ephialtes and Thermopylae); Hyp. 5.15 (Philip); Pl. *Resp.* 556e3–560b10 (revolutionaries). One episode contrasts the power of money with that of innate valor, a theme for the next chapter: in 394 Agesilaus reluctantly returned from Asia to fight the Corinthian War, with the comment that "a thousand archers" had driven him out of Asia (Plut. *Ages.* 15.6)—Persian coins were stamped with an archer.

104. Hdt. 5.63.

105. Pl. *Resp.* 362b7–d2; I take Glaucon's dichotomy of the tyrant and just man to be typical of sophistic argumentation. Cf. *Resp.* 362b7–d2 and *Euthphr.* 14e6–7, in which piety becomes a form of trade (ἐμπορικὴ τεχνὴ) between gods and mankind. The contrast between internal and external piety is made even more explicit in Theopompus' story (in Porph. *Abst.* 2.16) of how the rich Asian Magnes was told by the Delphic oracle that not he, but some indigent Arcadian (Clearchus of

Methudrion), makes the most pleasing sacrifices: thus, the gods "prefer before all temples the upright heart and pure."

106. Pind. *Ol.* 1.113–14.

107. Achilles: see esp. Hom. *Il.* 1.158–68. Midas: Tyrt. fr. 9.6 (Campbell). Gyges: Archil. fr. 22. Cinyras: Tyrt. fr. 9.6; Pind. *Pyth.* 2.15, *Nem.* 8.18. Croesus: Hdt. 1.30ff.

108. For example, Hdt. 3.89–97.

109. See, for instance, the Platonic *Alc.* I, 122b8–c4, 123b1–d4.

110. Solon, fr. 33 (West), in Plut. *Sol.* 14; cf. Theogr., 1.747–52.

111. Burning the Thinkery: Ar. *Nub.* 1506–1610. Aristophanes' *Plutus:* e.g., 780–81. Heracles: Haustash and Hunger, vol. 1, 113. Menander: *Mon.* 62 (ἀνὴρ δίκαιος πλοῦτον οὐκ ἔχει ποτέ); cf. *Kol.* fr. 9 (οὐθεὶς ἐπλούτησεν ταχέως δίκαιος ὤν).

112. *ME*, 195; cf. *GI* for a wide-ranging explication of the lasting association of greed with injustice.

113. Arist. *Rh.* 1390b32–1391a6. Cf. *GPM*, 110–11.

114. See Demosthenes' description of popular indignation at Meidias' ilk, 21.215–16, 21.226. Cf. 21.98 (wealth causes *hubris*), 21.123 (jurors ought to be enraged at Meidias), 21.158–59 (invidious consumption), 21.196 (Meidias deserves "hatred and envy and anger"). On Ariston and Konon, see Millet, *Lending and Borrowing in Ancient Athens,* 227–28.

115. See esp. Ar. *Vesp.* 1299–1325.

116. Pl. *Symp.* 215a4–b8 (ὑβριστὴς εἶ). In a previous conversation, Agathon used identical words (*Symp.* 175e7).

117. Thgn. 1.153–54 (Young): Τίκτει τοι κόρος ὕβριν, ὅταν κακῷ ὄλβος ἕπηται / ἀνθρώπῳ καὶ ὅτῳ μὴ νόος ἄρτιος ᾖ. Cf. 1.747–752 (ὑβρίζῃ πλούτῳ κεκορημένος), 1.1171–76.

118. Solon: fr. 6.3–4, 4.8–10, 4.32–35; cf. 13.9–12 (West) and *GI*, 92–94. Pindar: *Ol.*1.55–57, 13.10. Aeschylus: *Pers.* 821–82, *Ag.* 381–84; cf. *Ag.* 456–74. Sophocles: *OT,* 872–88. Herodotus: the principle pervades the *Histories,* but see for instance 1.32, 1.34.1, 3.80, 8.77.1. Euripides: *Tro.* 987–97, fr. 437, 438 (wealth rather than frugality of life breeds *hubris*). For a thorough analysis of the concept, see Fisher, *Hybris* (with 384–85 on the distinction of religious and secular *hubris*); cf. Solmsen, *Hesiod and Aeschylus,* 114–16.

119. Thuc. 3.39.4, 3.45.4.

120. Xenophon: *Mem.* 1.2.25, 3.5.5–6; cf. 3.5.13, 1.3.2 (gold, silver associated with tyranny). Isocrates: 7.1–7, 8.116–19 (contrasting Thessalian wealth, lack of self-restraint [ἀκολασία], and misfortune with Megarian poverty, temperance, and good fortune). Plato: *Leg.* 691c4, 679b5–c2, 728d6–e5. Others: Eub. fr. 88.

121. Lucian, *Timon,* 28; [Longinus], *Subl.* 44.6–12.

122. 1 Tim. 6:10. Cf. Col. 3:5; Luke 16:13 and Matt. 6:24 ("Ye cannot serve both God and Mammon"); Mark 10:17–26 (The story of the young rich man, and how it is harder for a rich man to enter heaven than a camel to pass through the eye of a needle).

123. Fr. 5 (West).

124. Soph. *Ant.* 293–303. It is interesting to note that Marx quotes the *Antigone* to support his assertion that "the ancients" feared the tendency of money to usurp all other values: "the ancients therefore denounced money as subversive of the economic and moral order of things" (*Capital,* part 1, chap. 3, "Money," 61.).

125. Excessive desire is the cause of war and all social evils: Pl. *Resp.* 373e5–9; *Phd.* 66c1–d5 is even more categorical. For the incompatibility of virtue and great wealth, see, e.g., *Resp.* 416e8–9, 550e4–551a2, 555c7–d1, *Lg.* 705b2–6, 836a1–2, 679b5–c3, 728e5–729a2, 742e4–743c4, 831c; cf. *GI*, 247–48. For elite communism as a bulwark of state unity, see the summary at Pl. *Resp.* 464a2–d5.

126. Crates: Diog. Laert. 6.50. Later instances of the sentiment: "Diogenes said that virtue could not dwell with wealth either in a city or in a house" (Stob. *Flor.* 3.93.35); "The desire for money is the cause of all evil" (*50th Letter* of "Diogenes" [Malherbe]).

127. Diog. Laert. 6.32 (spitting), 6.42 (Meidias), 6.39 (evil masters), 6.45 (temple officials), 6.51 (pale gold).

128. Diog. Laert. 6.41, taken with Cyrus' speech in Hdt. 1.153. Diogenes goes looking for a man, not for a "just" or "honest" man. The addition of these adjectives is true to the Cynic spirit, but only modern renderings have them (*CC*, 103–4).

129. See for example Hdt. 3.148 (king Cleomenes of Sparta the "justest of men" when he refused to take bribes of gold plate from Maeandrius, tyrant of Samos); Pl. *Resp.* 331c1–334b9 (justice defined as "repaying one's debts"); Plut. *Arist.* 5–6 (Aristides' nickname); cf. *GPM*, 170–71. Aristides was celebrated by Socratic thinkers (see Pl. *Grg.* 526b; Aeschin. Socr. 51; Plut. *Arist.* 25).

130. According to rumor, after the battle of Marathon, Callias accepted ransom from a captured Persian noble. But then, fearing that his venality might be discovered, he killed the man. The Persian had hidden his money in a ditch, and thereafter comic poets called Callias and his descendants λακκόπλουτοι, "enriched by the ditch." Subsequently, it became a term of opprobrium for the rich in general (Plut. *Arist.* 5; Alciphr. 1.9). Given the fact that they were cousins and gained their nicknames due to their conduct after Marathon, it is understandable that Aristides' just poverty was contrasted with Callias' unjust wealth. At least as old as Aeschines the Socratic is the story that after a public exchange between Aristides and Callias, "there was none who heard them that went not away desirous rather to be poor like Aristides than rich as Callias" (Plut. *Arist.* 25).

131. Hdt. 8.144. This moment was celebrated for generations after: see, e.g., Lys. 2.33 (those ancient patriots chose virtue, poverty, exile, freedom over vice, wealth, and slavery).

132. Aesch. *Eum.* 700–706.

133. Thuc. 2.60.5. Cf. 2.65.8

134. Dem. 18.298.

135. The motive that Plutarch attributes to Phocion for refusing Alexander's gift is redolent of the Socratic equation of wealth with the self: "so the treasure went back again from Athens, to prove to Greece, by a signal example, that he who could afford to give so magnificent a present, was yet not so rich as he who could afford to refuse it" (Plut. *Phoc.* 18). See *Phoc.* 21 for his refusal of Harpalus' "gift"; and *Phoc.* 19 for his wife's pride in "possessing" him over all jewelry.

136. Such figures serve to temper Ober's conclusion: "the Athenians never developed a topos of the 'unbribable poor man' which was a mainstay of the Roman ideology of wealth" (*ME*, 237n.65). It is true that this did not become a *commonplace* in classical literature. Yet judging from the relative plethora of such characters in the

fourth century (Agesilaus, Phocion, Epaminondas, Timoleon, as well as Xenophon's Cyrus and Plato's philosopher-kings), it seems that a strain of social asceticism was becoming more common, or at least more politically popular.

137. A loose adaptation of Aesch. *Ag.* 774–81.

138. Fr. 54, 55 (Nauck).

139. Isoc. 7.7; cf. 8.116–19.

140. For many examples from the orators, see *GPM*, 175–77.

141. Dem. 18.234.

142. See Dem. 14 and *EAG*, 378–81, 387–91 for more detailed references.

143. Xen. *Oec.* 2.6 (rich man's burdens), 2.2, 2.8–9 (Socrates' wealth, Critobulus' poverty).

144. Isoc. 8.128–29; cf. 15.159: "When I was a boy, it was not dangerous to be called rich and a man was proud of it; today he does all he can to hide the amount of his possessions, for it is more dangerous to pass for wealthy than to break the law." For other reasons for the phenomenon of hoarding, see *AET,* 159–62: without productive credit, "the hoarding of exchange value as coin, gold or silver, was precisely the most useful and sensible thing to do with it" (161).

145. For the power of the sycophant, see MacDowell, *The Law in Classical Athens,* 62–66; Cartledge, Miller, and Todd, *Nomos,* 83–121.

146. See Michell for detailed examples (*EAG,* 373–74).

147. Plut. *X orat.* 843d4–e1.

148. Arist. *Pol.* 1292a1–29 (on radical democracies governed by demogogues/flatterers and popular decrees rather than according to established laws), 1274a5–21 (tyranny of the Athenian *dêmos* after the introduction of political pay).

149. Ar. *Eq.* 773ff, 1111–20, 1158ff. Cf. *Ach.* 633–42.

150. Agoracritus on the table: As. *Eq.* 164–77. Cases from Arcadia and Ecbatana: *Eq.* 797–800, 1086–87. Dêmos crowned "king of the Greeks": *Eq.* 1333. Thundering Philocleon: *Vesp.* 620–30; cf. *Vesp.* 698–712 and Arist. *Pol.* 1274a5–21 (Athenian *dêmos* as *tyrannos*), 1292a1–12.

151. Xen. *Symp.* 4.29–32.

152. See Lucian, *Timon,* 36.3–37.6 on flatterers, sycophants, hostile assemblies, punitive decrees, etc.

153. For example, Plut. *De lat. viv.* (*Mor.* 1128a–30e).

154. Juv. *Sat.* 10.12–27, 10.57–58; cf. Hor. *Carm.* 3.16.7; Sen. *Ep.* 14.10.

155. Boethius, *De cons. phil.* 2.4 *ad fin.*

156. See the moral of Fable 263 (Hausrath and Hunger): better a fearless poverty than wealth with violence and hurt (κρεῖσσον πενία ἄφοβος ἢπλουσιότης μετὰ ἀναγκῶν καὶ ἐπηρειῶν).

157. Hdt. 5.92ζ; cf. Eur. *Supp.* 444–55.

158. Diog. Laert. 6.62.

159. Diog. Laert. 6.51.

160. Diog. Laert. 6.43.

161. Public care for Aristides' grandchildren: Plur. *Arist.* 27. Cleon the "watch-dog of the people": Ar. *Eq.* 1017–34, *Vesp.* 894ff. It may well have been a common metaphor: see Dem. 25.40 (Aristogeiton claims to be κύων τοῦ δήμου). If so, it could have given

inspiration to Plato, as well as the Cynic "dogs": see, e.g., Diog. Laert. 6.60 where Diogenes "fawns on those who give, barks at those who don't, and bites scoundrels." Perhaps here the recipients of Diogenes' affection or anger are the rich, who may be generous (τοὺς διδόντας), miserly (τοὺς μὴ διδόντας), and hubristic (τοὺς πονηρούς)? Concerning *possible* Cynic popularity in some quarters, Crates may have been nicknamed "the good *daimon*" during his lifetime, welcomed as a token of good luck in the houses he entered (Julian *Or.* 9.199c–200b); it is said that the citizens of Sinope erected a statue in honor of Diogenes after he died (Diog. Laert. 6.78).

162. Cf. Hopper, *Trade and Industry in Classical Greece*, chap. 2, esp. 48 ("cargoes were mixed") and 60.

163. *Phormophoroi*, fr. 63 (Kock) = Ath. 27e–28a. For the variety of goods, see Xen. [*Ath. pol.*] 2.7–11; Thuc. 2.38.2; Isoc. 4.42; Xen. *Vect.* 1.6-7, 3.1-2; Ar. *Pax,* 999ff. Braund writes: "There may have been a greater variety of luxuries in Athens than in other Greek states, but most of them will have been well beyond the pocket of most Athenians" ("The Luxuries of Athenian Democracy," 43). Michell notes how "most of the articles enumerated (as in Hermippus' list) are very distinctly in the luxury class" (*EAG*, 234). Cf. *CF*, 227–46 and *GC*, 320–31, 387–88, esp. 330–31 where he quotes Rev. 18:12 to underscore the sharp dichotomy in ancient markets between necessary and luxury goods, between the "old Jewish fisherman" and the merchant of "gold and silver and precious stones and of pearls and fine linen and purple and silk, and all manner of sweet wood and all manner of vessels of ivory and all manner of vessels of most precious wood and of brass and iron and marble, and cinnamon and odors, and ointments and frankincense and wine and oil and fine flour and sheep and horses and slaves and souls of men." Taking a slightly different approach in "Cargoes of the Heart's Desire," Foxhall tries to blur the distinction between basic and luxury goods, both theoretically (299–300, citing Berry's *The Idea of Luxury*) and by speculating that there were "semi-luxuries" or delicacies such as " 'good quality' imported wine, olive oil, wheat, fish sauce" and even certain textiles that the "less-well-off" could consume occasionally, in rituals, festivals, or other special occasions. Even so, heavy stress must be laid on "occasionally," as when Hesiod drinks Biblian wine only as a treat.

164. Mackerel mentioned also in Ar. *Eq.* 1007–10, fr. 414 (Edmonds). But cf. Lib. 32.1.28 on σκόμβροι as a Byzantine delicacy.

165. Scolia 890 (Campbell).

166. Hdt. 1.32–33.

167. Pl. *Resp.* 330d–331b.

168. This is true even of the praise of wealth in Aristophanes' *Plutus,* 802–22, where the house is filled with white flour, wine, oil, perfume, figs, garlic, and so forth; there is plenty of gold and silver, but it is used only for dining and to gamble. So too, Hermippus' list is not *primarily* a catalogue of consumer goods, but rather a catalogue of what the grape-god Dionysus has brought, "ever since he sailed the wine-dark sea."

169. Words such as τρυφή, δαπανή, σπατάλη, χλιδή, ἡδυπάθεια, ἁβρότης, and ἁβροσύνη. Cf. related ideas like ἀσωτία (wastefulness), ἀργία (laziness), ἀκρατία, ἀκολασία (lack of self-restraint), πολυτέλεια (expense), and ὀψοφαγία (eating luxuriously). Passages condemning these vices are legion; by contrast, temperance (σωφροσύνη) becomes a *canonical* virtue. In later medieval parlance, analo-

gously, *cupiditas, rex malorum,* is contrasted with *simplicitas* and *frugalitas.* Cf. Kurke, "The Politics of *Habrosune* in Archaic Greece"; Gribble, *Alcibiades and Athens,* 51–52; *FC,* 209–10 on ὀψοφαγία.

170. Aeschin. 3.240. Cf. 1.41–42, 1.95–97, 1.154.

171. Wasting an estate on boys: Isae. 10.25 (οἶκον καταπαιδεραστεῖν). Case of Athens vs. the peacock-owner: see Cartledge, "Fowl Play: A Curious Lawsuit in Classical Athens," in Cartledge, Millet, and Todd, *Nomos,* 41–62.

172. See Aeschin. 1.21, 30; Dem. 57.32; Diog. Laert. 1.55; and Harrison, *The Law of Athens,* 1:79–80.

173. Themistocles: See Plut. *Them.* 5. Alcibiades: Thuc. 6.12.2, 6.15.3–4, 6.27–28, and Gribble, *Alcibiades and Athens,* 69–82. Fish-mongers berating a customer for buying fish and seasonings (*hêdusmata*): Ar. *Vesp.* 486–507. Cf. *CF,* 278–308 and Sommerstein, *Aristophanes. Knights,* 175–76.

174. Aristotle: *Eth. Nic.* 1147b23–31; cf. *Pol.* 1257b1–1258a18 ("natural wealth" vs. the art of wealth-getting). Epicurus: *RS* 29 (Arrighetti); cf. Diog. Laert. 10.130–31, 10.144, 10.146, and esp. 10.149; Cic. *Fin.* 1.13.45, *Tusc.* 5.93; Ath. 12.511; Democr. DK 68 B 144, 223; Pl. *Resp.* 554a, 558c–559d (with Shorey's note), 571b3–c1, *Phd.* 64d–e, *Phil.* 62d7–e10; Xen. *Vect.* 6.1; Plut. *Lyc.* 9.

175. Pl. *Grg.* 491e6–492a3 (my translation).

176. Salvatore and Diulio, for instance, assume that "scarcity exists in every society *because human material wants are unlimited,* whereas the economic resources necessary to produce the goods and services to satisfy these wants are limited" (*Principles of Economics,* 11, italics added).

177. Cattle: Arist. *Eth. Nic.* 1095b19–22. Gourmand (ὀψόφαγος) who prays for a long throat: *Eth. Nic.* 1118a26–b1; cf. anecdotes about Melanthius the gourmand in Ar. *Pax* 801–12, 1009–15 (see also *CF,* 145-47). Melanthius was grandnephew of Aeschylus, who was surely more preoccupied with thoughts of Zeus' justice than with food.

178. Diog. Laert. 6.86.

179. Three obols was a proverbially paltry sum: see the phrase "not worth three obols" (Nicopho fr. 12); cf. Ar. *Av.* 1537–41, *Plut.* 124–26, 329–31.

180. Arist. *Met.* 981b20–25.

181. Pl. *Tht.* 172c2–173b7.

182. Diog. Laert. 5.40. Cf. Sen. *Ep.* 1.3 (omnia aliena sunt; tempus solum nostrum est).

183. Spending the day with Socrates: Xen. *Symp.* 4.44. Conversation is free: *Symp.* 4.41. Talking with Socrates: *Symp.* 4.30–32.

184. Socrates as philosophical peasant: Xen. *Symp.* 1.5 (αὐτουργὸς τῆς φιλοσοφίας). He talks with all sorts: Pl. *Ap.* 33a5–b3 and see *infra,* chapter 4, n.50 for more references. Pericles' statement: Thuc. 2.40 (φιλοκαλοῦμέν τε γὰρ μετ' εὐτελείας καὶ φιλοσοφοῦμεν ἄνευ μαλακίας).

185. In his "Political Pay Outside Athens," De Ste. Croix cites evidence (mainly from Aristotle's *Politics,* esp. 1317b30–38, 1320a17–22, 1299b38–1300a4) about assembly-pay at Rhodes, Iasus, and third-century Boeotia.

186. A common estimate for the number of festival days is 130–180 (JACT, *The World of Athens,* 118); cf. Thuc. 2.38.1; Pl. *Alc.* 2.148e5–149a1; Xen. [*Ath. Pol.*] 3.8; Gulick, *The Life of the Ancient Greeks,* 273–82, 306–10.

187. Arist. *Pol.* 4.6, 1293a (καὶ μάλιστα δὲ σχολάζει τὸ τοιοῦτον πλῆθος). The antidemocratic, antisocialist agenda of some nineteenth-century historians led them to depict the Athenian *dêmos* as a idle mob that watched plays and judged exciting cases all day while the slaves worked, subject cities paid tribute, and the rich paid protection-money: see chap. 1 of Wood, *Peasant-Citizen and Slave*, for a summary of the views of Fustel, Boeckh, Burckhardt, Mitford, and others. Given this, it would not be surprising if contemporary Greek "elites" entertained similar caricatures about an indolent *dêmos*. Ideas have a life of their own, and by a small adaptation could switch hosts and enter the Cynic vocabulary.

188. Cf. Democr. DK 68 B 251.

189. Teles, fr. 4 (Hense = Stob. 4.32a21).

190. Breakfast: Diog. Laert. 6.45. Clock: Diog. Laert. 6.104.

191. Diog. Laert. 6.51 (τὸν ἔρωτα σχολαζόντων ἀσχολίαν). Similarly Socrates was always "in love" (Xen. *Mem.* 4.1.2); cf. Pl. *Symp.* 177d7–e3 (Socrates knows only τὰ ἐρωτικά) and 203c6–d8 where the description of *erôs* is reminiscent of Socrates himself.

192. Crates: Plu. *De tranq. anim.* 466e, and cf. 477c3–6 for Diogenes' jocularity ("Diogenes, seeing a respected man in Lacedaemon getting himself ready for some festival asked the good man whether he did not consider every day a festival"). Cf. Plut. *Tim.* 15 (Diogenes and Dionysius); Pl. *Symp.* 216e2–5 (satyr-Socrates fooling and joking). Similarly, the first Franciscans were named *joculatores Dei* for their merriment.

193. Plut. *Per.* 20.

194. This was the contemporary rhetoric, though modern historians like Salmon are skeptical, and hold that Timoleon's constitutions were mixed, with only some democratic aspects ("Timoleon" in *OCD*, 3rd ed., 1528).

195. For this Stoic version of the first Cynic paradox, see Cic. *Paradoxa Stoicorum*, 8-9, 29; M.Ant. *Meditations*, 2.14. Cf. Diog. Laert. 6.105 (virtue alone is ἀναπόβλητος and cannot be lost).

196. Davies, *Wealth and the Power of Wealth in Ancient Athens*, 86. Cephalus' father, for instance, squandered *his* father's legacy, and Cephalus had to begin from scratch (Pl. *Resp.* 330b1–7). Demosthenes generalizes: "It is not usual for many citizens to maintain a continuous level of material prosperity" (42.4). For other examples, see *GPM*, 174–75; and Cohen on the short duration of most banking operations (*Athenian Economy and Society*, 215–16).

197. Andoc. *De Mys.* 131; Lys. 19.48.

198. Hes. *Op.* 1–10. Cf. Zeus in his role as *Zeus Ktêsios*, protector of a household's possessions (e.g., *Op.* 126). Nonagricultural wealth also has a divine origin: Pluto is god of the underworld's mineral wealth; Xenophon writes that rich veins of ore (like the silver mines at Laureum) are a divine allotment (θεῖα μοῖρα, *Vect.* 1.5). For Fortune, see Democr. DK 68 B 176 (Fortune makes great gifts, but also takes them away).

199. Hdt. 7.190.

200. Plut. *Tim.* 14.3–4. The entire passage is worth reading (*Tim.* 14–15).

201. Plut. *Tim.* 15.8–10.

202. Hes. *Op.* 493–95.

203. Hes. *Op.* 719–20.
204. Hes. *Op.* 455–56; cf. *Op.* 403.
205. Hes. *Op.* 638; cf. *Op.* 717–18 ("heart-rending poverty . . . gift of the ever-living gods").
206. Idleness of the golden age: Hes. *Op.* 43–46, 111–15. Pandora and Hope: *Op.* 90–105. The iron age of work: *Op.* 176–77.
207. Hes. *Op.* 476.
208. Hes. *Op.* 588–96.
209. Hes. *Op.* 1–10.
210. Hes. *Op.* 40–41 (νήπιοι, οὐδὲ ἴσασιν ὅσῳ πλέον ἥμισυ παντός / οὐδ' ὅσον ἐν μαλάχῃ τε καὶ ἀσφοδέλῳ μέγ' ὄνειαρ). Cf. Nelson who concludes that "the half is preferable, because one who strives for the whole is most likely to end up with nothing. . . . [I]n context, Hesiod's meaning clearly is that a small but honest living is better than great wealth unjustly earned" (*God and the Land,* 127). The proverb is quoted to the same effect in Pl. *Resp.* 466b–c.
211. Hungry idlers: Hes. *Op.* 302. Begging idlers: *Op.* 396–404.
212. Work, work, work: Hes. *Op.* 381–82. Hesiod's father: *Op.* 633–40. Envy is good: *Op.* 20–26. Zeus rewards the just materially: *Op.* 225–47.
213. Verg. *G.* 1.145.
214. Fr. 13.63–70 (West; my translation). For other examples of archaic pessimism, see Hom *Il.* 24.527–33 (Zeus' two urns); Thgn. 1.157–58 (Campbell).
215. Fr. 13.16–36 (West).
216. *CHCK* 25, 27 (italics added).
217. Thuc. 1.70.8–9.
218. For instance, Athenian hope, desire, confidence, daring, restlessness, greed, eagerness, risk-taking, ambition, experimentation, and quickness (ἐλπίς, ἔρως, θάρσος, τόλμα, πολυπραγμοσύνη, πλεονεξία, προθυμία, κινδυνεύτης, ἐπιχειρητής, φιλονικία, νεωτεροποιία, τό ὄξυ, and ταχύτης) vs. Spartan qualities like fear, lack of daring, safety, temperance, lack of activity, slowness, delay, and hesitation (φόβος, ἀτολμία, ἀσφάλεια, σωφροσύνη, ἀπραγμοσύνη, βραδύτης, ἀναβολή, διατριβή, μέλλησις, ὄκνος, and σχολαιότης). Thucydides confirms this programmatic dichotomy in 8.96.5. On this theme, Luginbill is most comprehensive (*Thucydides on War and National Character,* 82–215, esp. 87–94). Cf. Edmunds, *Chance and Intelligence in Thucydides,* 40–41, 89–90, 97–99; and Rood, *Thucydides: Narrative and Explanation,* 225–48.
219. Callicles: Pl. *Grg.* 491e2. Thucydides: "It has often been noticed that Thucydides never uses σωφροσύνη or a related word of the Athenians and that σωφροσύνη is not mentioned by Pericles in any of his speeches in Thucydides" (Edmunds, *Chance and Intelligence in Thucydides,* 76).
220. Do not flee *ponoi:* Thuc. 2.63.1. The *ponoi* of campaign, battle: 4.26.2, 4.14.4. The *ponoi* of war generally: 2.62.2 (ὁ πόνος ὁ κατὰ τόν πόλεμον), 5.110–11. The *ponoi* of plague and the unpredictable: 2.49.3, 2.51.6. Using one's σῶμα as a tool: 1.70.6. The "painless death": 2.43.6 (ἀναίσθητος θάνατος). Athens expending bodies and *ponoi* in war: 2.63.3. Athens the richest city: 2.64.4.
221. For instances of patriotic rhetoric outside the funeral oration, see, e.g., Aeschin. *In Ctes.* 181–3; Hyp. 9.31–37.

222. For a more detailed examination of how Thucydides' post-Periclean Athens lacked judgment (γνώμη) equal to its material resources (περιουσία χρημάτων), and for these themes in relation to the Sicilian Expedition, see Kallet-Marx, *Money and the Corrosion of Power in Thucydides,* especially 21–84, 147–82.

223. Thuc. 6.9.3.

224. Thuc. 6.18.

225. Thuc. 6.24.3–5 (δύναμις 'όθεν ἀίδιος μισθοφορά; ἡ ἂ γαν τῶν πλεόνων ἐπιθυμία).

226. Thuc. 6.24.3–4.

227. Thuc. 6.90. This rhetoric is not unique to Alcibiades or to his situation in Sparta: even when he is gone, the Athenians in Sicily continue frankly to acknowledge their habitual ambition and their right to empire. The ambassador Euphemus, for example, openly refers to the *polupragmosunê* that defines the Athenian nature, and warns the Camarineans that attempts to change this character will be in vain (Thuc. 6.87.1–3).

228. Thuc. 2.41.4.

229. Dem. 11.17–22. On Philip's *ponoi,* cf. Dem. 8.44.5. As a side note, there may be an echo of the imperial work-ethic in the anecdote that Diogenes went to Macedonia as a spy upon Philip's "insatiability" (κατάσκοπος τῆς σῆς ἀπληστίας: Diog. Laert. 6.43).

230. Plut. *Pyrrh.* 14.

231. Plut. *Alex.* 14.5.

232. Pl. *Meno* 81c9–d5; Arist. *De an.* 431b21 (ἡ ψυχὴ τὰ ὄντα πώς ἐστι πάντα), cf. *De an.* 405b15–17, 429a18–21.

233. Soph. *Ant.* 334ff.

234. See, e.g., Pl. *Ap.* 23a5–b4, 41e2–7 (ἐὰν δοκῶσί τι εἶναι μηδὲν ὄντες), *Symp.* 216d7–e5 (ἡγεῖται ... ἡμᾶς οὐδέν εἶναι).

235. See for instance Philemon, *Katapseudomenos,* fr. 37.2 (Kock): "It is possible to find out all things, so long as one does not flee the *ponos* which belongs to the searchers"; or Alexis, *Achaïs,* 30.7: "all things sought [rising and setting of stars, eclipses, etc.] are found out—so long as one does not give up or flee *ponos.*" Cf. *PRIA,* 192–221 for other examples and a detailed discussion.

236. Theoc. 2.76–80. Cf. Pl. *Phdr.* 248d6 (φιλόπονος ἡγυμναστικός).

237. See Ar. *Ran.* 818–89 for the ῥήματα γομφοπαγῆ of Aeschylus, φρενοτέκτων ἀνήρ, and for Euripides σμιλευματοεργός, στοματουργός with his πλευμόνων πολὺν πόνον. Pheidippides: Ar. *Nub.* 1397 (ὦ καινῶν ἐπῶν κινητὰ καὶ μοχλευτά). Cf. Eur. fr. 795 (χειρώνακτες λόγων) (Nauck) and Aeschin. 3.215 (δημιουργὸς λόγων).

238. DK 68 B 240. Cf. fr. 157, 182, 240, 241, 242 and 197.

239. Xen. *Mem.* 2.1.21ff.

240. Zeller, *Outlines of the History of Greek Philosophy,* 84; *CHCK,* 33.

241. Xen. *Mem.* 3.9.15.

242. Xen. *Mem.* 2.7.7.

243. Xen. *Mem.* 2.7.7–10, 2.7.12.

244. Xen. *Mem.* 2.1.3.

245. Xen. *Mem.* 2.1.17 (μοχθήσουσιν ἔκοντες).

246. Xen. *Mem.* 1.6.2–3 (κακοδαιμονίας διδάσκαλος).
247. See for example Xen. *Mem.* 2.1.19–20 (self-esteem) and 1.6.7–9.
248. For example, Xen. *Cyn.* 1.18, 12.9, 12.15–19, 13.10–18; *Mem.* 1.2.2.
249. Pl. *Ap.* 22a6–8.
250. See Pl. *Resp.* 535c1–d8. In other dialogues, the ascent to the Forms is described as one of *ponos,* for the body pulls the soul down, and the dark horse kicks wildly: see, e.g., *Phdr.* 247b, *Symp.* 210e. The "upper" realm, whatever it is, is a realm of perfection and, like Hesiod's golden age, is free of the need to toil (e.g., [*Ax*] 370d: ὁ ἄπονος βίος).
251. Pl. *Resp* 371e: hired laborers (*misthôtoi*) "sell the use of their strength." By analogy, merchants sell their time, because they have nothing else others want to buy. The guardian-class is referred to as *misthôtoi* or as *epikouroi* (mercenaries) in *Resp.* 419a–e, *Ti.* 18b1–7; cf. *Resp.* 347a1–b9, 416d7–e3, 463b1, 543b7–c3, et al. Such passages develop Socrates' analogies between the crafts and ruling in book 1 (and elsewhere): Socrates would ideally make politics as precise, rule-based, and undramatic as stitching a shoe; hence the philosophers are trained long in mathematics and dialectic. Such analogies would level difference, even though of course in other contexts the Platonic Socrates recognizes a non-economic realm in which poet, lover, philosopher, and others are not at all just "workers." Contrast Marx, who more univocally applauds bourgeois culture for exposing the idealism of the past as illusory: "The bourgeoisie has stripped of its halo every occupation hitherto honoured and looked up to with reverent awe. It has converted the physician, the lawyer, the priest, the poet, the man of science, into its paid wage labourers" (*Communist Manifesto,* 420).
252. See Arist. *Pol.* 1398b10–20 (all cities honor "the wise"; Athens, Sparta, and Thebes prospered under Solon, Lycurgus, and "philosophers," respectively). Cf. *Rh.* 1406b11–12 (Alcidamas: "philosophy is a bulwark for the law").
253. Pl. *Resp.* 370a7–b2, c3–5.
254. Pl. *Resp.* 371c5–8.
255. Pl. *Resp.* 460c.
256. Contrary to many previous assessments, this seems to me at least to be the inevitable thrust of the dialogue as a whole, with its emphasis upon free, voluntary labor. Slavery makes its first unambiguous appearance in the timarchic society, whose rulers are merciless towards the weak (Pl. *Resp.* 547c). The only other relevant passage is *Resp.* 469c—a conventional condemnation of enslaving fellow Greeks. This leaves open the possibility of enslaving foreigners, but the stated objection to Greek slavery here is that it would weaken the Greek race and expose it to subjection to barbarians (εὐλαβουμένους τὴν ὑπὸ τῶν βαρβάρων δουλείαν). By extension, enslaving foreigners would invite reprisals.
257. Pl. *Leg.* 846d4–e2, 847a5–6.
258. Pl. *Leg.* 807b7–e2.
259. No money-making: Pl. *Leg.* 847a3–7. No hunting with nets: 824a. City should be unwalled: 778e–779a. Festivals: 653c. Beggars: 936c1–7.
260. Arist. *Pol.* 1329a19–21.
261. Again, see Arist. *Pol.* 1.8 on modes of natural (vs. commercial) acquisition.
262. Arist. *Pol.* 1323a24–b21.

263. Arist. *Eth. Nic.* 11//b31–3.

264. Diog. Laert. 5.36; cf. Diog. Laert. 5.41.

265. Diog. Laert. 7.180.

266. Diog. Laert. 10.130, *RS* 15 (ὁ τῆς φύσεως πλοῦτος . . . εὐπόριστός ἐστιν) (Arighetti); and the third proposition of the Epicurean *tetrapharmakon* in the inscription of Diogenes of Oenanda: "the good is easily acquired" (τὸ ἀγαθὸν εὔκτητον). The adjective *euktêtos* is also by Crates concerning true wealth in fr. 18 (Giannantoni, V H 84.23).

267. Diog. Laert. 6.44.

268. Diog. Laert. 6.70–71. Höistad argues that this passage reflects Diogenes' own criticism of the popular admiration of the strength and athleticism of heroes like Heracles (*CHCK*, 37–47). The scope of Diogenes' critique is broader than this, however.

269. Bion, fr. 4.6ff; translated by Dudley, *HC*, 67.

270. Vegetables: Diog. Laert. 6.58; for other references, see *supra,* chapter 1, n.13. Cf. Lucian for the story of Diogenes as a latter-day Sisyphus. On the eve of Philip's attack, Corinth was in a furor of preparations. Diogenes decided to join in and began to roll his *pithos*-home up and down the Craneum-hill so that he would not seem "to be idle amidst such a great hubbub of work" (*Hist. Consecr.* 3). His *ergon* is of course as pointless as Sisyphus', but in a world ruled by *Tuchê,* most conventional work is "useless."

271. Diog. Laert. 6.31 (Diogenes' reported tutelage of Xeniades' sons) and 6.39 (his praise of Agesilaus and Epaminondas).

272. Dio. Chrys. 8.16. Cf. Epict. *Ench.* 29.6–7.

273. Diog. Laert. 6.34. Cf. Diog. Laert. 6.64: "defacing" customs is what Cynics always do.

274. Diog. Laert. 6.71.

275. Str. 15.1.64. Cf. Brown, *Onesicritus,* 38ff.

276. Str. 15.1.65.

277. Virtue as *ergon:* fr. 3 (Snell). Frugality as teacher: fr. 6. *Heracles*-fragment: fr. 7.

278. Antisthenes wrote four books on Cyrus and up to ten on the characters in the *Odyssey,* including one with the curious title, "Concerning Odysseus, Penelope and the dog" (Diog. Laert. 6.15–18). Diogenes' admiration for Agesilaus and Epaminondas: Diog. Laert. 6.39.

279. Arist. [*Ath. Pol*]. 43.4.

280. *FFS,* 154–64.

281. *FFS,* 148–49.

282. For many references, see *FFS,* esp. 141, 154–64; *GM,* 16 and 50.

283. Spread of gourmet dining: Gulick, "Preface," vii–viii; *CF* 6. Demetrius' legislation: see Williams, "The Ideology and Constitution of Demetrius of Phalerum," 335–38. Williams notes similarities between the sumptuary laws of Demetrius and Solon. One might add the potentially populist appeal of such laws for preventing conspicuous consumption and hubristic display of one's "good fortune." Binary oppositions between rich and poor appear commonly in both philosophical and nonphilosophical literature. Thus, Plato writes that most cities of the first quarter of the fourth century are in fact two cities—a city of the rich and a city of the poor—which struggle continuously for

dominance: *Resp.* 551d5–e4; cf. *Resp.* 422e8–423a1. In Marxist fashion, Aristotle makes class (rather than status or occupation) the prime criterion of social division: e.g. *Pol.* 1279b34–1280a5, 1290a13–29, 1291b7–13, 1295b1–5, 1296a10–13; cf. De Ste. Croix, *Class Struggle in the Ancient Greek World,* 69–80, 278–300. For similar ideas in the orators, see Finley, *Democracy Ancient and Modern,* 55–56; De Ste. Croix, *Class Struggle in the Ancient Greek World,* 69–80; and *ME,* 193, 195–96 (esp. 195n.7, citing Lys. 24.9; Dem. 22.53, 44.4, 45.80; Isae. 11.37, 6.59; Arist. *Rhet.* 1379a1–2, et al).

284. Thucydides describes the *stasis* in Corcyra as representative of the barbarities that occurred (3.81–84; cf. 3.46–48 and esp. 3.47.3 for hatred and cruelty). He also notes class-tension in Mytilene (3.27), and Syracuse (6.38).

285. Diod. Sic. 15.57–58; "The outrages of the *stasis* in Argos shocked the public opinion in Greece" (*SCAG,* 71n.66). For a fuller discussion, see *SCAG* 70–72.

286. Arist. *Pol.* 1310a8–10.

287. Thus, Fuks writes: γῆς ἀναδασμός and χρεῶν ἀποκοπαί "are the 'classical features' of the social revolution from the fourth to second centuries B.C." (*SCAG,* 70).

288. Demosthenes on past simplicity: 3.23–26, 3.29, 21.158–59, 23.206–10; cf. 13.28–31. Ober writes that "such statements were intended to have a specific impact on juries and cannot be taken on face value, but they exaggerate rather than falsify the reality of the situation" (*ME,* 118). There may be exaggeration, yet certainly the fact that they were designed to have this "specific impact" on popular audiences is highly significant.

289. Isoc. *Philippos,* 120–23. Cf. *SCAG,* 73–77.

290. Iambulus' Island of the Sun: Diodorus 2.55–60; Tarn, *Hellenistic Civilization,* 122.

291. Isocrates' slogan is "to work and be thrifty" (ἐργάζεσθαι καὶ φείδεσθαι, *Arpg.* 24). See *SCAG,* 52–79 for a full discussion, as well as a list of instances of Isocrates' opposition of ἀργία and ἐργασία (*Arpg.* 24–25, 31–36, 44–45, 55, et al.).

292. Arist. *Pol.* 1263a29–40. For a full discussion, see *SCAG,* 179–186; cf. *AET,* 153–57. With regard to Spartan customs, one is reminded of the medieval practice of leaving edges of a field in harvest-time, so that the poor could harvest it for themselves.

293. On Democritus and Archytas, see *SCAG,* 174–78 (I excerpt from his translations of Democritus, fr. 255 and Archytas, fr. 3). Demosthenes' *De Corona:* 18.268. On Theocles, Thrasonides, and Praxis, see Ael. *VH* 14.24; with *SCAG,* 182–84. For instances of the "amazing liberality of the wealthy" in the Hellenistic era, see Tarn, *Hellenistic Civilization,* 106–11.

294. Crates on lentil soup vs. shellfish and *stasis:* μὴ πρὸ φακῆς λοπάδ' αὔξων ἐς στάσιν ἄμμε βάλης (fr. 8). Aristophanes' poor eat lentil soup: e.g. *Eq.* 1007, *Vesp.* 811, *Plut.* 1004–5. The goddess *Metadoss:* Cerc. fr. 4.47–50 (Powell). Crates' republic of Pêra: fr. 6 (Snell).

295. Crates, fr. 9: κόγχον καὶ κύαμον σύναγ, <ὦ φίλε>, κἂν τάδε δράσῃς, ῥηϊδίως στήσεις <στάσεως> πενίας τε τροπαῖον. The κόγχος or κόγχη (mussel or cockle) was proverbially cheap; the phrase κόγχης ἄξιον means "cheap" or even "worthless" (Hsch., Suid.).

CHAPTER THREE

PRAISE OF POVERTY AND WAR

1. When Diogenes and Alexander meet, Alexander proclaims "I am Alexander the Great," to which Diogenes replies with equal pride, "And I am Diogenes the Dog" (Diog. Laert. 6.60., cf. 6.63). When Diogenes is being sold in the slave-market and is asked what he can do, he answers "Rule men" (Diog. Laert. 6.29). Many Hellenistic anecdotes juxtapose king and philosopher as if they were peers and rivals. In the anecdotes of the "Diogenes Legend," Diogenes defeats tyrant after tyrant with his sharp eloquence—Dionysius II, Philip, Alexander, Antipater, Craterus, Archidamus the Spartan king, Antigonus Gonatas, the Persian tyrants, and even mythic tyrants like Midas: for references, mainly from the Cynic Epistles, see Sayre, *Diogenes of Sinope,* 110–14. Other examples of the Cynic as "king": Diog. Laert. 6.55; Arr. *Epict. diss.* 3.22.76.

2. Diog. Laert. 6.13, 6.93, 7.40; *HC,* 39.

3. Hdt. 9.122.3.

4. Cf. Bowra: "The essence of the heroic outlook is the pursuit of honour through action. . . . Fame is the reward of honour, and the hero seeks it before everything else. This outlook runs through Greek history from Homer's Achilles to the historical Alexander" (*The Greek Experience,* 33). Bowra might have added that honor typically has a material manifestation: the Spartan kings, for instance, were served twice as much food as others (Hdt. 6.57). Lowry neglects the idealism of honor to apply the language of joint assets, transactions, cost-benefit analyses, and administrative rationality to the *Iliad,* as if the Homeric hero's motivation were "unmistakably a concern for gain, a kind of entrepreneurship in search of plunder that could be carried home" (*Archaeology of Economic Ideas,* 126). Certainly the heroes want spoils, but does the *Iliad* simply record the "economic and legal confrontation between Achilles and Agamemnon over the distribution of the returns of warfare" (131)? Such reductionism may be characteristic of a later age, of a Thucydides or Plato (whom Lowry cites)—or the Cynics—but *not* Homer.

5. Hom. *Il.* 1.161–62, 276, 355–56, 392.

6. "Hateful are his gifts": see Achilles' speech in Hom. *Il.* 9.378–418 (ἐχθρὰ δέ μοι τοῦ δῶρα). Generations of men: e.g., *Il.* 2.459–68, *Od.* 9.51. Achilles is honored by Zeus alone: *Il.* 9.607–10, with Whitman, *Homer and the Heroic Tradition,* 181–220. No business with the Trojans: *Il.* 1.152–60.

7. Lycaon: Hom. *Il.* 21.97–113 (νήπιε μή μοι ἄποινα πιφαύσκεο μηδ᾽ ἀγόρευε, κτλ). Hector: *Il.* 22.337–54. Priam: *Il.* 24.553–70.

8. The Homeric heroes often "drunk delight of battle" even in its worst carnage: see words like χάρμη (*Il.* 8.252, 12.203, 12.393, 13.82, et al., *Od.* 22.73), the phrase κύδεϊ γαίων (*Il.* 1.405, 5.906, 8.51), and longer passages as when Athena shakes the *aegis* over the Greek soldiers and war becomes sweeter to them than returning home (*Il.* 2.445–54), or when the earth itself laughs aloud in glee at the splendor of the army marching out (*Il.* 19.357–68).

9. Hybrias ap. Ath. 695e–696a.

10. Fr. 2 (West).

11. For references, see Campbell, *Greek Lyric Poetry,* 142.

12. For this summary, see Parke, *Greek Mercenary Soldiers,* 14–19.

13. For example, Tyrtaeus, 12.10–20 (West).

14. For example, Pl. *Ap.* 28d6–29a1.

15. Precise dates for the first and last funeral speech are unknown, but the major proposed dates for the first *epitaphios* (590, 511–509, 490, 456) mark an important phase in the emergence of the Athenian democracy (Solon, the Cleisthenic reforms, the battle of Marathon, Ephialtes' reforms). The rhetoric of the speech itself drew largely on democratic ideals. The genre seems to have faded away with the democracy itself: Hyperides delivered the last known funeral oration during the Lamian War, in 323. Hence the conclusion that it was essentially coterminous with the Athenian democracy, though its themes remained popular much later, at least until Sulla's siege in 86 (Plut. *Sull.* 13.4; cf. Cic. *Orat.* 151). Loraux's *The Invention of Athens* is the comprehensive work for the history, rhetoric, ideology, and other aspects of the *epitaphios.*

16. Myronides: Lys. 49–53; Thuc. 1.105.4–6. For the dichotomy of *aretê* and numbers, and the rhetorical *topos* that a few good soldiers defeated many enemies, see Lys. 15, 24, 27, 32, 36, 40, 41, 46, 63; Hdt. 6.109, 112. Athens fought "alone": Lys. 20; Hdt. 7.10, 9.27; Thuc. 1.18.1, 1.74.4; Pl. *Menex.* 240c6–7, 241b1; Isoc. *Paneg.* 86, *Panath.* 195. Cf. Loraux, *The Invention of Athens,* 158.

17. Corinth: Plut. *Tim.* 2 (πόλις φιλελεύθερος καὶ μισοτύραννος οὖσα ἀεί). Sparta: e.g., Hdt. 5.92, Thuc. 2.8.4, Isoc. 4.125; cf. Price, *Thucydides and Internal War,* 128.

18. See, for example, Thuc. 2.42.4; Lys. 2.33; Dem. 60.2, 60.18; cf. Ziolkowski, *Thucydides and the Tradition of Funeral Speeches at Athens,* 118–9.

19. Adapted from Thucydides, 2.42.4.

20. Hipponax, fr. 36 (West), Ar. *Plut.* 202–7. Cf. Th. 2.42.4, Ar. *Pax* 1172–78 (cowardice of a rich commander), and the quip attributed to Themistocles: "Of two that courted his daughter, Themistocles chose the brave man over the rich one, saying that he preferred a man without wealth, rather than wealth without a man" (Plut. *Them.* 18). Cf. Plut. *Ages.* 9 and Xen. *Ages.* 1.23–24 for instances of rich men avoiding personal service or sending hired soldiers as replacements, or the opening scenes of Aristophanes' *Acharnians* in which Dicaeopolis, "Honest Citizen," does his duty guarding the walls, while well-connected ambassadors report their "engagements" in hostile territory, forced to lie in pillowed carriages, drink wine from crystal goblets, and suffer other hardships (Ar. *Ach.* 61–93). For more references, see *GPM,* 111–12.

21. Thomas, *Oral Tradition and Written Record,* 207.

22. Hoplites relatively poor: Ar. *Vesp.* 1071–1121; Thuc. 3.16.1, 3.87.3; *CF,* 228–29. Aristotle on oxen: *Pol.* 1259b2–12.

23. Hdt. 7.9.2. Cf. Hdt. 1.82 (for the long-standing war between Sparta and Argos over Thyrea, a meager strip of land) and Isoc. 4.136–37, 5.125–26.

24. Hom. *Il.* 6.207–11 (αἰὲν ἀριστεύειν καὶ ὑπείροχον ἔμμεναι ἄλλων)— the line typically quoted as the epitome of the heroic spirit.

25. Hdt. 8.26. Cf. the story told of Themistocles realizing with admiration that cocks fight not for gods or country, but simply to win (Ael. *VH* 2.28).

26. Isoc. 5.133–36 (Philip should fight for honor and future fame, not power and wealth).

27. Plut. *Alex.* 21.

28. Plut. *Alex.* 29.

29. Plut. *Demetr.* 5.

30. Hom. *Od.* 9.27: ['Ιθάκη] τρηχεῖ', ἀλλ' ἀγαθὴ κουροτρόφος.

31. The one instance is the reference to the Abioi, milk-drinkers and "the justest of men" (Hom. *Il.* 13.6); cf. *PRIA,* 288.

32. Arcesilaus cited in Stob. 4.32.17: 'Αρκεσίλαος τὴν πενίαν λυπρὰν μὲν ἔλεγεν εἶναι ὥσπερ καὶ τὴν' Ἰθάκην, ἀγαθὴν δὲ κουροτρόφον ἐθίζουσαν συνεῖναι λιτότητι καὶ καρτερίᾳ, καὶ καθόλου γυμνάσιον ἀρετῆς ἔμπρακ–τον.

33. Hippoc. *Aer.* 16; cf. 23.

34. Hippoc. *Aer.* 24.

35. Xenophon: *Anab.* 3.5.16 (Carduchians), 5.2.2 (Drilae); *Hell.* 4.36 (the Spartan is poor and free). Aristotle: *Pol.* 1327b18–34. Herodotus: e.g., 1.66.2 where the Delphic oracle darkly warns the Spartans not to attack the "acorn-eating men" of Arcadian Tegea.

36. Hdt. 1.79.3.

37. Hdt. 1.155.4.

38. Hdt. 1.153.

39. Herodotus remarks that in the 490s the Ionians were "by far the weakest of the Greeks" (1.143.2); the battle at Mycale in 479 was the one great Ionian victory. Persian conquest and Ionian luxury: Thgn. 1103–4, Xenoph. fr. 3, with Bowra, "Xenophanes' Fragment 3." The proverb: πάλαι ποτ' ἦσαν ἄλκιμοι Μιλήσιοι (Anacr. 85, Ar. *Plut.* 1002, Pl. *Resp.* 614b, etc., as in *LSJ* under ἄλκιμος).

40. Aristophanes' overweight torchbearer: *Ra.* 1087–98, part of the critique of "Euripides" for corrupting the Athenians who once breathed pure valor under the influence of the Marathon-man "Aeschylus." Plato: *Leg.* 831c4-832a2 (love of money); *Resp.* 556b6–e1 (pale and fat oligarchs); *Leg.* 807a7-b3 (battening beasts); cf. Aristotle's generalization in *Pol.* 1310a22–25. Aristophanes' manly wasps: *Vesp.* 1090 et al.

41. See Thuc. 1.20–21 and 6.54–59. In 1.20.3, Thucydides takes Athenian ignorance of the fact that Harmodius and Aristogeiton only killed the brother of Hippias, and not the tyrant himself, as an illustration of how so very few people care about historical precision. Concerning the relatively undeveloped historical consciousness of the classical Greeks, see Nouhard, chapter 3, "La Connaissance de l'Histoire" in *L'Utilisation de l'Histoire par les Orateurs Attiques.*

42. Hdt. 8.77.

43. Hdt. 7.61–100.

44. Hdt. 7.83.

45. Mardonius makes the "barbarian's" typical mistake of assuming numbers and wealth to be superior to virtue: cf. Hdt. 7.9.

46. Hdt. 7.102.1.

47. Hdt. 7.210.

48. See, for instance, Diodorus Siculus, 11.11.2: Leonidas and his men "suffered bodily, but were undefeated in their souls" (ταῖς ψυχαῖς οὐχ ἡττήθησαν).

49. Greek armor: Hdt. 7.61.1, 9.63.2. Greek spears: 7.211.2. Persian bravery at Marathon and Plataea: 6.113.1, 9.62.3. Cythera as possible base: 7.235. Sea and land as enemies: 7.49.

50. At the Panathenaea, the Athenian state officially remembered the Plataeans' magnanimity, until Sparta razed it in 428 (Hdt. 6.111.2). But in many extant speeches, the Plataeans are not mentioned: see, for instance, Hdt. 6.108.1.

51. Hdt. 9.27.5–6.

52. For the tradition that the Athenians stood alone, see Thuc. 1.73.4, 6.83.2; Lys. 2.20–24; Xen. *Mem.* 3.5.10–11; Isoc. 16.27; Dem. 60.10–11. The boast of having overcome incredible odds is common in the funeral-speech tradition (Ziolkowski, *Thucydides and the Tradition of Funeral Speeches at Athens*, 116–17; Nouhard, *L'Utilisation de l'Histoire par les Orateurs Attiques*, 149-55); cf. Ar. *Ach.* 180–81, *Eq.* 565–80, 781, 1334, *Vesp.* 711, 1071–1100.

53. Dem. 60.10–11.

54. Thomas, *Oral Tradition and Written Record*, 225–26.

55. Pl. *Menex.* 240d1–d7 (italics added: πᾶν πλῆθος καὶ πᾶς πλοῦτος ἀρετῇ ὑπείκει); cf. Aspasia's similar comments on Salamis (241a6–b3). In a similar vein, Plutarch writes of Artemisum that "neither numbers of ships, nor riches and ornaments, nor boasting shouts, nor barbarous songs of victory are in any way terrible to men that know how to fight. . . . For the first step towards victory undoubtedly is to gain courage" (Plut. *Them.* 8).

56. Cic. *Orat.* 151.

57. Hdt. 9.122.

58. See the advice of the Lydian Sandanis to Croesus: " 'You are preparing, King, to attack men who wear leather pants and all leather clothes; who do not eat what they like, but what they can get from their harsh land; who drink water, not wine, and who have neither figs to eat nor any other good. If, then, you defeat them, what good will you get from them, since they have nothing? But if you are defeated, think of all that you will throw away. For having once tasted our luxuries, they will grasp for more and be very difficult to repulse. I myself, in fact, thank the gods for not inspiring the Persians to march against the Lydians.' His speech did not persuade Croesus, though he was right. For before the Lydians were subdued, the Persians did not have any delicacies or comforts" (Hdt. 1.71.2–4). For related material on the "wise advisor," primitivism, and the interplay between geography and *nomoi* in Herodotus, see Lattimore, "The Wise Advisor in Herodotus"; Redfield, "Herodotus the Tourist"; and Thomas, *Herodotus in Context*, 102–34.

59. Hdt. 1.34.1.

60. Poverty of Massagetae: The Massagetae "are unacquainted with the good things on which the Persians live and have never tasted the delights of life" (Hdt. 1.207.6). Cyrus' confidence: Hdt. 1.204.2. Cyrus ignores Croesus: Hdt. 1.207.2–208.

61. Hdt. 3.19–23.

62. Hdt. 3.21.3.

63. Hdt. 3.30.

64. Hdt. 3.25.2.

65. Hdt. 4.1.

66. No cities or farmland: Hdt. 4.127. Scythians cannot be conquered: Hdt. 4.83.

67. Hdt. 7.18.

68. Hdt. 9.82.

69. Hdt. 9.122 (my translation).

70. For the poverty of the Persians' mountain homeland, see, for example, Hdt. 1.126.

71. Herodotus gives many examples of the Persians' conspicuous splendor. The Immortals have gold trappings on their arms (7.41, 7.83.2); the general Mardonius has golden armor (9.22.2), a golden bit for his horse (9.20), as well as brass mangers (9.70.3). Xerxes ate from golden plates even in rough Thracian country (7.119). Herodotus does not say that Xerxes' traveling-throne (7.212.1, 8.90.4) was golden, although it seems that Xerxes did in fact sit on a golden throne at the foot of Mt. Aegaleus to watch the battle at Salamis (Plu. *Them.* 13). This throne was displayed as a victory trophy on the Athenian Acropolis until it was stolen over one hundred years later in the mid-fourth century (Dem. 24.129; cf. How and Wells, *A Commentary on Herodotus*, 2:266). Later historians were more eager than Herodotus to draw the appropriate moral from such details. Plutarch, for instance, attributes to Aristides a sermon on Xerxes' golden umbrella and the decadence of the Persians: "Themistocles, being desirous to try the opinion of Aristides, told him that he proposed to set sail for the Hellespont, to break up the bridge of ships, so as to shut up, he said, Asia a prisoner within Europe; but Aristides, disliking the design, said: 'We have hitherto fought with an enemy who has regarded little else but his pleasure and luxury; but if we shut him up within Greece, and drive him to necessity, he that is master of such great forces will no longer sit quiet with an umbrella of gold over his head, looking upon the fight for his pleasure; but in such a strait will attempt all things; he will be resolute, and will appear himself in person upon all occasions, he will soon correct his errors, and supply what he has formerly omitted through remissness, and will be better advised in all things'" (Plut. *Them.* 16). Such moralizing is not alien to the postwar environment with its sharp dichotomy between Greeks and "barbarians." In fact, the contrast between Greek poverty and Persian luxury may have been provided a regular spectacle for audiences in the Athenian Theater of Dionysus: based on passages in Pausanias, Plutarch, and Vitruvius, "It has been suggested that [the "luxurious marquee" of Xerxes (i.e. the tent of *Mardonius* displayed by Pausanias in Hdt. 9.82)] which may have been as much as 60 metres (197 feet) wide, was reassembled on the area next to the temple of Dionysus, and became both the backcloth and the backstage for the dramas that were performed after the war" (Connolly, *The Ancient City,* 92).

72. For dating, composition, recitations, and "publication" of the *Histories,* see Fornara, "Evidence for the Date of Herodotus' Publication"; Herodotus alludes, for instance, to "war between the Peloponnesians and the Athenians" (7.137.1) and the Theban attempt to seize Plataea in 431 (7.233.2). For pessimistic interpretations of the *Histories'* conclusion, see Moles, "Herodotus Warns the Athenians"; and Desmond, "Punishments and the Conclusion of Herodotus' *Histories.*"

73. See 5.78 for Herodotus' encomium of Athenian freedom.

74. On hatred of Athens, see for example Thuc. 2.11.2, 2.64.5, 3.37.2.

75. See *supra*, chapter 3, n.17 for references.

76. Thuc. 1.86 (Sthenelaidas), 2.63.2 (Pericles), 3.37.2 (Cleon); cf. 1.122.3, 1.124.3 (Corinthians).

77. Dion. Hal. *Thuc.* 37–41, esp. 39 (βασιλεῦσι γὰρ βαρβάροις ταῦτα πρὸς ῞Ελληνας ἥρμοττε λέγειν· κτλ.) and 42 (Thucydides' exile).

78. "Between ourselves and the Athenians alliance began, when you withdrew from the Median War and they remained to finish the business. But we did not become allies of the Athenians for the subjugation of the Hellenes, but allies of the Hellenes for their liberation from the Mede; and as long as the Athenians led us fairly we followed them loyally; but when we saw them relax their hostility to the Mede, to try to compass the subjection of the allies, then our apprehension began" (Thuc. 3.10.2–4). See Price, *Thucydides and Internal War*, 128–38 for a detailed discussion of the Mytilenians' speech and "frank equation between Athens and Persia" (135).

79. Thuc. 3.62.1–2, 3.64.

80. Thuc. 6.76.

81. Thuc. 1.121.3 (ὠνετὴ γὰρ ἡ Ἀθηναίων δύναμις μᾶλλον ἢ οἰκεία κτλ).

82. Thuc. 1.83.2.

83. Thuc. 1.86.3.

84. De Ste. Croix knows "of no parallel to this overruling of a king who was the leading Spartan of his day, except perhaps in 440" (*The Origins of the Peloponnesian War*, 143).

85. For Thucydides' revolutionary understanding of the role money in warfare, see Kallet-Marx, *Money, Expense, and Naval Power in Thucydides' History 1-5.24*, especially 11–16. For one application of the contrast between old and new, see her discussion of Archidamus and Sthenelaidas, 80–89.

86. See for example, Thuc. 2.13.2 and 2.13.9 (summarizing 2.13.5–9).

87. Thuc. 1.141.2–142.1.

88. Thuc. 2.13.9.

89. Thuc. 2.65.13.

90. Thuc. 2.65.7–13.

91. Thuc. 2.65.8 (Pericles as χρημάτων διαφανῶς ἀδωρότατος).

92. Thuc. 6.24.3 (ἔρως ἐνέπεσε τοῖς πᾶσιν ὁμοίως ἐκπλεῦσαι).

93. Thuc. 2.65.11. Kallet-Marx goes so far as to conclude that Thucydides' narrative of the Sicilian Expedition is specifically written "to impart lessons," though these are less moralistic than traditional tales of the fall of the mighty (*Money and the Corrosion of Power in Thucydides*, 181).

94. Thuc. 6.31.6.

95. See Plutarch's *Life of Nicias* for ambivalent reactions in Syracuse to Gylippus, uncouth and long-haired, yet the representative of the formidable Spartan army. According to Plutarch (and, he says, Thucydides and Philistus also), Gylippus' leadership was the primary cause of the eventual Syracusan victory (*Nic.* 19). Cf. Plutarch's comments on Sparta's high reputation in general: "For they [those cities that appealed to Sparta for aid] did not send petitions to them for ships or money, or a supply of

armed men, but only for a Spartan commander; and, having obtained one, used him with honour and reverence; so the Sicilians behaved to Gylippus, the Chalcidians to Brasidas, and all the Greeks in Asia to Lysander, Callicratidas, and Agesilaus" (*Lyc.* 30). Gylippus' name was still evoked, perhaps even revered, in fourth-century Syracuse— the city of the Cynic Monimus: see Plut. *Dio,* 49.

96. Xen. *Hell.* 2.2.23.

97. Xen. *An.* 6.1.26–28.

98. Xen. *Hell.* 2.4.40–41 (italics added). The rich detail of Xenophon's chapters on Thrasybulus' success and Pausanias' withdrawal from Athens suggest that Xenophon was particularly well informed on these events and that Thrasybulus in fact delivered such a speech.

99. Plut. *Ages.* 14. Plutarch records enough anecdotes with specifics of location, character, and conversation that it is difficult curtly to dismiss them all as later moralizing interpolations: (1) "When by Agesilaus' order the prisoners he had taken in Phrygia were exposed to sale, they were first stripped of their garments and then sold naked. The clothes found many customers to buy them, but the bodies being, from the want of all exposure and exercise, white and tender-skinned, were derided and scorned as unserviceable. Agesilaus, who stood by at the auction, told his Greeks, 'These are the men against whom you fight, and these the things we will gain by it'" (*Ages.* 9). (2) "Agesilaus coming first to the appointed place, threw himself down upon the grass under a tree, lying there in expectation of Pharnabazus, who, bringing with him soft skins, and wrought carpets to lie down upon, when he saw Agesilaus' posture, grew ashamed of his luxuries, and made no use of them, but laid himself down upon the grass also, without regard for his delicate and richly dyed clothing" (*Ages.* 12). (3) In Egypt, Agesilaus refused at first presents of sweetmeats, confections, and perfumes, then took them and gave them to the helots in his army, considering all such luxuries slavish (*Ages.* 36). These stories are not later inventions: see Xen. *Hell.* 4.29–38 (a meeting between Agesilaus and Pharnabazus), Xen. *Ages.* 1.28 (sale of Persian prisoners) and 1.34 (Persian nobles humbled).

100. Isoc. 5.124; cf. 4.143–49, 151–52, 154.

101. Arr. *Anab.* 7.9.2–6.

102. Curt. 6.2.1–3. Cf. Curt. 6.6.1–5, Diod. Sic. 17.77.4ff.

103. Plut. *Tim.* 11.6.

104. Plut. *Tim.* 29.4–6.

105. Arist. *Pol.* 1271a26–37.

106. Pl. *Resp.* 548a5–b2; see also *supra,* chapter 2, n.102.

107. For some historians' agreement, see Plutarch, *Lyc.* 30, *Agis,* 3, 5; cf. Forrest, *A History of Sparta,* 124. Despite his skepticism, Fine effectively accepts the ancient explanation (*The Ancient Greeks,* 157–61). The Delphic oracle, said to have been delivered to Lycurgus himself, became proverbial: ἁ φιλοχρηματία Σπάρταν ὀλεῖ, ἄλλο δὲ οὐδέν, "love of money, and nothing else, will destroy Sparta" (Diod. Sic. 7.12.5, Zen. 2.24, Plut. *Apophthegmata Laconica,* 239e13, and attributed to Aristotle's *Lacedaimonian Constitution* by the scholiast to Euripides' *Andromache,* 446).

108. Arist. *Rh.* 1398b18–20 (Alcidamas on the proven benefits of philosophical rule). On Epaminondas' social asceticism, see Plut. *Lyc.* 13.

109. Pl. *Symp.* 219e5–221c1.

110. Xen. *Mem.* 1.2.12–16, 24. Cf. *Mem.* 3.5.13 and Grote: "He [Socrates] is the semi-philosophical general; undervalued indeed as a hybrid by Plato—but by high-minded Romans like Cato, Agricola, Helvidius Priscus &c. likely to be esteemed higher than Plato himself" (*Plato and the other Companions of Sokrates,* 206–7).

111. Pl. *Chrm.* 153a1–d5.

112. On mercenaries playing tyrant, see, for example, Pl. *Resp.* 575a1–d2.

113. Paradox of the citizen-soldier: Pl. *Resp.* 375b9–d2; cf. Xen. *Mem.* 3.1.6. Dogs: Pl. *Resp.* 375e1–4.

114. Pl. *Resp.* 422a8–c10.

115. Pl. *Ti.* 19c2–c9.

116. Philosopher-rulers and their lifestyle: Pl. *Criti.* 112b3–c7, 112e2–6. Their intellectual studies: *Criti.* 110c5–d4, 112b3–e1. Athena and Hephaestus: *Criti.* 109c4–d2, 112b3–5.

117. Superlative wealth of Atlantis: Pl. *Criti.* 114d4–8. Center of trade: *Criti.* 117e4–8. Baths: *Criti.* 117a4–b5.

118. Eg. Hdt. 1.59.5, 2.168.2, 3.127.1; Pl. *Resp.* 566b5–8, 575b2; Arist. *Pol.* 1311a7–8, *Rh.* 1357b30–1358a1.

119. Pl. *Criti.* 120e6–121a3.

120. Note the verbal resemblances between Herodotus' opening sentence (ἔργα μεγάλα τε καὶ θωμαστά, τῷ χρόνῳ, ἀκλεᾶ / ἐξίτηλα γένηται) and *Timaeus* 20e4–6 (μεγάλα καὶ θαυμαστὰ ... ἔργα, ὑπὸ χρόνου, ἀνθρώπων ἠφανισμένα εἴη).

121. See Dunbabin, *The Western Greeks,* for detailed references to the legendary wealth and decadence of Sybaris (75–83) and its annihilation (361–68).

122. Persian poverty: Hdt. 1.71.2–4. Clearing thorny fields: 1.125–26.

123. Xenophon's Cyrus is a paladin, ever chivalrous and just, as Herodotus' was not. Thus Höistad writes: "In Herodotus, Cyrus appears as the indefatigable conqueror, who attacks without provocation one land after another [eg. I.178, 190, 201, 204]. Xenophon, on the other hand, makes the Assyrian and the Armenian wars begin with the foreigners' invasion of Median-Persian territory. [I.4.16ff] The Assyrian war is depicted as a diplomatically well-prepared war of aggression on the part of Assyria. Cyrus' campaigns against various peoples are presented as wars of liberation from Assyrian overlords" (*CHCK,* 84–85; square brackets in original).

124. See, for example, how the Persian officers are called *homotimoi,* similar to the Spartiate *homoioi* (Xen. *Cyr.* 2.1.9, 7.5.85).

125. Xen. *Cyr.* 7.5.74–85. Free agora: *Cyr.* 1.2.3. For Xenophon's conviction that superior virtue gives one the right to rule others, see passages like *Cyr.* 7.5.78, 7.5.83, 8.1.37–38.

126. In Crates' line, Pêra bears thyme and garlic and figs and bread (Diog. Laert. 6.85). θύμος means "thyme," but when accented on the last syllable (θυμός) "courage" or "spirit, mettle" as Dudley notes (*HC,* 57n.8γ). Thyme was a food eaten by Aristophanes' poor (*Plut.* 253, 283 and other references in *LSJ* under θύμος).

127. Diog. Laert. 6.23. For the standard demand that soldiers endure "heat and cold," see for instance Xen. *An.* 3.1.23; *Mem.* 1.2.1, 1.4.13, 1.6.2, 1.6.5, 2.1.1, 2.1.6, *Oec.*

5.4, *HG* 5.1.15, *Ages.* 5.3, 9.5, *Cyr.* 1.2.10, 8.1.36; Plut. *Ages.* 14.2 etc. On the heat of battle in summer, wearing armor, padding, etc., see Hanson, *The Western Way of War*, 79–81.

128. Diog. Laert. 6.59. Such praise may be begrudging, as in another anecdote, Diogenes can find "good men" nowhere, and even in Sparta only boys (Diog. Laert. 6.27); ἄνδρες ἀγαθοί is a standard phrase for heroes and patriots.

129. Arist. *Rh.* 1411a24.

130. Diog. Laert. 6.12. Cf. Heraclitus fr. 49 ("in my eyes, one man is worth ten thousand, if he is the best").

131. For the metaphor of the arrows of Fortune, see Cic. *Nat. D.* 3.83, 3.86; Dio Chrys. 64.18. One might compare the older conceit that the Persian bow never defeated the Greek hoplite (Aesch. *Pers.* 144–49).

132. Diog. Laert. 6.12. Cf. Dem. 60.1 (*aretê* is ἀνυπέρβλητον παντὶ λόγῳ).

133. Diog. Laert. 6.14, 7.30.

134. Diog. Laert. 6.13. Cf. Cic. *Paradoxa Stoicorum*, 27 (sapientis animus . . . virtutibus denique omnibus ut moenibus saeptus); Pl. *Leg.* (778d3–79a8) where following Sparta, the Cretan city will be unwalled, in order to force its citizens to train for war.

135. Diog. Laert. 6.93 (ἔχειν δὲ πατρίδα ἀδοξίαν καὶ πενίαν ἀνάλωτα τῇ τύχῃ). Cf. Arr. *Epict. diss.* 3.24.66. Following Cynic precedent, the Stoics would commonly say that virtue alone saves cities and lives (Diog. Laert. 6.14, 7.30) and compare philosophy to a well-walled city, ruled in accordance with reason (Diog. Laert. 7.40). Xenophon uses the word in a metaphorical way to praise Agesilaus' "unstormable soul" (Xen. *Ages.* 8.8: ψυχὴ ἀνάλωτος).

136. Crates, fr. 17 (Stob. *Flor.* 4.33.31 = Giannantoni, V H 83). Cf. Diog. Laert. 6.86; *HC*, 44.

137. Antisthenes wrote three books on Heracles (Diog. Laert. 6.15–18). For the Cynic emulation of Heracles, see, for instance, Diog. Laert. 6.71; *26th Letter* of Diogenes; Luc. *Vit. auct.* 10; Julian. *Or.* 6.187; Apul. *Flor.* 22.

138. Odysseus unarmed, unaided: Antisth. *Od.* 2, 14. Odysseus using weapons of a slave: Antisth. *Od.* 10. For the list of Antisthenes' works related to Odysseus and the Homeric poems, see Diog. Laert. 6.15–18. Cf. *7th Letter* of Diogenes (Malherbe); *19th Letter* of "Crates" (Malherbe); and Sayre, *Diogenes of Sinope*, 29 for many more references.

139. Diog. Laert. 6.53.

140. See, for instance, the Homeric leaders' repeated appeals to αἰδώς (Hom. *Il.* 5.787, 8.228, 13.95, 15.502, 16.422); or the standard appeal to the πρόγονοι and πατέρες.

141. Diogenes Laertius writes that Antisthenes fought with the Athenians at "Tanagra" (Diog. Laert. 6.1); this may be the Tanagra of 426, as in Thuc. 3.9.1. There is a remote possibility that Diogenes and Crates fought at Chaeronea, when Demosthenes was desperate to enlist all fighting men, including metics. Yet if so, they are not reported to have boasted of the fact later or touted any military service. For the Cynic condemnation of war and militarism as stupid and useless, see the anecdote of Diogenes rolling his *pithos* up and down prior to Alexander's attack on Corinth (Luc. *Hist. conscr.* 3); or his quip that generals are like mule-drivers, a witticism that plays on the etymology of στρατηγός, literally "army-driver" (Diog. Laert. 6.92); and most

of all, Crates' poem, *Pêra*. On the other hand, other anecdotes indicate the Cynics' interest at least in the moral aspects of contemporary wars: after the battle of Leuctra, Antisthenes said that the Thebans were as elated as little boys who have beaten their *paidagôgos* (Plu. *Lyc.* 30.6; cf. *CC*, 50).

142. According to Herodotus's Croesus, no one is so stupid as to pass over peace for war, in which parents bury their children rather than vice versa (Hdt. 1.87.4); cf. the "Persian" astonishment at Greek *nomoi*—why do these Greeks fight like this (Hdt. 7.9.2; *supra*, chapter 3, n.23)? For Plato's criticism of war as the ultimate expression of the body's aggressive greed, see *Resp.* 373e5–9, *Phd.* 66c1–d5, and *supra*, chapter 2, n.125. For Aristotle, war and κίνησις exist for the sake of peace and rest, the natural condition.

143. See Lys. 2.31, and Isoc. 4.92, 6.9.

144. Dem. 60.19–20, 60.21–22; cf. 18.300, 18.303 for similar language. In 18.247, Demosthenes boasts that "in my person, the city is invincible" (ἀήττητος): Demosthenes "triumphed" over Philip by refusing his bribes throughout his political career.

145. Lycurg. *Leoc.* 48. According to Hyperides' funeral oration, those who died in the Lamian war did not die at all: by benefiting their city, they have become famous and are therefore "born anew" (*Epit.* 27).

146. For the adjective ἀνίκητος used (1) of Heracles, see Tyrtaeus, fr. 11 (West); Soph. *Phil.* 77–78; (2) the Spartans, descendants of Heracles, see Tyrtaeus, fr. 11 (West), Diod. Sic. 15.56, 15.31; (3) of Alexander and the Macedonians, see Plut. *Alex.* 3, 14, *Pyrrh.* 19; Diod. Sic. 17.51, 17.93, 18.53; Dio Chrys. 4.24; (4) of the Cynic-Stoic philosopher, see Arr. *Epict. diss.* 1.18.21–23, 2.20.18 ("so powerful and ἀνίκητος is human nature"); (5) of Plato's spirited philosopher-kings, see *Resp.* 375a11–b2. In his essay on the adjective ἀνίκητος, Tarn does not consider its near synonym ἀήττητος, or the fact that the notion of the "undefeated" citizen-soldier and philosopher long preceded Alexander's career (*Alexander the Great*, 338–46).

CHAPTER FOUR
PRAISE OF POVERTY AND PHILOSOPHICAL WISDOM

1. Diog. Laert. 6.103. Dudley, for instance, repeats it (*HC*, ix).
2. Diog. Laert. 6.54.
3. *CHCK*, 103 and chapter 2, *passim*.
4. Zeller, *Socrates and the Socratic Schools*, 285.
5. "Only one account of the way is left—that Being exists. There are many proofs that Being is without birth and death, whole, alone of its kind, unmoving and without end. Nor does it have a past or future, since it is now together whole, one, continuous" (DK, 8.1–3).
6. For examples and an explanation of why Anaximander, Anaximenes, Heraclitus, Empedocles, Xenophanes, and other Pre-Socratics spoke of matter as "divine," see Jaeger, *The Theology of the Early Greek Philosophers*, 29ff; Guthrie, *A History of Greek Philosophy*, 1:67–68, 87–89, 402, 480.

7. DK B 67–9

8. See Dodds, *The Greeks and the Irrational*, chapter 5, and Guthrie, *A History of Greek Philosophy*, 2:11 with n.1 for further references. The comparison of Parmenides with shamans goes back at least to Diels' *Parmenides' Lehrgedicht, Griechisch und Deutsch*.

9. Pl. *Symp.* 174d3–175d2, 220c3–d5.

10. DK 28 B 1.1–3. Contrast DK 28 B 6.4 in which the nonphilosophical wander, "knowing nothing" (εἰδότες οὐδέν). Subsequent parenthetical citations in this chapter also refer to the Diels-Kranz text, unless otherwise noted.

11. Image of the road (ὁδός, πάτος, ἀταρπός): DK 28 B 1.1–2, 1.5, 1.27, 2.6, 6.3–7, 7.2–3, 8.1, 8.18, etc. Darkness to light: DK 28 B 1.8–10.

12. *The Science of Logic*, 83.

13. For Hegel's defense of the ontological argument, and for statements redolent of the Cynic indifference to externals, see *Science of Logic*, 89: "The reference back from particular finite being to being as such in its wholly abstract universality is to be regarded not only as the very first theoretical demand but as the very first practical demand too. When for example a fuss is made about the hundred dollars, that it does make a difference to the state of my fortune whether I have them or not, still more whether I am or not, or whether something else is or not, then—not to mention that there will be fortunes to which such possession of a hundred dollars will be a matter of indifference—we remind ourselves that man has a duty to rise to that abstract universality of mood in which he is indeed indifferent to the existence or non-existence of the hundred dollars, whatever may be their quantitative relation to his fortune, just as it ought to be matter of indifference to him whether he is or is not, that is, in finite life."

14. Diog. Laert. 9.21.

15. DK 59 B 17.

16. DK 68 B 9: νόμῳ γλυκύ, [καὶ] νόμῳ πικρόν, νόμῳ θερμόν, νόμῳ ψυχρόν, νόμῳ χροιή, ἐτεῆι δὲ ἄτομα καὶ κενόν; cf. DK 68 A 49. For the assertion that *tuchê* is merely a name for or an image of human ignorance, see DK 68 B 119.

17. DK 31 B 11. Cf. DK 31 B 2.3–6.

18. See esp. DK 31 B 2.3–6, 112, 113.

19. DK 31 B 120.

20. DK 31 B 112.4–5.

21. Comparing DK 31 B 29 and 134, Jaeger suggests that the primeval sphere of Love is also the "holy mind" whose thoughts dart quickly through the whole cosmos (*The Theology of the Early Greek Philosophers*, 153, 162). One suggestion has been that Empedocles equated the seer's enlightened condition with the initial state of the cosmos, when all things are united seamlessly by cosmic Love: knowledge is similar to love in that both unite disjoint particulars, the former in an intellectual, the later in a physical way.

22. DK 31 B 115.

23. DK 31 B 117.

24. DK 31 B 132.

25. DK 31 B 29.

26. DK 31 B 119.

27. For protreptic language, see DK 31 B 1, 2.8, 17.23; cf. Diog. Laert. 8.60–61.

28. DK 31 B 112.5–6; Cf. Diog. Laert. 8.73.

29. The phrase "meal of Syracusans" (Συρακόσιος τράπεζα) in Aristophanes was proverbial of luxurious living (fr. 216; cf. Pl. *7th Ep.* 326b5–d3; Julian. *Or.* 6.203a). Empedocles acknowledges the prosperity of Acragas in the opening of the *Katharmoi* when he alludes to the "great city" (μέγα ἄστυ) and its citizens "caring for their fine works" (ἀγαθῶν μελεδήμονες ἔργων) and "ignorant of evil" (κακότητος ἄπειροι). Guthrie here translates κακότης as "poverty" ("poverty or ill-fortune was a more likely meaning as applied to the wealthy, pleasure-loving [and meat-eating] Acragantines," *History of Greek Philosophy*, 2:246n.3); cf. Nelson's note on the word (*God and the Land*, 188n.19) and Diog. Laert. 8.63.

30. Diog. Laert. 9.3

31. Diog. Laert. 9.13–14.

32. Diog. Laert. 9.3.

33. Pl. *Prt.* 318a6–9.

34. Antisthenes, for instance, was a modest teacher of rhetoric before he met Socrates. Isocrates generalizes in his *Antidosis* (ca. 454) that most sophists live in poor or "very moderate circumstances": that is, Isocrates tries (disingenuously) to pass himself off as one of these undistinguished rhetoric-teachers (15.155). Cf. Lys. 33.3 ("sophists in dire straits and really in need of a livelihood").

35. Pl. *Ap.* 20b6–9. Skilled laborers made roughly a drachma a day: see *EAG*, 131–32. Socrates' statement that this is a very "reasonable price" probably expresses his own idealistic belief that virtue is worth any monetary sum.

36. Protagoras' hundred minas: Diog. Laert. 9.50, 9.52; cf. Quint. *Inst.* 3.1.10; Gellius, 5.3.7. Zeller writes that the sum is "no doubt greatly exaggerated" (*A History of Greek Philosophy*, 2:409n.2); the same fee of one hundred minas is ascribed to Gorgias (Diod. Sic. 12.53) and Zeno of Elea (Pl. *Alc.* I, 119a1–6). Hippocrates' hopes and despair: Pl. *Prt.* 310d8–e2.

37. For detailed references, Zeller, *A History of Greek Philosophy*, 2:409n.2, 410n.1, 415n.3, 417n.7, 421n.3.

38. Wood-carrier: Diog. Laert. 9.53 and Ath. 8.50, quoting a letter of Epicurus. Protagoras' wealth: Pl. *Meno* 91d2–5.

39. Pl. *Hp. mai.* 282d6–e8.

40. Isocrates writes that he knew no Sophist richer than Gorgias (15.155). Cf. Pl. *Hp. mai.* 282b4–c1, Xen. *Symp.* 1.5, Ath. 3.80 on the wealth of Protagoras and Gorgias. For Gorgias' statue, see Plin. *HN* 33.4, 33.83. Purple clothes: Ael. *VH* 12.32.

41. See the description of potential "transactions": if you give Protagoras money and persuade him to teach you, he will make you wise too (Pl. *Prt.* 310d6–8); Agathon thinks that if he sits next to Socrates, wisdom may be poured from one to the other like water from jar to jar, as if wisdom were a physical thing (Pl. *Symp.* 175c6–e6). Similarly, Pindar was intrigued by the notion of poems being transported as if they were physical goods: *logoi* become an imported delicacy, *opson* (*Nem.* 8.21) and *encômia* are shipped off like freight (*Nem.* 6.32–3); cf. *Pyth.* 2.67–68, *Nem.* 6.57–61, and Kurke, *The Traffic in Praise*, 58–59.

42. Pejorative: Ar. *Nub.* 331, 1111. Hippocrates: Pl. *Prt.* 312a1–7. Anytus: Pl. *Meno* 91c1–5.

43. For a summary of Plato's definitions of "sophist," see *Soph.* 231c–e. For other denigrations of sophists, see Pl. *Resp.* 493a6–9; Xen. *Cyn.* 13 ("the sophists hunt the rich and young, while philosophers are open and friendly with all; they neither honor nor dishonor the fortunes of men"), *Mem.* 1.6.13 (Socrates comparing sophists to prostitutes).

44. Arist. *Soph. el.* 165a21–22.

45. Philosopher, not sophist: Isoc. 10.6. Sophist's best pay: *Antid.* 220.

46. Prodicus' courses: Pl. *Cra.* 386a8–b8. Peasant-farmer of philosophy: Xen. *Symp.* 1.5.

47. Arist. *Pol.* 1259b2–12.

48. Socrates' house and total assets: Xen. *Oec.* 2.2–3. Sources are unanimous on Socrates' poverty: see, e.g., Pl. *Ap.* 23b7–c1, 31c2–3, 38b1–5; Xen. *Mem.* 1.2.1, *Oec.* 2.2, 11.3; cf. Zeller, *Socrates and the Socratic Schools*, 55n.1 for more references. Socrates' proposal of a one-mina penalty: Pl. *Ap.* 38b1–5.

49. See esp. Pl. *Ap.* 19e4–20a2. Cf. *Resp.* 600c2–d2, *Prt.* 316c5–d2; *Meno*, 91a1–b5, *Hp. mai.* 282b4–d3; Xen. *Mem.* 1.1.6.

50. Talking to everyone and anyone: Pl. *Ap.* 33a5–b3; Xen. *Symp.* 4.43, *Mem.* 1.1.10, 1.2.5–6, 1.2.60, 1.4.4, 1.6.13; cf. Xen. *Cyn.* 9, 13 and Pl. *Symp.* 216d7–e5. Socrates was not the only philosopher "in the market-place": Hippias also made displays among the stalls and bankers-tables of the *agora*. Compare Pl. *Hp. mi.* 368b2–5 with *Ap.* 17c7–d1; cf. Xen. *Mem.* 1.1.10, 4.1.1.

51. Epicharmus: Pl. [*Ax.*] 366c1–5. "Paying" Thrasymachus: Pl. *Resp.* 337d6–338b9.

52. Euthyphro's "wealth" of religious knowledge: Pl. *Euthphr.* 12a5–6. Thessaly's "wealth" of wisdom: *Meno*, 70a5–71b4. Xenophon attributes to this same Meno the tyrannical creed sketched by Glaucon in book 2 of the *Republic*: "Meno the Thessalian clearly had a fierce desire to be rich and to rule . . . so that he could commit injustice without having to suffer it" (Xen. *An.* 2.6.21–27). Compare the last phrase with Pl. *Resp.* 359a5–6. Callicles' view that philosophical λαλία makes the house "empty": *Grg.* 486c6–8, 485a4–e6. Socrates' response to Callicles: *Grg.* 486d2–d7. Socrates also calls Callicles a *hermaion* or lucky find (486e3). Phaedrus is golden: *Phdr.* 235d6–e4. Alcibiades on Socrates: *Symp.* 216e6–217a2. The external poverty and inner "wealth" of the philosopher king: see, e.g., *Resp.* 521a2–8, 547b5–7. The philosopher's prayer: *Phdr.* 279b8–c3, where Socrates prays that he might be made innerly beautiful and able to consider the "the wise man wealthy" (279c1). "Feast" or "gifts" of arguments: *Ly.* 211c10–d1, *Grg.* 447a3–6, *Soph.* 251b–c, *Ti.* 17a2–3, 20c1, 27b7–8. On the Greek love of talk, see the incident in the *Protagoras* when all eagerly draw their seats closer, delighted at the prospect of hearing the sophists speak. When Socrates gets up to leave early, the company all protest and Callias grabs him to prevent him from going (*Prt.* 335c8–d6). Old books as "treasure-troves": Xen. *Mem.* 1.6.14. Cicadas: Pl. *Phdr.* 259c2–d7. True Being as food for the soul: see esp. *Phdr.* 247e2–6, 248b5–c2. Rotten soul-food: *Prt.* 313a1–c3. For other instances of Socrates' use of such language, see *Ly.* 218c8, *Phd.* 69a, *Symp.* 218d6–219a1 (Alcibiades would exchange bronze for gold, as in the Homeric encounter between Diomedes

and Glaucon), *Cra.* 386a8–c2 (friends pooling knowledge when they cannot afford to hire the expert), *Grg.* 447a3–6, *Resp.* 458a1–2, 496c6, 521a2–6, *Plt.* 261e, *Hp. mi.* 364b2 (an offering of wisdom); Xen. *Mem.* 4.2.9 (wise thoughts "enrich" their possessor), *Symp.* 3.8–9, 4.2, 4.29–45 (esp. 34, 43–44), *Oec.* 2 (esp. 2.1–10 where poor Socrates is "rich" while rich Critobulus is "poor"). Cf. Democr. DK 68 B 40, 77, 171, 178 (Democritus would prefer to find one causal relation, *aitiologia*, than be king of Persia.

    53. Xen. *Symp.* 4.2, 4.43.

    54. Pl. *Ap.* 23b7–c1.

    55. Pl. *Symp.* 215c7.

    56. Esp. Pl. *Symp.* 215d1–216c3, 217e6–218b4.

    57. Pl. *Meno* 79e7–80b2.

    58. Aristodemus: Pl. *Symp.* 173b1–4, 174a3–d3. Apollodorus: Pl. *Symp.* 173c5–e3; cf. Xen. *Mem.* 3.11.17.

    59. Diog. Laert. 3.5, Ael. *VH* 2.30.

    60. Diog. Laert. 6.2; Cf. Jer. *Adv. Iovinian.* 2.14; *CC*, 52.

    61. Pl. *Symp,* 210e6–211a5.

    62. Compare Parmenides, fr. 8.3–33. Cf. Dover, *Symposium, ad loc;* and Palmer, *Plato's Reception of Parmenides,* 3–4, 17.

    63. Pl. *Symp.* 211c5–e4 (my translation). Compare Alcibiades' later description of Socrates' scorn for wealth and honor, and how he passes through the world laughing and playing—for nothing here is worth one's seriousness (216d7–e5).

    64. Pl. *Phdr.* 247c6–e2.

    65. The lover's infatuation: Pl. *Phdr.* 252a1–7. Nine types of *erôs*, ranked as stages of progressive enlightenment: *Phdr.* 248c5–e5. Intuiting "the really real": see, e.g., *Phdr.* 247c6–e2. Crippled souls, broken wings: *Phdr.* 248a–b. Despising lower reality: *Phdr.* 249c1–4. The "many" think the philosopher mad: *Phdr.* 249c5–d3.

    66. Philosophy as μελέτη θανάτου: Pl. *Phd.* 81a2. Body the locus of evil: *Phd.* 64–65a, 114e. Perfection is not here: *Phd.* 110a1–6. Soul curling into itself: see, e.g., *Phd.* 66a1–7.

    67. Pl. *Phd.* 78a1–9.

    68. Flight and ὁμοίωσις θεῷ κατὰ τὸ δυνατόν: Pl. *Tht.* 176a8–b2. Thinking the whole: *Tht.* 174d1–e5. Thracian maid and popular mockery: *Tht.* 174a4–176a2.

    69. The masses, wandering through the blooming confusion of the senses, cannot be philosophers: Pl. *Resp.* 484b3–7, 490a8–b7, and esp. 493e2–494a5 (φιλόσοφον πλῆθος ἀδύνατον εἶναι). What is Socrates' line of work: *Ap.* 20c4 (ἀλλ', ὦ Σώκρατες, τὸ σὸν τί ἐστι πρᾶγμα;).

    70. Philosopher as sea-captain and star-gazer: Pl. *Resp.* 489b3–c7. Philosopher, caught in storm of hostile culture: *Resp.* 496d2–e2. Persecution of the philosopher: *Resp.* 516e3–517a7; cf. *Grg.* 486a4–d1, 521c3–6.

    71. Wealth, glory and power are small: Pl. *Resp.* 485d10–486b2. The song of the Homeric Sirens: Hom. *Od.* 12.41–54, 12.153–200. Socrates as Siren: Pl. *Symp.* 216a. Archimedes' mathematical ecstasies: Plut. *Marc.* 17.11. Sirens and Fates: Pl. *Resp.* 617b–c. The "upper road" of philosophy and the Platonic "Way of Truth": *Resp.* 621b8–d3.

72. Socrates μετεωροσοφιστής: Ar. *Nub.* 360. Lampros: Phrynichus, fr. 69 (Kock). Euripides and dithyrambists: e.g., Ar. *Ach.* 395–401, *Pax*, 827–31.

73. Thales and the Thracian girl: Pl. *Tht.* 174a4–b7. Thales as man of affairs, engineer: Hdt. 1.75, 1.170.

74. *Hp. mai.* 281c3–8, 282e9–283b4.

75. Pl. *Symp.* 203c6–d8.

76. Why the gods and others do not philosophize: Pl. *Symp.* 204a1–7. Socrates has hardly ever been abroad: *Cri.* 51b1–52c3; cf. *Phdr.* 230d3–5. No one knows Socrates: *Symp.* 216c7–d1 (εὖ γὰρ ἴστε ὅτι οὐδεὶς ὑμῶν τοῦτον γιγνώσκει); cf. 215a2, 221c2–d6 (Socrates' strangeness, ἀτοπία).

77. For other anecdotes of the Cynics' rejection of the Platonic Forms, and of science itself, see Diog. Laert. 6.24 (Plato's classes a waste of time), 6.53 (I see a table, but not "tableness"), 6.103–5 (learning in general despised). Antisthenes himself is not typical of Diogenes' Cynics. Antisthenes wrote some sixty-two books (rolls): "From the titles of those works, we can identify treatises on logic, ethics, politics, history, music, biology, rhetoric, and other subjects, so that we would not be guilty of exaggeration in referring to him as an encyclopedic writer" (*CC*, 40).

78. See Arist. *Metaph.* 1024b32 (italics added). Cf. *CC*, 41.

79. See *CC*, 62–67: "Thus, the first proposition of Antisthenes' logic, having traveled a long road from Parmenides, and through the Sophists and Socrates, arrives at last at the doorstep of Cynicism and enters into it in the garb of an ethical proposition. Having shed along the way its Eleatic metaphysical trappings, it announces now an ethical program of action: the Cynic will have nothing to do with nothing, will not speak nothing or what is not, will not even attempt to understand nothing, and will begin to speak only what is. He will have no dealings with the lies and deceptions that constitute the structure that supports practically all human relationships and activities, from politics to religion, from public affairs to the most intimate sexual relations, from the most sophisticated educational endeavors to the noisy shouting of the crowd in athletic events" (65).

80. Diog. Laert. 6.13 (ἁπλοκύων).

81. For the Cynic's debunking of *tuphos*, see, for example, Diog. Laert. 6.72, 83.

82. Hor. *Sat.* 2.7.83–88.

83. See *supra*, chapter 4, n.21.

84. Aristodemus and Apollodorus: Pl. *Symp.* 172c3–173b2, 173d4–10. Philosophy and Socrates: Pl. *Grg.* 482a6–b1, 491a1–3, *Symp.* 221e5–6.

85. Compare with Navia on the sources of the unity of Cynicism: from the virtue of *atuphia* or clarity of mind, "all the other virtues of which the Cynics spoke flow naturally . . . : we become indifferent to inconsequential things and circumstances; we develop in ourselves a great deal of self-sufficiency and independence from others; we break asunder the fetters that tie us to the atavistic modes of thought and behavior manifested in blind political and nationalistic allegiances, in superstitious religious beliefs and practices, in the pointless pursuit of pleasures and wealth, and in many other manifestations of what the Cynics conceived of as human madness" (*CC*, ix).

1. The exception that proves the rule may be Cercidas of Megalopolis who writes of his "unshakeable heart" and of being "unconquered" by luxury (fr. 7, Powell): the politics and hoplite warfare that Cercidas knew were of a piece with those of mainland Greece in the fifth and fourth centuries.

2. "Of the bronze guts," for his endurance in writing 3500 rolls, more than any previous writer.

3. These, in Tarn's judgment, "expressed Hellenism as nothing else ever did—the whole tumult of the age, the meeting of civilization and barbarism, the conflict of good and evil, the striving with unfamiliar ways of expression, knowing no rest—all is there" (*Hellenistic Civilization,* 320).

4. Smith, *Hellenistic Sculpture,* 34, 36, referring to Vatican 288, an inscribed copy of the late third-century statue by Phyromachus of Athens.

5. Plin. *HN* 7.151; Val Max. 7.1.2. Cf. Levi, *The Cultural Atlas of the Greek World,* 182.

6. Euseb. *Hist. eccl.* 4.11.8, letter 9. For more references, see Boas, *Primitivism and Related Ideas in the Middle Ages,* 104–8.

7. See, for instance, Boyd, *Cynic, Sage, or Son of God;* Downing, *Cynics and Christian Origins;* Attridge, *First Century Cynicism in the Epistles;* and Martin, *Philosophy and Empty Deceit: Colossians as Response to a Cynic Critique.*

8. *HC,* 212.

BIBLIOGRAPHY

TEXTS

Greek texts are from the Oxford Classical Text (OCT) series, with the following exceptions:

Arrighetti, G. *Epicuro. Opere*. Turin: Einaudi, 1960.

Caizzi, F. *Antisthenis fragmenta*. Milan: Instituto Editoriale Cisalpino, 1966.

Campbell, D. A. *Greek Lyric Poetry*. Bristol: Bristol Classical Press, 1967.

Diels, H., and W. Kranz. *Die Fragmente der Vorsokratiker*. 6th ed. Berlin: Weidmann, 1951–1954.

Edmonds, J. M. *The Fragments of Attic Comedy*. Leiden: Brill, 1957.

Hausrath, A., and H. Hunger. *Corpus fabularum Aesopicarum*. 2nd ed. Leipzig: Teubner, 1970.

Hense, O. *Teletis reliquiae*. Tübingen, 1909; Hildesheim: Olms, 1969.

Jacoby, F. *Die Fragmente der griechischen Historiker*. 3rd ed. New York: E. J. Brill, 1993–1999.

Kock, T. *Comicorum Atticorum fragmenta*. Leipzig: Teubner, 1880.

Lobel, E., and D. L. Page. *Poetarum Lesbiorum fragmenta*. Oxford: Clarendon Press, 1955.

Malherbe, A., ed. *The Cynic Epistles: A Study Edition*. Missoula, Mont.: Scholars Press, 1977.

Nauck, A. *Tragicorum Graecorum fragmenta*. Leipzig: Teubner, 1889; Hildesheim: Olms, 1964.

Powell, J. U., ed. *Collectanea Alexandrina*. Oxford: Clarendon Press, 1925.

Snell, B. *Tragicorum Graecorum fragmenta*. Gottingen: Vandenhoeck, 1971.

Young, D. *Theognis*. 2nd ed. Leipzig: Teubner, 1971.

West, M. L. *Iambi et Elegi Graeci*. Oxford: Clarendon Press, 1971.

TRANSLATIONS

Translations are my own except for those excerpted from the following (unless otherwise indicated).

Adams, F., trans. *Hippocratic Writings*. Great Books of the Western World 10. Chicago: Encyclopaedia Britannica, 1952.

Brownson, C. L., trans. *Xenophon: Hellenica*. Cambridge, Mass.: Harvard University Press, 1961–1968.

Crawley, R., trans. *Thucydides: The History of the Peloponnesian War*. Great Books of the Western World 6. Revised by R. Feetham. Chicago: Encyclopaedia Britannica, 1952.

"Dryden" Translation of Plutarch's *Lives*. Great Books of the Western World 14. Chicago: Encyclopaedia Britannica, 1952.

Evelyn-White, H. G., trans. *Hesiod, the Homeric Hymns, and Homerica*. Cambridge, Mass.: Harvard University Press; 1982.

Jowett, B., trans. *The Dialogues of Plato*. Great Books of the Western World 7. Chicago: Encyclopaedia Britannica, 1952.

———. trans. *Politics*. In *The Works of Aristotle*, Great Books of the Western World 9. Chicago: Encyclopaedia Britannica, 1952.

Lamb, W. R., trans. *Lysias*. Cambridge, Mass.: Harvard University Press, 1976.

Marchant, E. C., trans. *Memorabilia*. In *Xenophon: Memorabilia, Oeconomicus, Symposium and Apology*. Cambridge, Mass.: Harvard University Press, 1979.

Miller, A. V., trans. *Hegel's Science of Logic*. New York: Humanities Press, 1969.

Moore, S., trans. *Manifesto of the Communist Party*. Great Books of the Western World 50. Chicago: Encyclopaedia Britannica, 1952.

Moore, S., and S. Aveling, trans. *Marx: Capital*. Great Books of the Western World 50. Chicago: Encyclopaedia Britannica, 1952.

Norlin, G., trans. *Isocrates*. 3 vols. Cambridge, Mass.: Harvard University Press, 1968.

Rawlinson, G., trans. *The History of Herodotus*. Great Books of the Western World 6. Chicago: Encyclopaedia Britannica, 1952.

Roberts, W. R., trans. *Rhetoric*. In *The Works of Aristotle*, Great Books of the Western World 9. Chicago: Encyclopaedia Britannica, 1952.

Ross, W. D., trans. *Nichomachean Ethics*. In *The Works of Aristotle*, Great Books of the Western World 9. Chicago: Encyclopaedia Britannica, 1952.

Tester, S. J., trans. *The Consolation of Philosophy*. In *Boethius*. Cambridge, Mass.: Harvard University Press, 1973.

Todd. O. J., trans. *Symposium* and *Apology*. In *Xenophon: Memorabilia, Oeconomicus, Symposium and Apology*. Cambridge, Mass.: Harvard University Press, 1979.

Secondary Sources

Adkins, A. *Merit and Responsibility*. Oxford: Clarendon Press, 1960.

Allison, J. *Power and Preparedness in Thucydides*. Baltimore: Johns Hopkins University Press, 1989.

Andreades, A. M. *A History of Greek Public Finance*. Translated by C. Brown. Cambridge, Mass.: Harvard University Press, 1933.

Arnold, E. V. *Roman Stoicism*. New York: Humanities Press, 1958.

———. "Stoicism." In *Encyclopaedia of Ethics and Religion*, ed. J. Hastings. New York: Charles Scribner's Sons, 1955.

Attridge, H., ed. and trans. *First century Cynicism in the Epistles of Heraclitus.* Missoula, Mont.: Scholars Press for the Harvard Theological Review, 1976.

Austin, M. M., and P. Vidal-Naquet. *Economic and Social History of Ancient Greece.* Translated by M.M. Austin. Berkeley: University of California Press, 1977.

Balme, M. "Attitudes to Work and Leisure in Ancient Greece." *Greece and Rome* 31 (1984): 140–52.

Balot, R. K. *Greed and Injustice in Classical Athens.* Princeton: Princeton University Press, 2001.

Barker, E. *Greek Political Theory: Plato and his Predecessors.* London: Methuen, 1979.

Beloch, K. J. *Griechische Geschichte.* 2nd ed. Strassburg: K.J. Trübner, 1912–27.

Berry, C. J. *The Idea of Luxury.* Cambridge: Cambridge University Press, 1994.

Bewes, T. *Cynicism and Postmodernity.* London: Verso Press, 1997.

Billerbeck, M. *Die Kyniker in der Modernen Forschung.* Amsterdam: B. R. Grüner, 1991.

———. "Le Cynisme idéalisé d'Épictète à Julien." In *Le Cynisme ancien et ses prolongements: Actes du Colloque International du CNRS,* ed. M. O. Goulet-Cazé and R. Goulet. Paris: Presses Universitaires de France, 1993.

Billot, M. F. "Antisthène et le Cynosarges dans l'Athènes des Ve et IVe siècles." In *Le Cynisme ancien et ses prolongements: Actes du Colloque International du CNRS,* ed. M. O. Goulet-Cazé and R. Goulet. Paris: Presses Universitaires de France, 1993.

Boas, G. *Primitivism and Related Ideas in the Middle Ages.* Baltimore: Johns Hopkins University Press, 1997.

Boedeker, D., and K. Raaflaub, eds. *Democracy, Empire, and the Arts in Fifth-century Athens.* Cambridge, Mass.: Harvard University Press, 1998.

Bolkestein, H. *Economic Life in Greece's Golden Age.* Edited by E. Jonkers. Leiden: E. J. Brill, 1958.

Bowra, C. M. *The Greek Experience.* New York: New American Library, 1957.

———. "Xenophanes' Fragment 3." *Classical Quarterly* 35 (1941): 119–26.

Boyd, G. *Cynic, Sage, or Son of God?* Wheaton, Ill.: Victor Books, 1995.

Branham, R. B., and M. O. Goulet-Cazé, eds. *The Cynics: The Cynic Movement in Antiquity and its Legacy.* Berkeley: University of California Press, 1996.

Braund, D. "The Luxuries of Athenian Democracy." *Greece and Rome* 41 (1994), 41–48.

Brown, T. S. *Onesicritus.* Berkeley: University of California Press, 1949.

Buchanan, J. *Theorika: A Study of Monetary Distributions to the Athenian Citizenry during the Fifth and Fourth Centuries B.C.* Locust Valley, N.Y.: J. J. Augustin, 1962.

Bury, J. B. *A History of Greece to the Death of Alexander the Great.* 3rd ed. Revised by R. Meiggs. London: Macmillan, 1963.

———. *The Idea of Progress.* New York: Dover Publications, 1960.

Butler, F. G. "Who are King Lear's Philosophers? An Answer with Some Help from Erasmus." *English Studies* 67 (1986): 511–24.

Campbell, D. A. *Greek Lyric Poetry.* Bristol: Bristol Classical Press, 1967.

Carter, L. B. *The Quiet Athenian.* Oxford: Clarendon Press, 1986.

Cartledge, P. "The Economy (Economies) of Ancient Greece." *Dialogus* 5 (1998), 4–24.

Cartledge, P., E. Cohen, and L. Foxhall, eds. *Money, Labour and Land: Approaches to the Economics of Ancient Greece.* New York: Routledge, 2002.

Cartledge, P., P. Millett, and S. von Reden, eds. *Kosmos: Essays in Order, Conflict, and Community in Classical Athens.* Cambridge: Cambridge University Press, 1998.

Cartledge, P., P. Millett, and S. Todd, eds. *Nomos: Essays in Athenian Law, Politics, and Society.* Cambridge: Cambridge University Press, 1990.

Casson, L. *The Ancient Mariners.* New York: Macmillan, 1959.

Chroust, A. H. *Socrates: Man and Myth; The Two Socratic Apologies of Xenophon.* Notre Dame: University of Notre Dame Press, 1957.

———. "On Bribery: Treason and Patriotism in Ancient Greece." *Journal of the History of Ideas* 15 (1954): 280–88.

Cohen, E. *Athenian Economy and Society: A Banking Perspective.* Princeton: Princeton University Press, 1992.

Connolly, P., and H. Dodge. *The Ancient City: Life in Classical Athens and Rome.* Oxford: Oxford University Press, 1998.

Connor, W. R. *Thucydides.* Princeton: Princeton University Press, 1984.

David, E. *Sparta between Empire and Revolution (404–243 B.C.): Internal Problems and Their Impact on Contemporary Greek Consciousness.* New York: Arno Press, 1981.

Davidson, J. *Courtesans and Fishcakes: The Consuming Passions of Classical Athens.* New York: St. Martin's Press, 1997.

Davies, J. K. "Ancient Economies: Models and Muddles." In *Trade, Traders, and the Ancient City,* ed. H. Parkins and C. Smith. New York: Routledge, 1998.

———. *Wealth and the Power of Wealth in Ancient Athens.* New York: Arno Press, 1981.

De Graaf, J., D. Wann, and T. Naylor, eds. *Affluenza: The All Consuming Epidemic.* San Francisco: Berrett-Koehler, 2001.

De Ste. Croix, G. E. M. *Class Struggle in the Ancient Greek World.* Ithaca: Cornell University Press, 1981.

———. "Political Pay outside Athens." *Classical Quarterly* 25 (1975): 48–52.

———. *The Origins of the Peloponnesian War.* London: Duckworth, 1972.

Denyer, N. *Language, Truth and Falsehood in Ancient Greek Philosophy.* London: Routledge, 1991.

Desmond, W. "Punishments and the Conclusion of Herodotus' *Histories.*" *Greek, Roman, and Byzantine Studies* 44 (2004): 19–40.

Diels, H. *Parmenides' Lehrgedicht, Griechisch und Deutsch.* Berlin, 1897.

Dillery, J. *Xenophon and the History of his Times.* London: Routledge, 1995.

Dodds, E. R. *The Greeks and the Irrational.* Berkeley: University of California Press, 1963.

Doloff, S. " 'Let Me Talk with this Philosopher': The Alexander Paradigm in *King Lear.*" *The Huntington Library Quarterly* 54 (1991): 253–55.

Donlan, W. *The Aristocratic Ideal in Ancient Greece: Attitudes of Superiority from Homer to the End of the Fifth Century B.C.* Lawrence, Kans.: Colorado Press, 1980.

Doribal, G. "L'image des cyniques chez les Pères grecs." In *Le Cynisme ancien et ses prolongements: Actes du Colloque International du CNRS,* ed. M. O. Goulet-Cazé and R. Goulet. Paris: Presses Universitaires de France, 1993.

Dover, K. J. *Greek Popular Morality in the Time of Plato and Aristotle.* Indianapolis: Hackett Publishing, 1994.

———. *Aristophanic Comedy.* Berkeley: University of California Press, 1972.

Dover, K. J., ed. *Aristophanes' Clouds*. Oxford: Clarendon Press, 1989.

————. *Symposium*. Cambridge: Cambridge University Press, 1980.

Downing, F. G. *Cynics and Christian Origins*. Edinburgh: T. & T. Clark, 1992.

————. *Christ and the Cynics: Jesus and Other Radical Preachers in the First Century Tradition*. Sheffield: JSOT Press, 1988.

Dudley, D. *A History of Cynicism from Diogenes to the 6th Century A.D.* London: Methuen & Co., 1937.

Dunbabin, T. J. *The Western Greeks*. Oxford: Clarendon Press, 1948.

Durant, W. *The Life of Greece*. New York: Simon and Schuster, 1939.

Edelstein, L. *The Idea of Progress in Classical Antiquity*. Baltimore: Johns Hopkins University Press, 1967.

Edmunds, L. *Chance and Intelligence in Thucydides*. Cambridge, Mass.: Harvard University Press, 1975.

————. "Thucydides' Ethics as Reflected in the Description of *Stasis*." *Harvard Studies in Classical Philology* 79 (1973): 73–92.

Ehrenberg, V. *The People of Aristophanes*. Oxford, 1943; New York: Schocken, 1962.

Figueira, T. "KREMATA: Acquisition and Possession in Archaic Greece." In *Social Justice in the Ancient World*, ed. K. D. Irani and M. Silver. Westport, Conn.: Greenwood Press, 1995.

Fine, J. *The Ancient Greeks: A Critical History*. Cambridge, Mass.: Belknap Press of Harvard University Press, 1983.

Finley, M. I. *The Ancient Economy*. Updated ed. Berkeley: University of California Press, 1999.

————. *Economy and Society in Ancient Greece*. Penguin Books, 1981.

————. *The World of Odysseus*. 2nd ed. New York: Viking Press, 1978.

————. *Democracy Ancient and Modern*. New Brunswick, N.J.: Rutgers University Press, 1973.

Fisher, N. *Hybris: A Study in the Values of Honour and Shame in Ancient Greece*. Warminster: Aris and Phillips, 1992.

————. *Social Values in Classical Athens*. London: Dent & Sons, 1976.

Flynn, T. R. "Foucault as *Parrhesiast*: His Last Course at the College de France." In *The Final Foucault*, ed. J. Bernauer and D. Ramussen. Cambridge, Mass.: MIT Press, 1991.

————. "Foucault and the Politics of Postmodernity." *Nous* 23 (1989): 187–98.

Fornara, C. "Evidence for the Date of Herodotus' Publication." *Journal of Hellenic Studies* 91 (1971): 25–34.

Forrest, W. G. *A History of Sparta, 950-192 B.C.* London: Duckworth, 1980.

Foxhall, L. "Cargoes of the Heart's Desire: The Character of Trade in the Archaic Mediterranean World." In *Archaic Greece: New Approaches and New Evidence*, ed. N. Fisher and H. Van Wees. London: Duckworth, 1998.

Frank, R. H. *Luxury Fever: Why Money Fails to Satisfy in an Era of Excess*. New York: Free Press, 1999.

Fuks, A. *Social Conflict in Ancient Greece*. Jerusalem: Magness Press; Leiden: E. J. Brill, 1984.

Gabrielsen, V. *Financing the Athenian Fleet: Public Taxation and Social Relations*. Baltimore: Johns Hopkins University Press, 1994.

Galbraith, J. K. *The Affluent Society.* New York: New American Library, 1969.

Garlan, Y. *Guerre et economie en Grèce ancienne.* Paris, 1989.

———. *War in the Ancient World.* Translated by J. Lloyd. London, 1975.

Garnsey, P. *Famine and Food Supply in the Greco-Roman World.* Cambridge: Cambridge University Press, 1988.

———. "Peasants in Ancient Roman Society." *Journal of Peasant Studies* 3 (1976): 221–35.

Geremek, B. *Poverty: A History.* Translated by A. Kolakowska. Oxford: Blackwell Press, 1994.

Giannantoni, G., ed. *Socraticorum Reliquiae.* 4 vols. Naples: Edizioni dell' Ateneo, 1983–1985.

Gladisch, A. *Einleitung in das Verständniss der Weltgeschichte.* Posen: Heine, 1841.

Glotz, G. *The Greek City and its Institutions.* Translated by N. Mallinson. New York: Alfred A. Knopf, 1930.

———. *Ancient Greece at Work: An Economic History of Greece from the Homeric Period to the Roman Conquest.* New York: Kegan Paul, Trench, Trubner & Co., 1926.

Goettling, C. W. "Diogenes der Cyniker oder die Philosophie des griechischen Proletariats." In *Gesammelte Abhandlungen aus dem classischen Alterthume.* Halle: Verlag, 1851.

Gomme, A. W., A. Andrewes, and K. J. Dover. *A Historical Commentary on Thucydides I–V.* Oxford: Oxford University Press, 1945–1981.

Goulet-Cazé, M. O. *L'Ascèse Cynique: Un commentaire de Diogène Laërce VI.70–71.* Paris: J. Vrin, 1986.

———. "Télès le Cynique." *Revue des Études Grecques* 94 (1981): 166–72.

Goulet-Cazé, M. O., and R.B. Branham, eds. *The Cynics: The Cynic Movement in Antiquity and its Legacy.* Berkeley: University of California Press, 1996.

Goulet-Cazé, M. O., and R. Goulet, eds. *Le Cynisme ancien et ses prolongements: Actes du Colloque International du CNRS.* Paris: Presses Universitaires de France, 1993.

Gribble, D. *Alcibiades and Athens.* Oxford: Clarendon Press, 1999.

Grote, G. *Plato and the Other Companions of Sokrates.* 4 vols. New York: Burt Franklin, 1974.

Guiraud, P. *La Main-d'oeuvre Industrielle dans l'Ancienne Grèce.* Paris: F. Alcan, 1900.

Gulick, C. B. "Preface" to *Athenaeus' The Deipnosophistae.* Cambridge, Mass.: Harvard University Press, 2003.

———. *The Life of the Ancient Greeks.* New York: D. Appleton, 1909.

Guthrie, W. K. C. *A History of Greek Philosophy.* 6 vols. Cambridge: Cambridge University Press, 1962–1981.

———. *Socrates.* Cambridge: Cambridge University Press, 1971.

———. *The Sophists.* Cambridge: Cambridge University Press, 1971.

Hamilton, C. D., and P. Krentz. *Polis and Polemos.* Claremont, Calif.: Regina Press, 1997.

Hansen, M. *The Athenian Democracy in the Age of Demosthenes: Structure, Principles, and Ideology.* Oxford: Blackwell Press, 1991.

Hanson, V. *The Other Greeks: The Family Farm and the Agrarian Roots of Western Civilization.* New York: Free Press, 1995.

————. *The Western Way of War*. Oxford: Oxford University Press, 1989

Harrison, A. R. W. *The Law of Athens*. 2 vols. London: Duckworth Press, 1998.

Hartog, F. *The Mirror of Herodotus: The Representation of the Other in the Writing of History*. Translated by J. Lloyd. Berkeley: University of California Press, 1988.

Harvey, D. *The Condition of Postmodernity: An Enquiry into the Origins of Cultural Change*. Cambridge, Mass.: Blackwell, 1989.

Hasebroek, J. *Staat und Handel im alten Griechenland*. Tübingen: J.C.B. Mohr, 1928.

Hastings, J., ed. *Encyclopedia of Ethics and Religion*. 13 vols. New York: Charles Scribner's Sons, 1955.

Havelock, E. *The Liberal Temper in Greek Politics*. London: Camelot, 1957.

Hegel, G. W. F. *The Science of Logic*. Translated by A. V. Miller. New York: Humanities Press, 1969.

Heitland, W. E. *Agricola*. Cambridge: Cambridge University Press, 1921.

Hemelrijk, J. *Penia en Ploutos*. New York: Arno Press, 1979.

Henne, D. "Cynique (École)." In *Dictionnaire des Sciences Philosophiques*, ed. A. Franck. Paris: Librairie Hachette, 1885.

Hock, R. "Simon the Shoemaker as an Ideal Cynic." *Greek, Roman, and Byzantine Studies* 17 (1976): 41–53.

Höistad, R. *Cynic Hero and Cynic King: Studies in the Cynic Conception of Man*. Uppsala: C.W.K. Gleerup, 1948.

Hopper, R. J. *Trade and Industry in Classical Greece*. London: Thames and Hudson, 1979.

Hornblower, S. *A Commentary on Thucydides*. Oxford: Clarendon Press, 1991–1996.

How, W. W., and J. Wells. *A Commentary on Herodotus*. 2 vols. Oxford: Oxford University Press, 1912.

Immerwahr, H. *Form and Thought in Herodotus*, by Henry R. Cleveland: Western Reserve University Press, 1966.

JACT (Joint Association of Classical Teachers). *The World of Athens*. Cambridge: Cambridge University Press, 1996.

Jaeger, W. *The Theology of the Early Greek Philosophers*. Translated by E. Robinson. Oxford: Clarendon Press, 1947.

Janko, R. *Books 13–16*. Vol. 4 of *The Iliad: A Commentary*, ed. by G. S. Kirk. Cambridge: Cambridge University Press, 1985–1993.

Joël, K. "Die Auffassung der kynischen Sokratik." *Archiv fur Geschichte der Philosophie* 20 (1907): 1–23, 147–70.

————. *Der echte und der xenophontische Sokrates*. 2 vols. Berlin: R. Gaertner, 1893–1901.

Johnstone, S. "Virtuous Toil, Vicious Work: Xenophon on Aristocratic Style." *Classical Philology* 89 (1994): 219–40.

Jones, A. H. M. *Athenian Democracy*. Baltimore: Johns Hopkins University Press, 1995.

Kallett-Marx, L. *Money and the Corrosion of Power in Thucydides: The Sicilian Expedition and Its Aftermath*. Berkeley: University of California Press, 2001.

————. *Money, Expense, and Naval Power in Thucydides' History 1–5.24*. Berkeley: University of California Press, 1993.

Kerferd, G. *The Sophistic Movement*. Cambridge: Cambridge University Press, 1981.

Kidd, I. G. "Antisthenes." In *The Encyclopaedia of Philosophy*, ed. P. Edwards. New York: Macmillan Press, 1967.

———. "Cynics." In *The Encyclopaedia of Philosophy*, ed. P. Edwards. New York: Macmillan Press, 1967.

———. "Diogenes of Sinope." In *The Encyclopaedia of Philosophy*, ed. P. Edwards. New York: Macmillan Press, 1967.

Kindstrand, J. "The Cynics and Heraclitus." *Eranos* 82 (1984): 149–78.

Knorringa, H. *Emporos*. Amsterdam: H. J. Paris, 1926.

Kurke, L. *Coins, Bodies, Games, and Gold*. Princeton: Princeton University Press, 1999.

———. "The Politics of *Habrosune* in Archaic Greece." *Classical Antiquity* 11 (1992): 91–120.

———. *The Traffic in Praise: Pindar and the Poetics of Social Economy*. Ithaca: Cornell University Press, 1991.

LaCapra, D. *Re-thinking Intellectual History: Texts, Contexts, Language*. Ithaca: Cornell University Press, 1983.

Langholm, O. *The Aristotelian Analysis of Usury*. New York: Universitetsforlaget, 1984.

Larre, J. P. *Diogène ou la science du bonheur*. Hélette: Editions Harriet, 1997.

Lattimore, R. "The Wise Advisor in Herodotus." *Classical Philology* 34 (1939): 23–35.

Levi, P. *The Cultural Atlas of the Greek World*. Alexandria, Va.: Stonehenge Press, 1992.

Lis, C., and S. Hugo. *Poverty and Capitalism in Pre-industrial Europe*. Hassocks: Harvester Press, 1979.

Little, L. *Religious Poverty and the Profit Economy in Medieval Europe*. Ithaca: Cornell University Press, 1978.

Livingstone, R. W. *The Mission of Greece: Some Greek Views of Life in the Roman World*. Oxford: Clarendon Press, 1928.

Long, A. A. *Stoic Studies*. Berkeley: University of California Press, 2001.

Loraux, N. *The Invention of Athens: The Funeral Oration in the Classical City*. Translated by A. Sheridan. Cambridge, Mass.: Harvard University Press, 1986.

Lovejoy, A. O., and G. Boas. *Primitivism and Related Ideas in Antiquity*. Paperbacks edition. Baltimore: Johns Hopkins University Press, 1997.

Lowry, S. T. *Archaeology of Economic Ideas*. Durham: Duke University Press, 1987.

Luginbill, R. D. *Thucydides on War and National Character*. Boulder, Colo.: Westview Press, 1999.

Lutz, C. "Democritus and Heraclitus." *The Classical Journal* 49 (1954): 309–14.

MacDowell, D. M. *The Law in Classical Athens*. London: Thames and Hudson, 1978.

Malherbe, A. *The Cynic Epistles: A Study Edition*. Missoula, Mont.: Scholars Press, 1977.

Martin, T. *By Philosophy and Empty Deceit: Colossians as Response to a Cynic Critique*. Sheffield: Sheffield Academic Press, 1996.

McCarthy, G. *Marx and the Ancients: Classical Ethics, Social Justice, and Nineteenth-century Political Economy*. Savage, Md.: Rowman & Littlefield, 1990.

McEvilley, T. "Early Greek Philosophy and Madhyamika." *Philosophy East and West* 31 (1981): 141–64.

McKirahan, R. D. *Philosophy before Socrates*. Indianapolis: Hackett Publishing, 1994.

McKirahan, V. T. "Cynicism," In *Ethics*, ed. J. K. Roth, 1: 208–9. Pasadena: Salem Press, 1994.

Meiggs, R. *The Athenian Empire.* Oxford: Clarendon Press, 1972.

Meijer, F., and O. van Nijf. *Trade, Transport, and Society in the Ancient World.* New York: Routledge, 1992.

Meikle, S. *Aristotle's Economic Thought.* Oxford: Clarendon Press, 1995.

Meyer, G. "Laudes Inopiae." PhD diss., Göttingen, 1915.

Michell, H. *The Economics of Ancient Greece.* Cambridge: Cambridge University Press, 1940.

Miller, D., ed. *Acknowledging Consumption: A Review of New Studies.* New York: Routledge, 1995.

———. *Material Culture and Mass Consumption.* New York: Blackwell, 1987.

Millett, P. *Lending and Borrowing in Ancient Athens.* Cambridge: Cambridge University Press, 1991.

Moles, J. "Herodotus Warns the Athenians." *Papers of the Leeds International Latin Seminar* 9 (1996): 258–84.

———. "Le cosmopolitisme cynique." In *Le Cynisme ancien et ses prolongements: Actes du Colloque International du CNRS*, ed. M. O. Goulet-Cazé and R. Goulet. Paris: Presses Universitaires de France, 1993.

Momigliano, A. "Sea Power in Greek Thought." *Classical Review* 58 (1944): 1–7.

Morris, I. "Foreword." In *The Ancient Economy*, ed. M. I. Finley, updated edition. Berkeley: University of California Press, 1999.

———. "The Athenian Economy Twenty Years after *The Ancient Economy*." *Classical Philology* 89 (1994): 351–66.

Mossé, C. *The Ancient World at Work.* Translated by J. Lloyd. London: Chatto & Windus, 1969.

Müller, K. O. "Antisthenes and the Cynics." In *A History of the Literature of Ancient Greece.* 3 vols. Translated by G. C. Lewis and J. W. Donaldson. London: Longman, Green & Co., 1884.

Munn, M. *The School of History: Athens in the Age of Socrates.* Berkeley: University of California Press, 2000.

Murray, O. *Early Greece.* 2nd ed. London: Harper Collins, 1993.

Murray, O., and S. Price, eds. *The Greek City. From Homer to Alexander.* Oxford: Clarendon Press, 1990.

Nakhov, I. M. "Der Mensch in der Philosophie der Kyniker." In *Der Mensch als Mass der Dinge: Studien zum Griechischen Menschenbild in der Zeit der Blüte und Krise der Polis*, ed. R. Müller. Berlin: Akademie-Verlag, 1976.

Navia, L. E. *Antisthenes of Athens: Setting the World Aright.* Westport, Conn.: Greenwood Press, 2001.

———. *Diogenes of Sinope: The Man in the Tub.* Westport, Conn.: Greenwood Press, 1998.

———. *Classical Cynicism: A Critical Study.* Westport, Conn.: Greenwood Press, 1996.

———. *The Philosophy of Cynicism: An Annotated Bibliography.* Westport, Conn.: Greenwood Press, 1995.

Nelson, S. *God and the Land.* New York: Oxford University Press, 1998.

Newman, W. *The Politics of Aristotle.* 4 vols. Oxford: Clarendon Press, 1887–1902.

Niehues-Pröbsting, H. *Der Kynismus des Diogenes und der Begriff des Zynismus.* Munich: Wilhelm Fink Verlag, 1979.

Nietzsche, F. *On the Genealogy of Morality*. Translated by C. Diethe. Cambridge: Cambridge University Press, 1994.

Nouhard, M. *L'Utilisation de l'Histoire par les Orateurs Attiques*. Paris, 1982.

Ober, J. *Political Dissent in Democratic Athens: Intellectual Critics of Popular Rule*. Princeton: Princeton University Press, 1998.

———. *Mass and Elite in Democratic Athens: Rhetoric, Ideology, and the Power of the People*. Princeton: Princeton University Press, 1989.

Ober, J., and C. Hedrick, eds. *Dēmokratia: A Conversation on Democracies, Ancient and Modern*. Princeton: Princeton University Press, 1996.

Olmstead, A. T. *History of the Persian Empire*. Chicago: University of Chicago Press, 1948.

O'Neill, E. *Teles: The Cynic Teacher*. Missoula, Mont.: Scholars Press, 1977.

Onfray, M. *Cynismes: Portrait du philosophe en chien*. Paris: B. Grasset, 1990.

Palmer, J. *Plato's Reception of Parmenides*. New York: Oxford University Press, 1999.

Paquet, L. *Les Cyniques grecs: Fragments et témoignages*. Ottawa: Les Presses de l'Université d'Ottawa, 1988.

Parke, H. W. *Greek Mercenary Soldiers*. Oxford: Clarendon Press, 1933.

Pöhlmann, R. von. *Geschichte der Sozialen Frage und des Sozialismus in der antiken Welt*. 2 vols. Munich: C. H. Beck, 1925.

Polanyi, K. "Aristotle Discovers the Economy." In *Primitive, Archaic, and Modern Economies*. Edited by G. Dalton. Boston: Beacon Press, 1968.

Polanyi, K., C. M. Arensberg, and H. W. Pearson, eds. *Trade and Market in the Early Empires*. Glencoe, Ill.: Free Press, 1957.

Price, J. *Thucydides and Internal War*. Cambridge: Cambridge University Press, 2001.

Rankin, H. D. *Antisthenes Sokratikos*. Amsterdam: Hakkert, 1986.

———. *Sophists, Socratics, and Cynics*. London: Croom Helm, 1983.

———. " 'Ouk estin antilegein.' " In *The Sophists and their Legacy*, ed. G. B. Kerferd. Weisbaden: Steiner, 1981.

Reden, S. von. *Exchange in Ancient Greece*. London: Duckworth, 1995.

Reed, C. M. *Maritime Traders in the Ancient Greek World*. Cambridge: Cambridge University Press, 2003.

Redfield, J. "Herodotus the Tourist." *Classical Philology* 80 (1985): 97–118.

Reeve, C. D. C. *Philosopher-Kings: The Argument of Plato's Republic*. Princeton: Princeton University Press, 1988.

Rich, A. "The Cynic Conception of *autarkeia*." In *Die Kyniker in der modernen Forschung*, ed. M. Billerbeck. Amsterdam: B. R. Grüner, 1991.

Riis, T., ed. *Aspects of Poverty in Early Modern Europe*. Florence: Publications of the European University Institute, 1981.

Robert, R. *The Classic Slum*. Harmondsworth: Penguin, 1973.

Robinson, D. M. *Ancient Sinope*. Baltimore: Johns Hopkins University Press, 1906.

Romilly, J. de. *The Rise and Fall of States According to Greek Authors*. Ann Arbor: University of Michigan Press, 1977.

———. *Thucydides and Athenian Imperialism*. Oxford, 1963.

Rood, T. *Thucydides: Narrative and Explanation*. New York: Clarendon Press, 1998.

Rostovtzeff, M. *The Social and Economic History of the Hellenistic World*. Oxford: Clarendon Press, 1953.

Runciman, W. G. "Doomed to Extinction: The *polis* as an Evolutionary Dead-end." In *The Greek City: From Homer to Alexander*, ed. O. Murray and S. Price. Oxford: Clarendon Press, 1990.

Russell, B. *A History of Western Philosophy*. New York: Simon and Schuster, 1972.

———. *In Praise of Idleness and Other Essays*. New York: W. W. Norton, 1935.

Sage, M. *Warfare in Ancient Greece*. London: Routledge Press, 1996.

Salvatore, D., and E. Diulio. *Principles of Economics*. 2nd ed. Schaum's Outline Series. New York: McGraw Hill, 1996.

Sayre, F. *The Greek Cynics*. Baltimore: J. H. Furst, 1948.

———. *Diogenes of Sinope: A Study of Greek Cynicism*. Baltimore: J. H. Furst, 1938.

Schumpeter, J. *History of Economic Analysis*. New York: Oxford University Press, 1954.

Seaford, R. *Reciprocity and Ritual: Homer and Tragedy in the Developing City-state*. Oxford: Clarendon Press, 1994.

Sealey, R. *Demosthenes and His Time: A Study in Defeat*. New York: Oxford University Press, 1993.

Seltmann, C. T. "Diogenes of Sinope, Son of the Banker Hikesias." In *Transactions of the International Numismatic Congress*, ed. J. Mattingly and E. Robinson. London: B. Quaritch, 1938.

Simmel, G. *Philosophy of Money*. Translated by T. Bottomore and D. Frisby. New York: Routledge, 1990.

Sinclair, T. *A History of Greek Political Thought*. London: Routledge, 1967.

Sloterdijk, P. *Critique of Cynical Reason*. Translated by M. Eldred. Minneapolis: University of Minnesota Press, 1987.

Smith, R. *Hellenistic Sculpture: A Handbook*. New York: Thames and Hudson, 1991.

Snell, B. *The Discovery of the Mind*. Translated by T. Rosenmeyer. Cambridge, Mass.: Harvard University Press, 1953.

Solmsen, F. *Hesiod and Aeschylus*. Ithaca: Cornell University Press, 1949.

Sommerstein, A., ed. *Aristophanes: Knights*. Warminster: Aris & Phillips, 1981.

Starr, C. G. *The Economic and Social Growth of Early Greece*. New York: Oxford University Press, 1977.

Stewart, Z. "Democritus and the Cynics." *Harvard Studies in Classical Philology* 63 (1958): 179–91.

Tarn, W. W. *Hellenistic Civilization*. 3rd ed. Revised by G. T. Griffith. New York: New American Library, 1961.

———. *Alexander the Great*. Boston: Beacon Press, 1956.

Thomas, K. *The Oxford Book of Work*. Oxford: Oxford University Press, 1999.

Thomas, R. *Herodotus in Context: Ethnography, Science, and the Art of Persuasion*. Cambridge: Cambridge University Press, 2000.

———. *Oral Tradition and Written Record*. Cambridge: Cambridge University Press, 1989.

Trever, A. A. *A History of Greek Economic Thought*. Chicago: University of Chicago Press, 1916.

Vernant, J.-P. *The Origins of Greek Thought*. Ithaca: Cornell University Press, 1982.

Voss, B. R. "Die Keule der Kyniker." *Hermes* 95 (1967): 441–46.

Warry, J. *Warfare in the Classical World*. Norman: University of Oklahoma Press, 1995.

Weber, M. *Economy and Society: An Outline of Interpretative Sociology.* Edited by G. Roth and C. Wittich. Translated by E. Fischoff. Berkeley: University of California Press, 1978.

Wenley, R. "Cynics." In *Encyclopaedia of Ethics and Religion,* ed. J. Hastings. New York: Charles Scribner's Sons, 1955.

Whitman, C. H. *Aristophanes and the Comic Hero.* Cambridge, Mass.: Harvard University Press, 1964.

———. *Homer and the Heroic Tradition.* Cambridge, Mass.: Harvard University Press, 1958.

Williams, J. "The Ideology and Constitution of Demetrius of Phalerum." In *Polis and Polemos,* ed. C. D. Hamilton and P. Krentz. Claremont, Calif.: Regina Press, 1997.

Wood, E. M. *Peasant-citizen and Slave: The Foundations of Athenian Democracy.* London: Verso Press, 1988.

Zeller, E. *Outlines of the History of Greek Philosophy.* Trans. L. R. Palmer. New York: Dover Publications, 1980.

———. *Socrates and the Socratic Schools.* London: Longmans, Green & Co., 1885.

———. *A History of Greek Philosophy.* Translated by S. F. Alleyne. London: Longmans, Green & Co., 1881.

Zimmern, A. *The Greek Commonwealth.* New York: Modern Library, 1956.

Ziolkowski, J. E. *Thucydides and the Tradition of Funeral Speeches at Athens.* New York: Arno Press, 1981.

INDEX

WILLIAM DESMOND

is a lecturer in the Department of Classics
at Trinity College Dublin.